KAGAWA TOYOHIKO'S
WAR RESPONSIBILITY CONFESSION

Kagawa Toyohiko's War Responsibility Confession

MIKIO MIYAGI

WIPF & STOCK · Eugene, Oregon

KAGAWA TOYOHIKO'S WAR RESPONSIBILITY CONFESSION

Copyright © 2025 Mikio Miyagi. All rights reserved. Except for brief quotations in critical publications or reviews, no part of this book may be reproduced in any manner without prior written permission from the publisher. Write: Permissions, Wipf and Stock Publishers, 199 W. 8th Ave., Suite 3, Eugene, OR 97401.

Wipf & Stock
An Imprint of Wipf and Stock Publishers
199 W. 8th Ave., Suite 3
Eugene, OR 97401

www.wipfandstock.com

PAPERBACK ISBN: 979-8-3852-0039-9
HARDCOVER ISBN: 979-8-3852-0040-5
EBOOK ISBN: 979-8-3852-0041-2

06/24/25

Scripture quotations marked NRSV are from the New Revised Standard Version, copyright @ 1989, Division of Christian Education of the National Council of the Churches of Christ in the United States in the United States of America. Used by permission. All rights reserved.

Scripture quotations marked NRSVUE are from the New Revised Standard Version, Updated Edition. Copyright © 2021 National Council of Churches of Christ in the United States of America. Used by permission. All rights reserved worldwide.

To Miyagi Taeko and family:
Mika, Key, Ayaka, Ken, Nao, and Kaho

Contents

List of Tables, Charts, Photos, and Map | *viii*

Acknowledgments and Preface: Why I Was Led to Write Kagawa Toyohiko's Confession of War Responsibility | *xiii*

List of Abbreviations | *xviii*

1. Introduction | 1
2. Japan against Christianity | 17
3. Kagawa's Evangelical Work, Patriotism, and Repentance | 32
4. Kagawa Resonated with First-Generation Christians' Heritage of Reverence for the Emperor and Patriotism | 63
5. The Emperor | 88
6. Theological Perspective on a Response to the State | 108
7. Kagawa's War Responsibility | 123
8. Conclusion | 157

Bibliography | 169

Index | 177

List of Tables, Charts, and Photos

1: Introduction	Photos: Kagawa at a slum in Kobe, Japan, early 1900s (left); support for victims of the Great Kanto Earthquake (right)
1: Introduction	Table: Evangelical work in Japan and the US
1: Introduction	Chart: Kagawa's rhetoric for Japan's invasion of Asian countries (West dominates Asia; Japan is the only state that stands against the West)
1: Introduction	Table: Chronology during the wars
2: Japan against Christianity	Table: Chronology of anti-Christianity in Japan
2: Japan against Christianity	Table: The edicts of Toyotomi Hideyoshi (excerpt from *Expulsion of Missionaries*, 1587)
2: Japan against Christianity	Table: The edict of 1635 ordering the closing of Japan, addressed to the joint *bugyō* (magistrate) of Nagasaki
2: Japan against Christianity	Table: The Five Public Notices (Mar. 1868)

LIST OF TABLES, CHARTS, AND PHOTOS

2: Japan against Christianity	Photo: The Public Notices for the common people; five notices were written on each wooden board (see the right side, banning Christianity).
2: Japan against Christianity	Table: The Charter Oath
3: Kagawa's Evangelical Work	Table: Chronology related to the NEMM
3: Kagawa's Evangelical Work	Table: Results of the NEMM's ecumenical activities
3: Kagawa's Evangelical Work	Table: Chronology related to the KGM
3: Kagawa's Evangelical Work	Table: Result of the KGM's ecumenical activities
3: Kagawa's Evangelical Work	Chart: Japanese church history in relation to WWII
3: Kagawa's Evangelical Work	Chart: Japanese church history in relation to WWII
3: Kagawa's Evangelical Work	Table: Results of the NJCCM (1946–48)
4: Kagawa Resonated with First-Generation Christians	Table: Chronology of sociopolitical context
4: Kagawa Resonated with First-Generation Christians	Table: Christians of first and second generations
4: Kagawa Resonated with First-Generation Christians	Table: Treaty of Amity and Commerce between the United States and the Empire of Japan, article 8
4: Kagawa Resonated with First-Generation Christians	Photo: Yanaihara states, "I love Japan with my whole heart" (*Tokyo Asahi Shimbun* [東京朝日新聞], Dec. 2, 1937)

ix

LIST OF TABLES, CHARTS, AND PHOTOS

5: The Emperor	Table: Chronology related to the emperor
5: The Emperor	Chart: The emperor as the state's sovereign
5: The Emperor	Chart: Social reformation: Percentage of population by status at the beginning of the Meiji era (thanks to the social reformation of the Charter Oath in the Five Articles of 1868)
5: The Emperor	Table: Ministers who were killed or suffered assassination attempts by the ultra-nationalistic army youth officers
5: The Emperor	Table: Relationship between Christian faith and patriotic sentiment
6: Theological Perspective on a Response to the State	Table: Kagawa's theological perspective on a response to the state
6: Theological Perspective on a Response to the State	Chart: Romans 9:3: Interpretation of Moses and Paul
6: Theological Perspective on a Response to the State	Chart: Romans 9:3: Interpretation of Kagawa
6: Theological Perspective on a Response to the State	Chart: Romans 9:3: Interpretation of the Author
6: Theological Perspective on a Response to the State	Chart: Romans 9:3: Another Interpretation of the Author
6: Theological Perspective on a Response to the State	Chart: Romans 9:3: Final Interpretation of the Author

LIST OF TABLES, CHARTS, AND PHOTOS

7: Kagawa's War Responsibility	Table: Chronology of war responsibility confession
7: Kagawa's War Responsibility	Supplementary explanation for the above table
7: Kagawa's War Responsibility	Chart: Kagawa's apology and criticism of US during and after war
7: Kagawa's War Responsibility	Table: The structure of paragraph 3 and its explanatory diagram
7: Kagawa's War Responsibility	Chart: Kagawa's understanding of the IEEW (Aug. 15, 1945) and subjects' response to emperor's demands (through the open letter to MacArthur)
7: Kagawa's War Responsibility	Table: Chronology related to *Direction for New Lives*
8: Conclusion	Chart: Path to confession of war responsibility
8: Conclusion	Table: Japanese churches' war responsibility confessions

Acknowledgments and Preface

Why I Was Led to Write Kagawa Toyohiko's Confession of War Responsibility

APOLOGY FOR COLONIZING THE UNDEVELOPED COUNTRIES

When I attended the United Methodist Mission Bicentennial Conference (UMMBC) in Atlanta in 2019, after a presentation by an African scholar on the history of missions in his country, I asked whether a suzerain country had made an apology of colonization to his country, referring to the United Church of Christ in Japan, who made a war responsibility confession in 1967. There was a short moment between when I asked him and when I received his reply. He confessed that they received economic assistance for state development but no apology for colonization from the suzerain.

He might have felt confused about how to reply, given that most of the conference attendees came from Western countries. However, this reply surprised me, as I expected suzerain countries to make statements of apology for colonization, so I was shocked to realize the relationship between the invaded country and the colonizing country.

It was Dr. Dana L. Robert, my academic professor during my master of theological studies program at Boston University School of Theology, who suggested I apply to present at UMMBC, as I was a visiting scholar at the Center for Global Christianity & Mission. I would like to express my great gratitude to her for allowing me to present at the conference and for the above experience.

ACKNOWLEDGMENTS AND PREFACE

THE GAP BETWEEN FIRST- AND SECOND-GENERATION CHRISTIANS AND THIRD-GENERATION CHRISTIANS ON WAR RESPONSIBILITY

Is the above experience at the UMMBC related to Kagawa Toyohiko's war responsibility confession? Seven years after Kagawa, a second-generation Japanese Christian (b. 1888), passed away in 1960, the UCCJ confessed its war responsibility in the name of UCCJ's moderator, Suzuki Masahisa, a third-generation Christian (1912–69). This paper will examine the theological gap between the Kagawa generation of Christians—the so-called second-generation Christians—and the third-generation Christians by whom the church confessed its responsibility for the war, as well as the continuity that transcends the gap.

In reviewing the gap and continuity of both Christian generations, I am convinced of the importance of analyzing Japanese Christians' theological attitude toward the state authorities and feelings of apology toward Asian people. After the end of WWII, the leaders of the UCCJ consisted of second-generation Christians such as Tomita Mitsuru (1883–1961), Kozakai Michio (1888–1973, Congregationalist), Abe Yoshimune (1886–1980, Methodist), who were forced to cooperate with the government during the war and excused of war responsibility immediately afterward.[1]

It is necessary to consider that the faith, theology, and attitude toward the nation of first-generation Christians such as Uemura Masahisa (Presbyterian), Uchimura Kanzo (non-church movement), and Ebina Danjo (Congregationalist) influenced the second-generation Christian leaders of the church. In particular, it is clear that second-generation Christians' response to the wartime government's forcible suppression of national policies, such as worship of the emperor, was a continuation of the attitude of first-generation Christian leaders.

In particular, the first generation of Christians who came from the samurai class that supported the Tokugawa shogunate during the Meiji Restoration were those who served the feudal lord based on their education in Confucianism, Shinto, and Buddhism, but who became Christians, including Inazo Nitobe, Uchimura Kanzo, Uemura Masahisa, and Ebina Danjo; so, I needed to have academic knowledge of Japan's religious and spiritual climate. I received guidance from the assistant dean of Boston University's School of Theology and was able to write a master's thesis entitled

---

1. UCCJ, *History of the UCCJ*, 4.

"First-Generation Japanese Protestant Indigenization into Japan's Spiritual Formation" in April 2010 with guidance from Dr. John Berthrong, an assistant dean. I would like to express my heartfelt gratitude to Dr. Berthrong and offer my condolences, as Dr. Berthrong passed away in August 2022.

THE SIMILARITY BETWEEN THE INHUMAN OPPRESSION OF THE RULED BY THE RULERS AND THE RESPONSIBILITY FOR WAR BY THE RULERS

During my PhD program at International Christian University (ICU) from 2010 to 2014, Dr. Anri Morimoto, the assistant president of ICU, advised me to write a dissertation entitled, "Theology of Social Justice in Okinawa: Hope amid Calamity (1945–1972)," based on social justice issues during the US administration period from 1945 to 1972, such as the farmers' land confiscation by the US military authorities and the Yumiko-chan incident by the US soldier who raped and killed a six-year-old girl, and the Hansen's disease matter.

Through the facts of the unjust treatment of the ruled population by foreign domination and the work of Christians who stood up against these social problems, I learned that God's work is amid calamities. Thus, I would like to express my gratitude to the entire doctoral thesis review committee members and Dr. Morimoto, as the content of the dissertation is related to Kagawa's war responsibility; I referred to the atrocities Japanese military authorities committed in Japan in colonized and invaded countries in Asia.

CONFESSION OF WAR RESPONSIBILITY BASED ON MY GRANDMOTHER'S GUILT TOWARD CHINA

While I was a researcher at the Institute for the Study of Christianity and Culture of the ICU, the Oriental Theological Seminary (OTS) in Nagaland, India, invited me to lecture at OTS and to give a public lecture at Nagaland City Hall in December 2017. Bokali Chishi, an Indian friend at the Boston University STH, arranged for me to give a speech with two female Indian attorneys at the Tenth Youth Peace Fest 2017.

Considering that India was a colony of Britain, which exploited Indian people, I told the story of what my grandmother did just after WWII. Though my grandfather, the leader of the Tianjin Japanese Church, had

ACKNOWLEDGMENTS AND PREFACE

gained significant profits thanks to his pharmacy in Tianjin, China, with my grandmother, after he died, the grandmother did not transmit the profit to the Japanese mainland near the end of the war, because she as a Christian decided to leave the money he had earned in China. After the war, she and her family returned to Japan without treasure. I recognize what she did in China was a war responsibility confession.

I REALIZED MY GUILT FOR THE SINS COMMITTED BY JAPAN DURING ITS COLONIAL RULE WHEN I ATTENDED A WORSHIP SERVICE AT YOUNGNAK PRESBYTERIAN CHURCH

I visited South Korea as an employee of a joint venture between the Mitsubishi Corporation and an American construction manufacturer and was involved in a project to purchase electronic components from Samsung Electronics in Korea, so I attended a development meeting in Korea. As the meeting finished on Friday, I extended my visit two days in order to attend a Korean church on Sunday. As I am a member of Cumberland Presbyterian Church, I asked the taxi driver on Sunday to take me to any Presbyterian church.

It was Youngnak Presbyterian Church to which the driver took me. I was overwhelmed by the majestic and gigantic chapel, and I still clearly remember how the attendees wore their overcoats during the service in the cold December weather. During the service, I listened to a Japanese interpreter through headphones, but I don't remember the sermon clearly. I say this because, as a Japanese person, I felt a sense of atonement and guilt for worshiping in a church in a country that Japan had colonized during the war.

APOLOGIZE FOR THE ATROCITIES JAPAN COMMITTED DURING THE MILITARY INVASION OF CHINA

In the late 1990s, I stayed for a few days to observe the missionary activities of the San Francisco Chinese Church of Cumberland Presbyterian Church. During my stay, I attended a service centered around elderly people who spoke Mandarin. I apologized for the atrocities committed during the military invasion of China.

ACKNOWLEDGMENTS AND PREFACE

THE FIRST-GENERATION CHRISTIANS' HERITAGE HAS BEEN CARRIED DOWN TO MY GENERATION

Dr. John Berthrong, the adviser for my master's thesis, also helped me to consider that the heritage of the first-generation Christians, such as Uemura Masahisa (Presbyterian), Uchimura Kanzo (Non-Church movement), Ebina Danjo (Congregation), has been carried down to my generation.

"Presentation of the "Kagawa Toyohiko's War Responsibility for Dr. Thomas John Hastings, EDITOR, INTERNATIONAL BULLETIN OF MISSION RESEARCH, at Princeton Theological Seminary. Dr. Hastings recommended I contact WIPF & Stock for publication.

GRATITUDE TO TAEKO MIYAGI

Finally, I would like to express my gratitude to my wife, Taeko Miyagi. When I started studying theology at Boston University STH, I lived with her during the first semester. She helped me prepare for classes, and she was the first reader of my PhD papers at ICU in Tokyo, who assisted with explaining abstract theological content such as social justice, eschatology, dialectical theology, etc. I believe these conversations are common to all conversations between researchers and their spouses in the world.

LAST WORDS TO WAR VICTIMS, ESPECIALLY ASIAN VICTIMS

I confess that through my life and that of my family, God has led me to feel guilty for the inhumane and brutal acts committed by Japan in Korea and China and to confess my responsibility for the war.

List of Abbreviations

Abbreviation	Formal Form
COFA	Charter Oath in Five Articles
FPN	Five Public Notices
IASA	Institute for Advanced Studies on Asia
ICU	International Christian University
IEEW	Imperial Edict of the End of the War
IEPNS	Imperial Edict on the Promotion of National Spirit
IRE	Imperial Rescript of Education
JCP	Japanese Communist Party
KGM	Kingdom of God Movement
KKS	*Kamino Kuni Sinbun* (KGM's newspaper)
LN	League of Nations
MEJG	Ministry of Education (of the Japanese government)
MSP	Military Special Office
NEMM	National Ecumenical Missionary Movement
NJCCM	New Japan Construction Christ Movement
NPMM	National Spiritual Mobilization Movement
NRSV	New Revised Standard Version
OTS	Oriental Theological Seminary
PD	Potsdam Declaration
POW	Prisoners of war

LIST OF ABBREVIATIONS

PPL	Peace Preservation Law
RCA	Reformed Church in America
RJACLC	Riverside Japanese American Christian Leaders Conference
ROL	Religious Organization Law
SCAP	Supreme Commander for the Allied Powers
SHP	Special Higher Police
TACUJ	Treaty of Amity and Commerce between the United States and the Empire of Japan
UCCJ	United Church of Christ in Japan
UMMBC	United Methodist Mission Bicentennial Conference
WCC	World Council of Churches

1

Introduction

KAGAWA TOYOHIKO, A WELL-KNOWN CHRISTIAN LEADER

There is no doubt that Kagawa Toyohiko (賀川豊彦, 1888–1960) was well known in the world as a Japanese Christian leader due to his sacrificial commitment to social reforms for the underprivileged in establishing cooperatives and unions for industrial workers, fishermen, and farmers; credit cooperatives; hospital cooperatives; and other social organizations. He reformed society to eliminate an inequitable commonwealth based on his theology of redemptive love and nonviolent spirit. We should not forget his work helping the devastated victims of the Great Kanto Earthquake of 1923, even moving his mission base from Kobe to Tokyo.

Kagawa at a slum in Kobe, Japan, early 1900s (left);
support for victims of the Great Kanto Earthquake (right)

What made him best known in the world was perhaps first the semi-autobiographical novel about his life in the slum area of Shinkawa (新川),

Kobe, *Shisen wo Koetsu* (死線を超えて, Across the Deathline), as it was translated into non-Japanese several languages; and second his missionary works as a mass evangelist in both Japan and the world, especially for the *Kami no kuni Undo* (神の国運動, Kingdom of God Movement, 1928–34), *Sin Nippon Kensetsu Kirisuto Undo* (新日本建設キリスト教運動, New Japan Construction Christian Movement, 1946–49), and the US and European tours in 1924, 1936, and 1950.

Kuroda Shiro (黒田四郎), who traveled with Kagawa, reported the result of the KGM as follows. Looking at the data, we can see how great Kagawa's work in evangelism was. See also the result of the lecture tour in the US in 1950, just five years after the Pacific War.

Kagawa's Evangelical Work

In evangelical meetings in Japan, Kagawa delivered God's message as an evangelist, mainly in peripheral areas, such as in lands for farmers and foresters, where the number of Japanese Christians was small.

Table 1.1: Evangelical work in Japan and the US

Name	Kingdom of God Movement[1]	New Japan Construction Christian Movement[2]	US lecture tour[3]
	(1928–34)	(1946–49)	1950
Total years or months	4.5 years	3.5 years	5 months
Number of days	734	733	165
Number of meetings	1,859	1,384	(not available; Kagawa visited 137 places)
Number of attendees	787,223	754,428	300,000
Number of decision cards	62,410	200,987	(not available)

---

1. Kuroda, *Research on Kagawa Toyohiko*, 204–5.
2. Kuroda, *Research on Kagawa Toyohiko*, 204–5.
3. Bradshaw, *Unconquerable Kagawa*, 18.

INTRODUCTION

KAGAWA'S MISSION FOR THE POOR:
KAGAWA IS INFLUENCED BY REV. NAGAO MAKI

It was Catholic priests who brought both Catholic theology and faith in the sixteenth century. On the other hand, Protestant Christianity was introduced by Western missionaries in the middle of the nineteenth century. Christianity in Japan was rooted in the sacrificial love of Western Catholic priests and Protestant missionaries, including women; "in this period, the Women's Foreign Missionary Society did not send married women missionaries to Japan; they sent missional-related information to America and required single women missionaries for Japan" (as a missionary's wife was considered unable to devote herself to full-time missionary work).[4]

Though Kagawa criticized *Shimabara no Ran* (島原の乱, the Revolt of Shimabara-Amakusa in 1637–38 during the end period of the Tokugawa Bakufu) as a determined resistance against the state, it was not an uprising when hidden Japanese Catholics appeared to visit the Basilica of the Twenty-Six Holy Martyrs of Japan, the so-called Oura Cathedral (大浦天主堂), which was rebuilt by the Catholic Church thanks to the Treaty of Amity and Commerce between Japan and France in 1864. Nine years before the Meiji government was established, Catholics were recognized in public.[5]

The Tokugawa government caught 3370 hidden Catholics, as the law banning Christianity was still legal. The Tokugawa government banished them from Nagasaki to thirty-three feudal domains, to force them into apostasy from their faith. Nagao Hachiinomon (長尾八乃門), the samurai of Kanazawa Han (金沢藩, Kanazawa domain), was installed as a chief for supervising the performance of the hidden Christians' rigorous duties.[6]

In 1889, as Nagao Hachiinomon was moved by the faith of the hidden Catholics, who "kept faith even though they had been forced to work hard, he and other five other Japanese were converted to Christianity by an American Presbyterian missionary, Rev. Thomas Clay Winn. The next year in 1881, Rev. Thomas C. Winn baptized Nagao's son, Nagao Maki (長尾巻, 1852–1934), who became a minister of the Kanazawa Kyokai of the Nihon Kirisutōky Kyokai (日本基督教会) after studying at the Department of Theology of Hokuriku Eiwa School (北陸英和学校).

---

4. Saito, *Contribution of Missionaries' Wives*, 96–97.
5. National Archives of Japan, "Grand Council of State Proclamation 68."
6. Amemiya, *Kagawa Toyohiko in Youth*, 286–87.

What was Kagawa's motive for sacrificing all his life for the socially unprivileged in a slum in Shinkawa? What moved him to the Shinkawa slums? In July 1907, after graduating from Meiji Gakuin, Kagawa was scheduled to enter Kobe Singakkou (Kobe Seminary) in September.[7] Kagawa met Rev. Nagao Maki, who welcomed him at Toyohashi Church in Aichi Prefecture, where Nagao Maki was pastoring the congregation. While assisting a mission work at the Toyohashi Church for a little more than a month, Kagawa was inspired and influenced by Rev. Nagao Maki. In 1936, at the third memorial service of Rev. Nagao Maki, Kagawa made a statement.

> Rev. Nagao did not have any status in this world. A pastor is poor, but I have never met the poorest pastor like Rev. Nagao. He was a Christian samurai who had broken through poverty, persecution, and suffering by faith. He neither complained nor was dissatisfied with anything in his life. Rev. Nagao inspired me the most among the pastors in Japan. After knowing Rev. Nagao, I was convinced that the New Testament had indigenized Christianity in Japan through him.[8]

Kagawa confessed Rev. Nagao Maki as a Christian minister he should imitate all his life, as Kagawa decided to move into the Shikana slum after he had met Rev. Nagao Maki.

Kagawa's statement improved the spirit of Japanese Christianity's continuation from Catholic to Protestant. Rev. Nagao Maki had decided to follow the Japanese Catholic Christians' thorny path through his father, Nagao Hachinomon. Though Kagawa criticized the Shimabara Uprising of Catholic Christians, those Christians never committed apostasy but delivered the message to Protestant Christians. It was an irony that Kagawa's story transcended his criticism of Catholic believers.

SOCIOPOLITICAL CONTEXT OF JAPAN

We must look at the sociopolitical context of Japan when Kagawa met Rev. Nagao Maki in 1907. As the Empire of Japan defeated Russia, one of the Western empires, thanks to *fukoku kyouhei seisaku* (富国強兵政策, a policy of increasing wealth and military strength), Japanese people felt a heady sense of victory in the Russo-Japanese War (1904–5). At this period, a young man's dream was to become a soldier, and it was precisely at this

---

7. Amemiya, *Kagawa Toyohiko in Youth*, 283.
8. Amemiya, *Kagawa Toyohiko in Youth*, 283.

time that Kagawa decided to devote his life to the weak as he met Rev. Nagao Maki, who influenced him and changed his life until his death. This means Kagawa's mission of devoting himself to the socially unprivileged transcended the local state's sociopolitical context in the world.

Then, how did Kagawa's mission relate to the war? Did Kagawa ignore war affairs? Did he keep a distance from being involved in them, including in the Japanese military invasion of Asian countries? We should review how Kagawa faced and responded to the reality of war by focusing on the so-called Fifteen War, which started from the Liutiaohu incident in 1931 up to the end of the Pacific War on August 15, 1945.

Furthermore, we need to clarify why Kagawa was respected by Christians in non-Japanese countries, such as the US and European countries, more than the Japanese Christians who criticized Kagawa because of what he did during the war. And I try to conclude that Kagawa's mission for loving the socially poor transcended the sociopolitical context of Japan and the world.

Japanese Christians had been under persecution by state authorities since the Toyotomi government (1585–1603), which issued the edict in 1587 that demanded the expulsion of Christianity from Japan; and the Tokugawa shogunate (1603–1867) succeeded the anti-Christianity policy of the Toyotomi government.

The Edict of Toyotomi Hideyoshi (豊臣秀吉): Expulsion of the Missionaries, 1587

How did the Japanese spiritual climate become anti-Christian? To examine Japan's anti-Christian climate, we must see that the Toyotomi government (豊臣政権, 1585–1868) enacted an anti-Christianity edict based on Western military aggression and colonial policy in Asia.[9] Moreover, the policies of the Toyotomi government were inherited by the Tokugawa shogunate (徳川幕府, 1603–1868) and the Meiji government (明治政府, 1868–1912).

> The Tokugawa government issued a more strict edict than Toyotomi in 1635; it established the *danka* (檀家, temple parishioner) system, by which the *bakufu* (幕府, shogunate) ordered that certificates of temple registration be issued for every Japanese in 1638.[10]

---

9. Asia for Educators, "Edicts of Toyotomi Hideyoshi," 1–2.
10. Tamamura, "Local Society and Temple-Parishioner Relationship," 262.

In the first stage of the Meiji period, the newly established Constitution in 1889 specified freedom of religion in article 28, which specified that "Japanese subjects shall, within limits not prejudicial to peace and order, and not antagonistic to their duties as subjects, enjoy freedom of religious belief," Christians had been forced to show loyalty to the state, which revived Shintoism and forced the population to worship the emperor. After the Russian Revolution in 1917, the Meiji government enacted the Peace Preservation Law in 1925, 1928, and 1941[11] to clamp down on left-wing groups. Article 1 of the law is specified below.

> Any person who organizes an association with the object of changing the national polity or who attempts to do or who participates in such association shall be punished with death or penal servitude.[12]

As the prewar Japanese national polity (国体, *kokutai*) was firmly built on the emperor system by the Meiji government through establishing the Constitution of the Empire Japan and the Imperial Rescript of Education in 1890, Christians had to live in a Japanese spiritual climate that demanded selfless loyalty and patriotism to the emperor and the state. How did Christians accept Christianity during this period? Did they despise this feudalistic climate as paganism? Did they resist the government's legal demand to worship the emperor and resolve to die as traitors to the state? We cannot so simply categorize Christians and churches that survived during this period because as the leaders of first-generation Christians such as Uemura Masahisa (植村正久, 1858–1925), Uchimura Kanzo (内村鑑三, 1861–1930), and Nitobe Inazo (新渡戸稲造, 1862–1933), came from a samurai-class family that valued selfless loyalty to their local domain, it had been not only totally difficult for them to reject selfless loyalty, but they justified the selfless loyalty by interpreting it theologically and applying it for survival.

Anti-Immigration Act of 1924

In addition to the above-mentioned anti-Christian climate of Japan, we should recognize the external factor that drove the Japanese population,

---

11. After 1945 it was revoked as part of the US occupation's (SCAP's) attempts to dismantle the structures that had given rise to Japanese militarism.

12. Laverge, "Peace Preservation Law."

including Christians, to become patriotic citizens was the unequal treaties between Japan and Western countries and the so-called Anti-Immigration Act (Johnson-Reed Act) of 1924 enacted by the United States.

Since the sociopolitical context at the time was as described above, prewar Christians had the feeling of loving their country, which coexisted with their Christian faith, and their patriotic spirit developed into anti-Western sentiment. When the first Protestant church was organized by an American missionary, James Hamilton Ballagh (1832–1920), who was sent from the Reformed Church in America (Dutch), with eleven Japanese believers in 1872, the church installed Rev. Ballagh not as a senior pastor but as a provisional pastor, nor did it belong to Rev. Ballagh's homeland denomination of the RCA. This history of the first Protestant church in Japan tells us that even when Christianity was brought by American missionaries, their congregation had to be the church of Japan.

How did Kagawa react to the anti-Japanese immigration act? Kagawa commented on his travels in America for a lecture tour as follows.

> The trip to the US was unpleasant. The US gave me uncomfortable feelings, who am like a man of *ai minzoku shugi sha* [愛民族主義者, an affectionate nationalism]. . . . I cannot understand but I was shocked at America's unreasonably incomprehensive nature. However, it is appreciable that American missionaries in Japan have made every effort, more than the Japanese, to protest the American anti-Japanese issue. The core members, Axling [William Axling] and Gulick [Sidney L. Gulick], . . . have been protesting furiously. . . . We should never forget their work.[13]

Though Kagawa criticized the anti-Japanese sentiment of the US but expressed gratitude to missionaries protesting anti-Japanese immigration laws in their mission to Japan, it is clear that he was not just an anti-American, ultranationalistic Japanese Christian.

KAGAWA'S NATURE OF LOVING THE COUNTRY COEXISTS WITH HELPING THE SOCIALLY POOR

How did Kagawa receive Japanese Christians' sentiment of loving the country? If we could acknowledge that Kagawa was like the other prewar Christians who had a loving sentiment for their country, we could reasonably postulate that he was a patriotic Christian. And then, we could conclude

---

13. Kagawa, *Complete Set*, 24:43.

that Kagawa's commitment to sacrificial love for the socially poor coexisted with his patriotic nature.

How did Kagawa face the state's authority? I believe that Kagawa's attitude toward the state was shaped by Rom 13:1, which demands:

> Let every person be subject to the governing authority, for there is no authority except God, and those authorities that exist have been instituted by God. (NRSV)

If a state authority governs based on justice, by protecting the human rights of the people, Kagawa might have unreservedly accepted this message of the Romans. The question is whether Kagawa kept this message even when the Japanese military invaded Asian countries during the so-called Fifteen-Year War (1931–45).

If Kagawa protested the state when the Japanese military invaded Asian countries during the war, we could justify the above assumption that "Kagawa's commitment to sacrificial love for the socially poor coexisted with his patriotic nature." However, if Kagawa did not protest the state, or if his confession of war responsibility was unsatisfactory, or if war victims could not accept his apology for the atrocity the Japanese military committed on Asian people, we could not defend the above assumption.

The Conflict between Asia and the West

As Protestant Japanese Christians converted to Christianity during the period when Western countries were colonizing Asian countries, we should recognize the conflict between the West and Asia. Maruyama Masao (1914–96), a Japanese political scientist, commented:

> Oriental countries were unaware of themselves within international society but were drawn into "it" coercively—by armed power or threats of armed force. So, unsophisticated national sentiments in the Oriental countries arose at first in reaction to the pressures of European forces from outside.[14]

Maruyama continued to state, based on Sanai Hashimoto's thought:

> Instruments and technology will be introduced from the West, but benevolence, loyalty, and filial piety should remain in Japan.[15]

---

14. Maruyama, *Japanese Nationalism*, 10.
15. Maruyama, *Japanese Nationalism*, 12.

INTRODUCTION

And Maruyama claimed:

> Japan had no choice but to choose one path, i.e., Japan should limit the adoption of European civilization to so-called "material civilization" such as industry, technology, and military, and prevent the infiltration of ideological and political principles such as Christianity, individualism, and liberal democracy to a minimum.... As is well known, Japan succeeded in a revolution by the Meiji Restoration and established *the first centralized nation-state in the East*. It has grown to become a comparable imperialist state.[16]

Does Maruyama's account of the political context of the conflicted relationship with Western countries explain how Kagawa positioned the Japanese in the Asia countries that had been exploited by the Western powers during the Fifteen-Year War? Kagawa is seen as having aligned with Japanese government policy during the war. See the chart below.

Chart 1.1: Kagawa's rhetoric for Japan's invasion of Asian countries		
(West dominates Asia; Japan is the only country that stands against the West.)		
Exploiting nations		**Exploited nations**
(A) Western countries: US, UK, France, Netherlands, etc.		(B) Asian countries, including Japan, which was the only country that could fight against the West.

We will discuss this issue in a later chapter. However, loyalty came too late for Kagawa and Japanese Christians, as the state authorities did not trust Kagawa.

Like the first-generation Christians, second-generation Christians like Kagawa and all prewar Christians were people whose existence was denied to the nation. During the war, in 1943, a document of the Special Higher Police (SHP) exposed the government's anti-Christianity policy. It reported:

> The Bible teaches Christianity to be rebellious to the state and the national polity. Without denying the Bible, it is hard to eradicate Christianity in Japan. Thus, the time is ripe for destroying Christianity in times of war.[17]

---

16. Maruyama, *Japanese Nationalism*, 12; emphasis added.
17. Institute for the Study of Humans and Society, *Movement of Christianity*, 3:52.

KAGAWA'S WAR RESPONSIBILITY AFTER THE WAR

To show that Japanese Christians were not traitors to their country, Christians confirmed their history of proving themselves to be patriots. However, the government enacted the Peace Preservation Law in 1925, revised it in 1928, and finally in 1941, cracked down on people and groups that violated the national polity, most severely. The state established the United Church of Christ in Japan (UCCJ) in 1941 with the aim of cracking down not only on anti-national policy thinkers but also on religion.

In such a context, Kagawa, based on his biblical interpretation and theology, did not take a critical stance toward the state but acted cooperatively. The purpose of this book is to scrutinize how Kagawa confessed his responsibility for the war afterword, based on his words and deeds that had gone along with the government.

Romans 9 and 13: Relation to the State

How did Kagawa relate to the state authorities based on his theological understanding of the Pauline Letter to Romans? Was Kagawa against the state during the war or for the state? If he was for the state, was Kagawa forced by the military government, or did he cooperate voluntarily with propaganda? Kagawa-related materials show that he worked for the state by delivering critical radio messages against Western countries and by visiting China as a member of pacification units. He did work to send Christians to Manchuria to carve out new farmland in the last stage of the Pacific War; we cannot judge Kagawa as an ultranationalistic Christian.

Kagawa believed that a Japanese Christian should be a real patriot, just like Paul, who loved the people of Israel so much that he would even be cursed and cut off from Christ for their sake (Rom 9:3). After the war, since Kagawa referred to Rom 9:3 in justifying his deeds during the war, we should understand his interpretation of the Pauline letter correctly.

By contrast, Yanaihara Tadao (1893–1961), a contemporary of Kagawa and a well-known Japanese Christian leader due to his critical protest of Japanese military for the Marco Polo Bridge incident in 1937, commented:

> When we obey political power while abhorring evil and clinging to good according to our faith, for the first time our obedience becomes not hypocritical but rather free and conscientious. We are called to be prophets who condemn the corruption of the

state, and, at the same time, we are always to be in conscientious submission to the politics of the state. Because we know that the state's political power comes from God and because we put great importance on this point, we as prophets do not keep silent when power is abused.[18]

Yanaihara's above statement represents his faith attitude as a prophetic interpretation of Paul's Letter to Romans by protesting that the Japanese military committed atrocity in invading the Chinese domain in the 1930s. How did the Japanese military government then recognize both Kagawa and Yanaihara? Did the government judge Kagawa as a trustworthy Christian to the state, as Kagawa interpreted Romans that a Christian should not be rebellious against the state? How did the SHP judge Kagawa's radio message, titled "Destruction of America," which aired on September 7, 1944. The SHP reported:

> It is difficult to admit that Kagawa's criticism of the United States was necessarily based on a desire to complete the war or animosity toward the destruction of the United States and Britain. Rather, Kagawa is concerned that a finger-pointing attack on the enemy against Japan, the United States, which is a Christian nation, will turn into an attack on Japanese Christianity among the Japanese people in general; and from the standpoint of exclusively defending Japanese Christianity, he is acting against the United States in the hope of having a domestic effect.[19]

The SHP also judged Yanaihara as rebellious to the state authorities after Yanaihara finished lecturing at Sendai and Nagoya on November 11, 1941. The SHP recorded the content of his speech as follows:

> Yanaihara's idea is that, based on his utopian and self-righteous view of peace, he is now disseminating theories that slander and obliterate the purpose of our holy war. Thus, we should take extra strict precautions against non-churchless movements.[20]

So, the state authorities regarded both Kagawa and Yanaihara as traitors to the state.

---

18. Miyata, *Authority and Obedience*, 133.
19. Institute for the Study of Humans and Society, *Movement of Christianity*, 3:217–18.
20. Institute for the Study of Humans and Society, *Movement of Christianity*, 2:120–21.

Repentance of War Responsibility to Asian People

Before discussing the repentance of war responsibility to Asian people, I need to introduce the confession of war responsibility of the UCCJ, as the confession specifically asks for the forgiveness of the people of nations, particularly in Asia.

The UCCJ issued the statement "Confession on the Responsibility during WWII" in 1967, including the following:

> Indeed, even as our country committed sin, so we too, as a church, fell into the same sin. We neglected to perform our mission as a "watchman." Now, with deep pain in our hearts, we confess our sins and ask the Lord for forgiveness. We also seek the forgiveness of the people of all nations, *particularly in Asia*, and of the churches therein and our brothers and sisters in Christ throughout the world, as well as the forgiveness of the people in our own country.[21]

The Japanese Christian Delegation to the Chinese Church in 1957

Matsutani Yosuke stated:

> A visit to China by the Japanese Christian Mission to China, consisting of fifteen representatives from various Christian circles in Japan, has been realized.[22]

Why was Kagawa not selected as one of those delegates to China? I believe that Kagawa might have been convinced that visiting China in 1957 was not good timing for him because of the two reasons below. First, Kagawa, in October 1944, was convinced that "the sense of redemptive love was born in China. The day when a large number of those who bear the disadvantages of the weak and poor emerge, China will realize that it has been forever restored."[23] This means that through the redemptive love of Jesus, China would realize that everlasting restoration could be achieved. If China rejected following the redemptive message of Jesus, Kagawa could not give any alternative message to the Chinese people, including asking

---

21. UCCJ, "Confession on the Responsibility," para. 7; emphasis added.
22. Matsutani, "Crossing the Bamboo Curtain," 249.
23. Kagawa, *Complete Set*, 13:27.

for forgiveness from them, and Kagawa, during a lecture tour in the US in 1950, stated:

> The communist attack on me was serious. They claimed I was the tool of the capitalists, trying to pacify workers and peasants so they would not organize properly and revolt. Many people listened to them and began to believe what they said. So, I fought back. In the presence of truth, persecution, and oppression are powerless, I attacked the false philosophy of the Russian communists and their dependence on violence.[24]

Based on these two reasons, Kagawa might have remained uninvolved in visiting China in 1957.

Finally, I will discuss how Kagawa's goal of serving the socially vulnerable should be evaluated based on Japan's political and social context and the world, especially the relationship between the emperor and the people.

The Tension between the Emperor and Christians

After Protestant foreign missionaries introduced Christianity during the Meiji Restoration in the middle of the nineteenth century, respecting the emperor and the imperial house was important for Japanese Christians because the emperor was the state's sovereign.

The Constitution of the Empire of Japan, the so-called Meiji Constitution, which was established in 1889, specified that "the Empire of Japan shall be reigned over and governed by a line of Emperors unbroken for ages eternal" (art. 1); "the Emperor is sacred and inviolable" (art. 3), and "the Emperor has the supreme command of the Army and Navy" (art. 11).[25]

---

24. Bradshaw, *Unconquerable Kagawa*, 116.
25. National Diet Library, "Constitution of the Empire."

Table 1.2 Chronology during the wars

(Z)

Criticized Western states for their colonization of Asian states

1937 Second Sino-Japanese War
Aug. 1940: Kagawa is detained at Sugamu Prison by Shibuya SHP due to anti-war acts (P1).
1941: Riverside Japanese American Christian conference in the US
Jan. 1943: Kagawa devotes to writing *Cosmic Purpose*.
Mar. 1943: Kagawa devotes to writing *Cosmic Purpose*.
May 1943: Kagawa is detained at Kobe Aioibashi Police Station for anti-war and socialist thoughts (P2).
Nov. 3, 1943: Kagawa is interrogated at Tokyo Military Police Headquarters for anti-war acts (P3).
Nov. 6, 1943: Greater East Asia Declaration is adopted.
Mar. 1944: Kagawa devotes to writing *Cosmic Purpose*.
Aug. 1944: Kagawa sends a radio message entitled "Prophecy of America's Demise" through NHK (Japan Broadcasting Corporation).

(X)

Help the weak

Patriotism

Venerate emperor

(E)

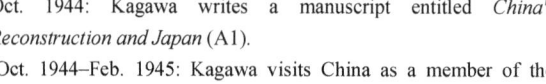
Turning Point: Redemptive Love with Brotherhood Economics

Oct. 1944: Kagawa writes a manuscript entitled *China's Reconstruction and Japan* (A1).
Oct. 1944–Feb. 1945: Kagawa visits China as a member of the religious envoy (A2).
July 1945: Kagawa is detained at SHP headquarters in Kudanshita, Tokyo, for nine days. He makes war repentance of humankind's sin of war to God (P4).
Aug. 15, 1945: IEEW (E1).
Aug. 22, 1945: Kagawa is evacuated to Mamada Tochigi Prefecture, as there is a rumor of Kagawa's assassination because the US planned to install a political leader after the war.
Aug. 30, 1945: Kagawa sends an open letter to General MacArthur.
Aug. 1946: Kagawa confesses war repentance at Sapporo Hokkaido. He criticizes Japan for not trusting God but the gods of myth and idolatry (C).
1950: Lecture tour of US; American people accept Kagawa.
1955: Kagawa sends an open letter to Syngman Rhee, the president of Korea, who accepts Kagawa's statement of war responsibility.

(Y)

Repent of human evils, including of Japan to God

INTRODUCTION

Remarks:

1. P1–4 represent Kagawa having been detained by the SHP four times during the 1940s.
2. E1 represents Kagawa's reverence to the emperor and imperial house.
3. A1–2 represent Kagawa's message that exhorted the recovery of China through brotherhood economics in the Asian world, based on the Declaration of Great East Asia.
4. C represents Kagawa's exorting repentance to God for Japan's having committed atrocities in Asia.

The issue of Kagawa's responsibility for the war will be discussed in detail in the chapter on war responsibility and the conclusion of the final chapter. In response to the central issue of this book, the confession of Kagawa's war responsibility, I explain that Kagawa was consistent throughout his life from the time he became a Christian.

God gave Kagawa the gift of serving the socially vulnerable, and Kagawa contributed to the work of helping the weak in society, in the nation and the world. At the same time, Kagawa was a Christian who preached the gospel of Christ with patriotism toward Japan and reverence for the emperor and the imperial family. In other words, I argue that Kagawa's work of helping the weak, patriotism, and reverence for the emperor and the imperial family coexisted with Kagawa's faith.

Finally, regarding his responsibility for the war, Kagawa sharply criticized the West for militarily invading, exploiting, and colonizing Asian countries. From 1937, even when Japan militarily invaded China, to the end of the Pacific War in late 1944, Kagawa remained critical of the West.

Kagawa had been working on the eradication of social evils in society since he was young, and from 1943 to early 1944 he completed a dissertation on cosmic purpose. In his essay, Kagawa asserted that the evils of humanity in society and nation can be overcome through the atonement of the cross of Christ. For this reason, not only the West but also Japan and Kagawa himself must repent of their sins to God.

It was in July 1945, one month before Japan lost the Pacific War, that Kagawa was detained for nine days at the SHP headquarters in Kudanshita, Tokyo, where Kagawa was enlightened to notice unforgiven sins human sins of war, not only of the West but also of Japan.

Japan invaded and controlled the following Asian countries and territories during the Fifteen War:

- Taiwan comes under Japanese rule in 1895.
- Southern Sakhalin is annexed in 1904.
- Korea is annexed in 1910.
- Manchuria is established in 1932.
- Southern French Indochina comes under Japan's control in 1940.
- Singapore comes under Japan's control in 1942.
- Burma comes under Japan's control in 1932.
- Netherlands' East Indies Dutch (Indonesia) comes under Japan's control in 1942.
- Manila (Philippines) comes under Japan's control in 1942.

2

Japan against Christianity

INTRODUCTION

Understanding the problem with Japan's anti-Christianity has to do with how Japan faced the colonial policies of Western Christian nations against Asian countries. It is clear from the chronology that Japan's national governing authorities viewed Japanese Christians, who were deeply connected to Western Christianity, as destructive beings who would betray Japan. See the chronological table below.

Table 2.1: Chronology of anti-Christianity in Japan	
1549	F. Xavier, a Catholic priest of the Jesuits, introduces Christianity to Japan.
1587	Toyotomi Hideyoshi issues the edict expelling Catholics from Japan.
1612	Tokugawa Bakufu issues the edict expelling Catholics from Japan.
1635	Tokugawa Bakufu issues the edict closing Japan.
1638	Tokugawa Bakufu orders temple registration for all Japanese.
1858	Treaty of Amity and Commerce between the United States and the Empire of Japan
1868	*Shinbutsu Bunri Rei*: Shinto and Buddhism Separation Order for establishing Shintoism as a state religion
1868	FPN
1873	Meiji government withdraws its prohibition of Christianity. After that, the Meiji government tacitly recognizes Christianity.

1881	Buddhist monk Shimoji Mokurai's petition, that worshipping an emperor is a subject duty and not a religious one, is accepted later by the Meiji government.
1889	Constitution of the Empire of Japan (Meiji government): article 28, freedom of religion
1899	Meiji government officially recognizes Christian missions.
1904–5	Russo-Japanese War
1912	Sankyo Godo (three religions: Shinto, Buddhism, and Christianity) denomination is arranged by the Meiji government.
1914–18	WWI: Japan joins the Allied Forces.

Francisco de Xavier, a Catholic priest of the Society of the Jesuits, introduced Christianity to Japan in 1549, while Protestantism was introduced before the Meiji Restoration in the mid-nineteenth century thanks to the Treaty of Amity and Commerce between the United States and the Empire of Japan in 1858. The character of Japanese spirituality when Protestantism was brought to "Japan" was based on the syncretistic nature of Buddhism, Shintoism, and Confucianism. Though the Tokugawa shogunate reinforced the concept of Confucianism, precisely neo-Confucianism, for administering the regime, the Meiji government revived Shinto to justify Japanese modernization, which expanded into Japanese imperialism in the early twentieth century.

At this time, the first generation of Protestant Christians tried to embed their faith in the spiritual dominance of the state authorities. Christianity had been proscribed as harmful by the Tokugawa shogunate, which judged it as a religion rebellious against the state. In 1873, five years after the establishment of the Meiji era, the government had to withdraw its prohibition of Christianity due to the demands of Western countries. The strong suspicion of the Tokugawa and the Meiji government that Christianity was a dangerous form of rebellion against the state lasted until World War II.

ANTI-CHRISTIANITY: TOYOTOMI AND TOKUGAWA GOVERNMENTS

How did the Japanese spiritual climate become anti-Christian? To examine Japan's anti-Christian climate, we must see that the Toyotomi government (豊臣政権, 1585–1603) enacted an anti-Christianity edict based on Western military aggression and colonial policy in Asia. Moreover, the policies of the Toyotomi government were inherited by the Tokugawa shogunate (徳川幕府, 1603–1868) and the Meiji government (明治政府, 1868–1912). See the Edicts of Toyotomi Hideyoshi, 1587, below.

Table 2.2: The edicts of Toyotomi Hideyoshi (excerpt from *Expulsion of Missionaries*, 1587)[1]	
1	Japan is the country of gods but has been receiving false teachings from Christian countries. This cannot be tolerated any further.
2	The [missionaries] approach people in provinces and districts to make them their followers and let them destroy shrines and temples. This is an unheard-of outrage. When a vassal receives a province, a district, a village, or another form of a fief, he must consider it as property entrusted to him on a temporary basis. He must follow the laws of this country and abide by their intent. However, some vassals illegally [commended part of their fiefs to the church]. This is a culpable offense.
3	The padres, by their special knowledge [in the sciences and medicine], feel that they can entice people to become their believers. In doing so they commit the illegal act of destroying the teaching of Buddha prevailing in Japan. These padres cannot be permitted to remain in Japan. They must prepare to leave the country within twenty days of the issuance of this notice.
4	The black [Portuguese and Spanish] ships come to Japan to engage in trade. Thus, the matter is a separate one. They can continue to engage in trade.

The above proclamation expressed how the Toyotomi government ruled Japan. In other words, Toyotomi ruled Japan based on a Japanese spiritual climate of Buddhism, indigenous Shintoism, and Confucianism. It denied Catholicism as a Western religion, since Christianity would destroy the Japanese religious foundation and would shake the country.

In 1612, the Tokugawa government issued a stricter edict by which Tokugawa expelled Catholics from Japan, and it finally issued the edict of 1635 below ordering the closing of Japan. In 1638, it established the *danka* (檀家, temple parishioner) system, in which the *bakufu* (幕府, shogunate) ordered that certificates of temple registration be issued for every Japanese in 1638.[2] It is known throughout the world that the Tokugawa shogunate's severe oppression of Catholics resulted in many victims and martyrs in the Shimabara Rebellion (1637–38). Furthermore, the *danka* system is an anti-Christian system that took advantage of the family system that spans all

1. Asia for Educators, "Edicts of Toyotomi Hideyoshi," 2.
2. Tamamuro, "Local Society and Temple-Parishioner Relationship," 262.

of Japan, and to this day Christians have been subject to harsh scrutiny in local communities. See the proclamation closing Japan by the Tokugawa government below.

	Table 2.3: The edict of 1635 ordering the closing of Japan, addressed to the joint *bugyō* (magistrate) of Nagasaki[3]
1	Japanese ships are strictly forbidden to leave for foreign countries.
2	No Japanese is permitted to go abroad. If there is anyone who attempts to do so secretly, he must be executed. The ship so involved must be impounded and its owner arrested, and the matter must be reported to the higher authority.
3	If any Japanese returns from overseas after residing there, he must be put to death.
4	If there is any place where the teachings of padres (Christianity) are practiced, the two of you must order a thorough investigation.

The Tokugawa shogunate continued to trade with foreign countries (only with the Netherlands and China) as it implemented the edict mentioned above, which thoroughly rejected the conversion of the people to foreign ideologies and religions, especially to Christianity. It also implemented a policy of thoroughly excluding Christians from families and local communities through the temple parish system.

We will examine whether the Meiji government inherited the national governance of Toyotomi and Tokugawa for expelling Christians. In 1868, the emperor issued the FPN in five articles, in which article 4 specified the ban on Christianity. However, due to the Western countries' criticism of the issue of freedom of religion, in 1873, the Meiji government had no alternative but to withdraw its prohibition of Christianity; and in 1889, the Constitution of the Empire of Japan, the so-called Meiji Constitution, was established, in which article 28, freedom of religion, was specified.

These three political decisions by the emperor and the Meiji government brought about decisive trials for Japanese Christians and the church during the war. At the same time, Christians had been forced to cooperate with the Showa government's military actions of invading Asia states. Thus, Japanese Christians had formed a core of questions about how both Christians and the church faced the state's authorities during the war.

---

3. Asia for Educators, "Edicts of Tokugawa Shogunate," 1.

ATTACK ON CHRISTIANITY BY BUDDHISM: CLAIM THAT SHINTO IS NOT A RELIGION

On March 27, 1868, the Meiji government attacked Buddhism to break up the traditional syncretism of Shinto and Buddhism with the edict of the *Daijokan* (太政官, the Grand Council of State, the Cabinet). The anti-Buddhist movement took place across the country based on the government's initiative. Marra states that this period's social context is as follows:

> Modernization started with a shock for Japanese Buddhism. After more than a millennium of religious dominance and political influence, the newly established Meiji government chose to favor Shinto, as Japan's indigenous religion was better suited to support the reinstallation of imperial rule and to instill a mood of national enthusiasm, which would help to win greater acceptance for both, the new government and the severities of rapid industrialization and militarization which were to come.[4]

Hand Marin Kramer quoted the conventional statement of Shimaji Mokurai (島地黙雷, 1838–1911), a priest of the Jodo Shinshu Hongwanji-ha (浄土真宗本願寺派, true pure land Hongannji) sect of Buddhism as follows.

> I have not penetrated this thing called Shinto completely yet, but what I can say for sure is that it [Shinto] is not a so-called sectarian teaching [religion]. If one now nonetheless attempts to make it into a sectarian teaching, the harm for Japan and the shame from the outside will be enormous. In olden times, when Buddhism had not entered Japan, only a civic teaching [*jikyo*, 治教] existed in our country. There is thus no obstacle to the coexistence of sectarian teaching and civic teaching, but how could one person possibly have two sectarian teachings at the same time?[5]

Shimaji called religion doctrine, used the word "teaching" (*jikyo*, 治教) to describe its function, and saw its characteristic as being universal. Based on this view, Shimaji argued that Buddhism, typified by Jodo Shinshu, is a religion that leads to a higher level of civilization and also treats Shinto and the imperial way as non-religions. Shinto is not a "doctrine" and cannot compete with the "doctrine" of Christianity. Preaching reverence of God to the people brings out the superiority of Christianity.

4. Marra, "Anti-Buddhism Movement," 173.
5. Kramer, "How 'Religion' Came," 91.

How did Shimaji's assertion that Shinto was not a religion develop, based on the sociopolitical context when Japan struggled to survive with Western countries?

The Meiji Government's Introduction of Freedom of Religion

Hayasida Kojun (林田康順), a faculty member of the Buddhist University of Taisho University, states how the government and legal scholars positioned Shinto's nature based on Shimaji's recognition that Shinto is not religious.

> The imperial Japanese government and legal scholars of the time set aside the fact that State Shinto was a religion, that it was a state ritual system, not a religion defined by law, but was expected to be recognized as a public institution and to be revered by the people, but that this did not violate the principle of religious freedom.[6]

Hayashida argues that the imperial Japanese government did not consider it a violation of freedom of religion to instill a spirit of worship of the emperor as a duty for subjects. In discussing the viewpoint of war responsibility, the postwar Japanese Christians, including myself, recognize that this does not justify the imperial Japanese government's order of emperor worship to Japanese subjects and also to citizens of Korea, Taiwan, Manchuria, etc., where Japanese military authorities ruled during the wars.

Hayashida claims:

> Japan rushed to establish an emperor-centered state to oppose the Western powers by adopting a policy that made the state's economy grow and encouraged the reinforcement of military forces.[7]

Based on Hayashida's statement, we should examine how the Meiji government coped with opposing Western regimes within the international political context.

---

6. Hayashida, "Acquisition and Acceptance," 194.
7. Hayashida, "Acquisition and Acceptance," 187.

THE FIVE PUBLIC NOTICES

The Five Public Notices: Declared by the Emperor in March 1868

The emperor declared the Five Public Notices (FPN) below on March 15, 1868, and they were posted to the ordinary people as follows.

	Table 2.4: The Five Public Notices[8]
1.1	As a person, you should follow the five principles of morality.
1.2	It would be best if you pitied those who are widowed, lonely, or ill.
1.3	It is unacceptable to commit evil deeds such as killing people, burning down houses, and stealing.
2	There have been many consultations regarding various matters, but they have been treated as if they were just a lie and have been neglected. In other cases, people have been told they will be forced to leave towns and villages, which is strictly prohibited. If you find such a situation, please report it to the relevant government office immediately. We will give a reward for your report.
3.1	The Christian sect is strictly prohibited.
3.3	Heretical sects are strictly prohibited.

The FPN implies that to counter the military power of Western countries due to the Meiji Restoration, the Meiji government promoted modernization, but it also sought religious aspects in the spiritual culture of Japan and declared that it would continue to reject Christianity from the Toyotomi and Tokugawa governments. However, the West seeks religious freedom, and Buddhism, especially Shingon Buddhism, which has the emperor at its apex, would be trusted by the Meiji government and continue to exist in the government; it promised to pay respect to Shinto, with the emperor at its apex, as a duty of the people. Unfortunately, the UCCJ leaders also promised to worship the emperor, not as a religion but as a duty of the people to pay respect to the state power.

How did the Meiji government deliver the content of the FPN to the people? The government used the *kosatsu* (高札, official bulletin board) which had been used during the Tokugawa period for things such as the Bateren Edict (expelling the Catholics from Japan), thanks to the high literacy rate.

---

8. National Graduate Institute for Policy Studies and Institute for Advanced Studies on Asia, "Five Public Notices."

Photo 2.1: The Public Notices for the common people; five notices were written on each wooden board (see the right side, banning Christianity).

We recognize that the Meiji government proclaimed that the Japanese state authorities regarded Christianity as a religion against the state by inheriting the state polity from the Toyotomi and Tokugawa governments. Thus, the Meiji government sent *interfaith spies* to Nagasaki, Osaka, Tokyo, Yokohama, and Hakodate to infiltrate missionaries and gather inside information. It seems that there were quite a few Jodo Shinshu (浄土真宗, the true pure land sect of Buddhism) monks among them. Still, it was also desirable for Hongan-ji (本願寺) to stop the spread of Christianity as soon as possible, and

> Hongan-ji probably demonstrated to the Meiji government the significance of their existence by cooperating with dangerous work. It seems that there was a purpose to creating it.[9]

Foreign settlements in Nagasaki, Osaka, Tokyo, Yokohama, and Hakodate, were permitted freedom of religion due to the Treaty of Amity and Commerce between the United States and the Empire of Japan in 1858, later with France and other Western countries.

9. Obinata, "Early Meiji Government and Christianity," 15.

The FPN and the Charter Oath (CO) below are closely related as comparative studies, as the former represents the Tokugawa period's feudal system, while the CO has been called a model of democracy. From a missiological perspective, I recognize the tremendous difference between them because the anti-Christianity article was completely deleted from the FPN in the CO.

THE MEIJI GOVERNMENT'S LEGAL MEASURES TO ESTABLISH THE EMPEROR SYSTEM: THE CHARTER OATH

	Table 2.5: The Charter Oath[10]
1	Deliberative Assemblies shall be widely established, and all matters shall be decided by public discussion.
2	All people, high and low, shall unite their minds to conduct the affairs of the state.
3	All people, civil and military classes as well as commoners, shall be encouraged to achieve their respective wishes so as not to keep them frustrated.
4	Old, corrupt customs shall be abolished, and everything shall be based on the just way of nature.
5	Knowledge shall be sought throughout the world so as to strengthen the foundations of imperial rule.
Emperor's words	In order to implement reforms unprecedented in our country, I, ahead of the people, pray to gods of heaven and earth and decree these national principles in order to establish the way of security for all. So, my people, based on this intention of mine, make efforts cooperatively among yourselves.

If I conclude that the reason the Meiji government deleted the anti-Christianity article was due to the international political background, I should review the current postwar Japanese government's historical understanding of this issue. The Ministry of Education, Culture, Sports, Science and Technology of the Japanese government presents the religious administration in the early Meiji period as follows:

---

10. National Graduate Institute for Policy Studies and Institute for Advanced Studies on Asia, "Charter of Oath."

> The various treaties that had been concluded with foreign countries since the Ansei era (1855–1860) were unequal, and the government and people demanded that they desired these treaties be changed to equal treaties. By the way, the major obstacles to this treaty revision were the treatment of Christianity and the special treatment of shrines. Therefore, in May 1899, the government officially recognized the mission of Christianity.[11]

It can be seen that the current Japanese government's view on the above issue is to prioritize a historical perspective that places greater emphasis on international relations with Western countries when it comes to handling Christianity, rather than on Shimaji's insisting that Shinto is not a religion. This means that the Meiji government had to permit Christianity, in order for Japan to obtain international equal status with Western powers. It is a historical irony that the UCCJ followed the imperial Japanese government's order to worship the emperor, if emperor worship was not a religion, as Shimaji claimed.

The Japanese Christians' response to state authority in the Sankyo Godo (三教合同, three religions: Shinto, Buddhism, and Christianity) denomination is also needed to review their attitude toward the government.

The Meiji Government's Emperor-Centered Religious Policy in the Sociopolitical World Context

Japan won the Russo-Japanese War (1904–5) and participated as an Allied power in World War I (1914–18), achieving victory and making it possible to lay the foundations for imperialism. It can be judged that the 1910 Treaty of the Annexation of Korea, which placed Korea under Japanese control, marked a significant step forward in Japan's subsequent military expansion strategy in Asia.

In the above political context, how did Japanese Christians respond to the Meiji government's emperor-centered religious policies? In 1912, the Sankyo Godo denomination was arranged by the Meiji government. Doi Akio (1928–2008), in his book *The History of Japanese Protestant Christianity*, commented:

> The ideology of the imperial system is one in which the emperor does not exercise force over the people and demand their obedience

---

11. Ministry of Education, "Religious Administration in Early Meiji."

but instead praises the emperor's blessings to the people, and the people reciprocate with their gratitude.

The national consciousness of the Meiji people, who believed that Japan had achieved independence many times in Asia and had become a wealthy and powerful nation, was believed to have come about as the Meiji emperor shared the hardships with the people and devoted himself to the development of the nation's fortunes. It became a strong foundation supporting the imperial national polity, connected to the emperor's consciousness of praising its magnificent and boundless blessings.

The Sankyo Godo was an application of the ideology of the imperial system to the religious world. Thus, this was shown as an expression of the blessings of the imperial system to the religious leaders, including Christianity, and they accepted it as a chance to praise the imperial fortune to repay his blessing. This was particularly felt by Christians, who had previously been treated poorly and discriminated against both socially and institutionally.[12]

Doi commented that,

> although the majority of Christians agreed to the Sankyo Godo, some Christians such as Kashiwagi Gien (柏木義円), Uchimura Kanzo (内村鑑三), Takagi Mizutaro (高木壬太郎), and Akashi Shigetaro (赤司繁太郎) expressed their opposition to the Sankyo Godo.[13]

As Doi stated, the majority of Christians agreed to the Sankyo Godo, but a few of the above Christians rejected joining the government-arranged project. In particular, Kashiwagi claimed that recognizing the union of three religions as the government's use of religion meant that

> religions colluding with the government would inevitably become corrupted and degraded. Religions should engage in missionary work based on their truth and should not live under the government's protection.[14]

The religious stance that arose in the early Meiji period, in which a small number of Japanese Christians confronted the government, continued into the wartime period when the government severely suppressed Christians. Considering that Kagawa had a religious attitude that defended

---

12. Doi, *Japanese Protestant Christianity*, 132–35.
13. Doi, *Japanese Protestant Christianity*, 136.
14. Doi, *Japanese Protestant Christianity*, 136.

state power while Yanaihara, who was a disciple of Uchimura, had a prophetic calling and an attitude that confronted the military government, the religious attitudes of both men conflicted. This difference relates to postwar confessions of war responsibility, but this important issue will be discussed in a later chapter.

CONCLUSION: JAPAN AGAINST CHRISTIANITY

Through this chapter, we learned that in Japan's history, up to the Toyotomi, Tokugawa, Meiji, and Showa periods, the government of each time saw Christianity as opposed to the spiritual climate of the nation. Thus, it was natural that Japanese Christians and churches had been cautious of becoming subservient to Western states and Christianity.

Japan's Christian leaders were recognized as traitors by the government at the time, but they contributed to Japan with patriotism and reverence for the emperor. Kagawa, like other Christian leaders, had a sense of patriotism and reverence for the emperor, but his uniqueness was in serving the socially unprivileged based on Christian brotherhood economics with redemptive love, and in the work of mass evangelism, especially delivering the message to peripheral areas, such as places where farmers, fishermen, and foresters had never heard the gospel.

The following chapters will review how Kagawa faced government authorities during the war period.

Kagawa Protested against the Anti-Christian Spiritual Climate in Japan

> The Kobe Prefecture brought Kagawa to the military police office for interrogation as he denounced our State Shintoism [Shrine Shinto]. As the authority recognized that Kagawa had not intended to denounce Shinto and he exhibited remorse for his criticism, the authority of the prosecutor's office released Kagawa after receiving his submissions of written oath in which he pledged to refrain from critical statements in public.[15]

---

15. Yanaihara, *Japanese Spirit*, 23.

Kagawa's testimony—"Kagawa did not intend to denounce Shinto and he exhibited remorse for his criticism"—shows that Kagawa was critical of Shinto during the war.

On October 2 and 3, forty-eight days after the end of the Pacific War (Aug. 15, 1945), Yanaihara presented a speech entitled "A Reflection on the Japanese Spirit," as one of the Christians who had been criticized by the SHP as having been anti-Christian, anti-imperial, anti-nation, and nationalist during the war.

> If the Japanese people change their traditional arrogant attitude toward Christianity, abandon their prejudices and misunderstandings, stop hating them, become humble, listen to the gospel of Christ, and study the Christian Bible, this will save Japan. This is a path that makes use of the Japanese spirit.[16]

Yanaihara's speech exactly refuted the SHP's above report that demonstrated the Japanese government authorities' intention to drive Christians to the verge of extinction. Thus, we can recognize that both Kagawa and Yanaihara as Christians had been amid calamity during the war because of sociopolitical oppression. Nonetheless, we cannot judge whether an antagonistic attitude to the state authorities and the anti-Christianity holding the Japanese majority population in its sway was a faithfully Christian way or not.

Based on the sociopolitical context we studied previously, we should review how Japanese Christians responded to the government's legal demand for the unification of all Protestant churches.

Lamentation by Yanaihara in 1945 immediately after the war

> The people wept before His Majesty, and they cried together.
> Bow down before the Creator of heaven and earth.
> God, we have sinned, and we have transgressed, and You have not forgiven us . . .
> Defeat in war does not necessarily mean exile.
> We will stop relying on force and financial power,
> Rather, learn faith through suffering.
> So, Jehovah will judge the world on the day of judgment,
> Let us sing with joy of eternal peace and freedom.[17]

---

16. Yanaihara, *Japanese Spirit*, 57.
17. Yanaihara, *Japanese Spirit*, 59–61.

When Kagawa was being interrogated at the SHP headquarters one month before the end of the war, he, like Yanaihara, believed that the sins committed by Japan and other foreign countries were against God's will, and he accepted God's judgment. However, the emperor's attitude of confessing that the emperor would share in the suffering with the people could make it possible for both Kagawa and Yanaihara to feel a shadow of God's judgment. This is indicated by Yanaihara, before he recited the above poem, saying,

> I believe that the Christian faith will not destroy Japan's national polity either practically or ideologically, but on the contrary, it will make it even more beautiful and more secure.[18]

Through the poem, Kagawa and Yanaihara delivered the message of God's judgment, but both concluded with the message of hope in Christ's love to the devastated Japanese people.

Let's take a closer look at the emperor's views on war. The content of the Imperial Edict of the End of the War (hereafter IEEW) represented the justification of the war, as it declared Japan engaged in a war for "assuring Japan's self-preservation and stabilization of East Asia."[19] This means Japan had no alternative but to engage in the war to eradicate the American economic blockage and the Hull Note requirement that demanded withdrawal from the territories Japan had evaded.[20]

Then how did Kagawa interpret the emperor's claim that it was "far from our thought either to infringe on the sovereignty of other nations or to embark on territorial aggrandizement"[21]—despite that the Japanese Empire had invaded Manchuria, Korea, and Taiwan during the war and made offensive operations in South East Asian countries such as Singapore,

---

18. Yanaihara, *Japanese Spirit*, 58.

19. National Archives of Japan, "Imperial Rescript Ending the War."

20. The Hull Note was delivered by US Secretary of State Hull to Ambassadors Nomura Kisaburo and Kurusu Saburo on Nov. 26, 1941 (US time). It listed the items that the US considered necessary to improve US-Japan relations, such as the conclusion of (1) a mutual nonaggression treaty between Japan, the US, Great Britain, the USSR, the Netherlands, the Chongqing Nationalist government, the Netherlands, and Thailand; (2) the complete withdrawal of Japanese troops from "China and all of French Indochina"; (3) a commitment by both Japan and the US not to support any government in China other than the Chongqing Nationalist government; and (4) the conclusion of a trade treaty between Japan and the US based on most-favored-nation treatment (Japan Center for Asian Historical Records, "Hull Note").

21. National Archives of Japan, "Imperial Rescript Ending the War."

the Dutch East Indies, and Malaya in December 1941 for securing natural resources in the name of establishment of the Daitoa Kyōeiken (大東亜共同宣言, Greater East Asia Co-prosperity Sphere).

We notice the emperor's words by which Kagawa was moved as the emperor declared:

> We have resolved to pave the way for a grand peace for all generations to come by enduring the unendurable suffering that is insufferable.[22]

---

22. National Archives of Japan, "Imperial Rescript Ending the War."

3

Kagawa's Evangelical Work, Patriotism, and Repentance

EVANGELICAL WORK

In this chapter, first, I review how Kagawa as an evangelist preached Christianity to Japanese people, especially to the socially underprivileged such as farmers, fishermen, and forestry workers, by confronting a deep-rooted anti-Christian spiritual climate in the local area during the period of the war through the *Kami no Kuni Undo* (Kingdom of God Movement, 1928–34, hereafter KGM), and after the Pacific War through the *Shin Nihon Kensetsu Kristo Undo* (New Japan Construction Christian Movement, 1946–49, hereafter NJCCM).

Though Kagawa was not involved in the *Zenkoku Kyodo Undo* (全国協同運動, National Ecumenical Missionary Movement, 1915–17, hereafter NEMM), due to his studying at the Princeton Theological Seminary, since first-generation Christians led the movement, including Uemura Masahisa, a leader in the Presbyterian Church, I review how the NEMM contributed to the development of Japanese Christianity. Kagawa led evangelical meetings of the KGM while Japan was invading by force of arms neighboring Asian countries, and for the NJCM after Japan surrendered to the Allied forces in 1945.

Second, I review how Japanese local churches accepted newcomers who handed in a decision card from three evangelical meetings to local churches.

Third, I review why Japanese Christians failed to accept newcomers to their local congregations.

Fourth, I review why Japanese Christians failed to protest atrocities done by the Japanese government authorities in Asia, especially in Korea, Taiwan, and China, especially in northern China. To deal with this issue, I will examine what Kagawa stated in these as he visited the US in 1936, Korea in 1938–39, and China in the 1930s and 1944.

Fifth, I review the meaning of Kagawa's repentance while he was detained at the SHP headquarters in July 1945, one month before Japan's surrender.

National Ecumenical Missionary Movement (1915–17)

The NEMM led evangelism by mobilizing Japan's various denominations.

> As the past missionary system was reflected at the 1910 World Missionary Conference, the Edinburgh Missionary Conference decided that various denominations would carry out cooperative evangelism. Then, in 1913, John Raleigh Mott (1865–1955) was dispatched to Japan, and the NEMM was carefully planned.[1]

Three first-generation Japanese Christians, Ibuka Kajinosuke (1854–1940, Presbyterian) as chair of the NEMM and Uemura Masahis (1858–1925, Presbyterian) and Miyakawa Tsuneteru (1857–1936, Congregational) as senior leaders led the NEMM.

As we can see from the chronology below (table 3.1), NEMM acted under circumstances that were greatly influenced by Japan's domestic and global political contexts. In particular, the Meiji government, faced with the threat of communists due to the Russian Revolution of 1917, enacted the Peace Preservation Law in 1925 to crack down on dangerous leftist elements. Furthermore, to counter political and military threats to the Western powers, Japan used its strengthened military power to invade Taiwan, Korea, Manchuria, and northern China, with the policy of *fukoku kyohei* (富国強兵, enriching the country and strengthening its military) as the pillar of its national policy. The imperial edict in 1923, called *Kokumin Seishin Sakko ni Kansuru shosho* (Imperial edict on the promotion of national spirit), "based on the educational system for all the population, aimed to increase the national prosperity and the military strength, and cultivate loyal subjects to the emperor."[2]

---

1. Kurokawa, "Christian Mission in Japan," 61.
2. Ministry of Education, Culture, Sports, Science and Technology, "Imperial Edict."

	Table 3.1: Chronology related to the NEMM
1894–1945	Sino-Japanese War (Taiwan is under Japanese rule)
1904–45	Russo-Japanese War (Korea is annexed to Japan in 1904)
1910	World Missionary Conference, Edinburgh Missionary Conference
1914–18	World War I
1915–17	NEMM
1916	Yoshino publishes the thesis "Mankan wo Shisatsu site" (Visiting Manchuria and Korea), in which he criticizes Japanese colonialism.
1917	Russian Revolution
1919	March 1, the 3.1 Movement (Korea calls for independence from imperial Japan)
1921	Kawasaki Mitsubishi Shipyard Strike. Kagawa is imprisoned in the Tachibana police branch of Kobe Prison.
1923	September, Great Kanto Earthquake
1923	IEPNS
1924	The US issues the anti-Japanese immigration law
1925	Peace Preservation Law (治安維持法)

Then reviewing the result of the NEMM ecumenical activities, Kurokawa commented on the result of the NEMM as follows (table 3.2).[3]

Table 3.2: Results of the NEMM's ecumenical activities		
1. Number of meetings	4,788	
2. Number of attendees	777,000	
3. Number of decision cards	27,000	
	1. Number of Christians	
(A)	82,638	In 1912, three years before NEMM
(B)	123,222	In 1916, during NEMM
(C)	142,346	In 1921, four years after NEMM

3. Kurokawa, "Christian Mission in Japan," 61. For number of churches, see Statistics Japan; *Statistical Yearbook*; for number of baptisms, see Kirisuto Shinbun, *Christianity Yearbook 1960*, 320–21.

Result by percentage	(B)/(A) =	49.1 percent increase
	(C)/(A) =	72.3 percent increase
2. Number of churches		
(A)	1,321	In 1912, three years before NEMM
(B)	1,434	In 1916, during NEMM
(C)	1,538	In 1921, four years after NEMM
Result by percentage	(B)/(A) =	8.6 percent increase
	(C)/(A) =	16.4 percent increase
3. Number of baptisms		
(A)	6,839	In 1912, four years before NEMM
(B)	10,133	In 1916, during NEMM
(C)	10,764	In 1921, four years after NEMM
Result by percentage	(B)/(A) =	47.9 percent increase
	(C)/(A) =	57.4 percent increase
4. Number of church ministers		
(A)	2,190	In 1912, three years before NEMM
(B)	2,439	In 1916, during NEMM
(C)	2,593	In 1919, two years after NEMM
Result by percentage	(B)/(A) =	11.4 percent increase
	(C)/(A) =	18.4 percent increase

Kurokawa admitted that

> the difference between the National Ecumenical Missionary Movement and the Kingdom of God Movement is that while the former met the target of evangelism with the general congregation even in Korea, Taiwan, and China, the latter focuses on the method of evangelism, first, evangelism to the poor, and the second point is liberation from social problems.[4]

However, that the NEMM succeeded in attracting Japanese people to Christianity can be seen by the chart above. But, why could leaders of the NEMM not reach the socially unprivileged of both Japan and the people of Taiwan, Korea, and Manchuria, which were placed under imperial Japan's rule? Leaders might have been aware of the discriminatory treatment of these people by the Japanese imperial government. This is indicated by

4. Kurokawa, "Christian Mission in Japan," 61.

Yoshino Sakuzo having published his essays "Mankan wo Shisatsu site" (Visiting Manchuria and Korea) and "Explaining the True Meaning of Constitutional Government and Discussing the Way to Achieve Its Final Beauty" in 1916, one year before the NEMM was launched. The discriminatory treatment was made public through the national magazine *Chuokoron*. In these essays, Yoshino criticized the colonial policy of the Japanese imperial government.

Though the NEMM brought excellent results for the development of Japanese Christianity, the KGM, in which Kagawa committed to the development of mass evangelical work during the period Japan started heading to the Pacific War in 1941, is significant in examining Japanese Christians, including Kagawa, as to whether their faith was damaged because of the military government's oppression or whether they survived faithfully.

Kingdom of God Movement (KGM, 1928–34)

Before reviewing the results of the KGM, we need to recognize the domestic and international political problems that Japanese Christians faced, which had pushed them into a corner. See the chronological table below (table 3.3).

		Table 3.3: Chronology related to the KGM
	1923	Great Kanto Earthquake (Kagawa goes from Kobe to Tokyo to help victims)
	1924	The US issues the anti-Japanese immigration law.
	1925	Peace Preservation Law
KGM	1928–34	KGM
	1931	Kagawa visits China, where he apologizes for what the military did.
	Sept. 1931	Manchurian incident (Fifteen Years War: 1931–45)
	1932	League of Blood incident and May 15 incident (coup d'état)
	1933	Japan withdraws from the League of Nations.

1936	Kagawa's America lecture tour
July 1937	Second Shino-Japanese War

The government of Japan recognized why the National Spiritual Mobilization Movement was established:

> With the outbreak of the second Sino-Japanese incident [war in 1937], it became necessary to further expand and strengthen educational activities for the people. Therefore, at a cabinet meeting held on August 24, 1937, the government decided on the outline for implementing the National Spiritual Mobilization Movement.[5]

As the Japanese government recognized, the purpose of the National Spiritual Mobilization Movement was to strengthen the people's loyalty to the nation and reverence for the national Shinto spirit, from the "Imperial Edict on the Promotion of National Spirit" due to the outbreak of the Second Sino-Japanese War. For Japanese Christians, including Kagawa, this meant that the Japanese military government transitioned to a military system in which elements dangerous to national policy, especially those with anti-war ideology, were eliminated by law. Kagawa was taken into police custody.

Before discussing the above three objectives, we need to see the results of the KGM, though I do not discuss the theological and missional meaning of the numbers, as my main point is Kagawa's war responsibility. As far as the result of the number of new followers who accepted Christianity is concerned, Kagawa might have succeeded in gaining great results for the KGM. Kuroda Shiro, who accompanied Kagawa in the KGM, recorded:

> The number of meetings was 1,859, the number of attendees was 787,223, and the number of attendees who submitted decision cards was 62,410.[6]

We need to analyze the result of the KGM (1928–34) statistically by considering the sociopolitical context both inside and outside. See the analyzed data below.

Table 3.4: Results of the KGM's ecumenical activities

---

5. Ministry of Education, Culture, Sports, Science and Technology, "National Spiritual Mobilization Movement."

6. Kuroda, *Research on Kagawa Toyohiko*, 192.

	1. Number of Christians		
(A)	161,240	In 1926, two years before KGM	
(B)	193,937	In 1930, during KGM	
(C)	204,588	In 1935, the following year after KGM	
(D)	232,463	In 1939, five years after KGM	
Result by percentage	(B)/(A) =	19.5 percent increase	
	(C)/(A) =	20.1 percent increase	
	(D)/(A) =	39.3 percent increase	

	2. Number of churches		
(A)	1,595	In 1926, two years before KGM	
(B)	1,795	In 1930, during KGM	
(C)	2,066	In 1935, the following year after KGM	
	2,156	In 1937, three years after KGM	
Result by percentage	(B)/(A) =	12.5 percent increase	
	(C)/(A) =	29.5 percent increase	
	(D)/(A) =	35.4 percent increase	

	3. Number of baptisms		
(A)	11,979	In 1926, two years before KGM	
(B)	18,059	In 1930, during KGM	
(C)	10,074	In 1935, the following year after KGM	
	8,409	In 1940, six years after KGM	

Result by percentage	(B)/(A) =	50.8 percent increase
	(C)/(A) =	15.9 percent increase
	(D)/(A) =	28.8 percent increase

4. Number of church ministers

(A)	2,348	In 1926, two years before KGM
(B)	2,512	In 1930, during KGM
(C)	3,001	In 1935, the following year after KGM
(D)	2,965	In 1937, three years after KGM
Result by percentage	(B)/(A) =	7.1 percent increase
	(C)/(A) =	27.8 percent increase
	(CD/(A) =	26.3 percent increase

As the above-analyzed data shows, the number of Christians and churches increased after the KGM finished, while the number of baptized and church ministers decreased after the KGM. I recognize that the decrease could be because of political issues. Thus, what Kurokawa claimed was reasonable. He said:

> In 1931, the Manchurian incident broke out, and in 1932, both the League of Blood incident and the May 15 incident [both nationalist movements] occurred domestically, Japan rapidly entered a wartime regime, and the Kingdom of God Movement came to a rapid end. I had no choice but to do it.[7]

After the war, many scholars completely rejected Kagawa, saying that he had fallen and turned into a nationalist with State Shinto at its peak. However, in response to Kagawa's statement defending national policy during the government's wartime regime, I do not agree with the arguments

---

7. Kurokawa, "Christian Mission in Japan," 62.

of scholars who criticize Kagawa based on how Japan's state power viewed him during the war. The SHP recorded:

> As the authority recognized that Kagawa did not intend to denounce Shinto and he exhibited remorse for his criticism, the authority of the prosecutor's office released Kagawa after receiving his submissions of written oath in which he pledged to refrain from critical statements in public.[8]

The SHP recognized that "Kagawa did not intend to denounce Shinto." Thus, this statement testifies that Kagawa rejected the State Shinto.

Kagawa committed to the evangelical work of the KGM existentially by loving the Japanese people who might have been hearing the Christian message for the first time in their lives at the meetings in local areas where marginalized groups such as farmers, fishermen, foresters, and workers lived. Kagawa also reached people through publishing books even during the KGM in plain language rather than in Christian jargon. He was a pastor and an evangelist.

Whenever Kagawa visited places of the KGM, he always stayed with local Christian ministers and/or leaders to pray together for the meetings. He also donated all the offerings dedicated at the meetings to them. I recognize that Kagawa encouraged local churches that stood and survived in a place where Christianity, as a Western religion, was not welcomed.

My conclusion is to value Kagawa's contribution to the KGM. Though Kurokawa states that "as Japan moved toward wartime status, KGM had to quickly come to an end,"[9] Kagawa played his Christian role by standing through one of the worst times in Japanese history.

To achieve the above analysis, first, we should use Kagawa's comments for replying to questions during his US lecture tour in 1936, in which American reporters asked Kagawa about his Christian understanding of Japan's military aggression, its withdrawal from the League of Nations, disarmament issues, the US economic blockade, whether the US is a Christian nation, and the issue of world evil. Second, we should recognize discussions between leaders of both countries at the Riverside Japanese American Christian Leaders Conference in April 1941, in which the US leaders warned that the Japanese government's forced worship of the emperor violates religious freedom and could be considered idolatry. They also questioned whether

---

8. Institute for the Study of Humans and Society, *Movement of Christianity*, 3:23.
9. Kurokawa, "Christian Mission in Japan," 62.

the United Church of Christ in Japan was being established under pressure from the Japanese government.

Look at the chart below (3.1) showing the chronological flow of Japanese church history toward the Pacific War, Kagawa's works, such as mass evangelism, lecture tours in the United States, the Japan-US Christian conference at Riverside, and the foundation of the UCCJ, in which all Protestant denominations were jointly inscribed by the government's legal force. See the chart for understanding why Japanese Christians may have gone along with the *kokutai* (国体, national polity).

Chart 3.1: Japanese church history in relation to WWII

Adoption of NJCCM of UCCJ at the General Assembly (June 1946)

NJCCM (June 1946–December 1949)

Kagawa's lecture tour in America (1950)

Kagawa's open letter to Korean president (1955)

War responsibility apology by UCCJ's delegation in China (1957)

War responsibility statement of UCCJ (1967)

EVANGELICAL WORK IN THE US, KOREA, AND CHINA

Kagawa's Visit to the US in 1936

Based on the above-mentioned sociopolitical context, we should review Kagawa's statements while he was in America in 1936 for a lecture tour. He commented to the reporters as follows:

> Q1. Dr. Kagawa, do you represent the Japanese government in your tour of America?
>
> A1. I do not represent my government, but I represent 99 percent of our people because I know that they want peace.
>
> Q2. What is the attitude of your people toward the military activities of the Japanese government?
>
> A2. We look upon the militarists in the same way as you look upon one or two mosquitoes in a room at night. They are very troublesome, even though they are not large in number.
>
> Q3. Do you take a position that Japan should not expand?
>
> A3. The Dutch expanded when they took Formosa; I suppose the French expanded when they took Indochina. In a sense, the British expanded when they obtained such large control of Chinese ports and Chinese trade. You see, we have excellent precedents for expansion, and we, also, have serious problems caused by overpopulation and unemployment.
>
> Q4. Do you think that to expand by a process of military conquest is Christian?
>
> A4. No, decidedly not. But you must remember that Japan has not gotten wholly away from the feudal system. While we are living in a machine age, many of the feudal ideas still linger. I think we have made some mistakes in the Orient, but I think other nations have also made their own mistakes.
>
> Q5. Is there any thought in Japan of seizing the Philippines?
>
> A5. Such a thing is farthest from our minds. As a matter of fact, the feeling of our people is that granting freedom to the Philippines was one of the noblest steps that America ever took. It must be recorded as a great achievement.[10]

---

10. Bradshaw et al., *Kagawa in Lincoln's Land*, 45.

Kagawa's reply comments on Japan's military expansion in Asia (A4) and the potential occupation of the Philippines (A5) expressed his honest reflections on the atrocities committed by the Japanese military and respected US political decisions regarding Philippine autonomy. In Kagawa's comments, during Japan's invasion of Manchuria, there was no prejudice against American national policy toward Asians. However, we should not overlook that Kagawa referred to the historical fact that Asian countries had been colonized by the Netherlands, France, and England. Kagawa severely criticized the United States and Britain during the Pacific War and referred to the colonization of Western countries.

With the West colonizing Asia, Kagawa might have recognized that Japan was the only country to counter the West against an oppressed Asia militarily to liberate the oppressed Asian states. Kagawa's discourse on his lecture tour to the United States in 1936 is the prototype of his rhetoric to justify Japan's invasion of Asia even after the war. However, I wondered whether Kagawa's justification for Japan's participation in the war was born out of coercion by the military, or whether it reflected Kagawa's intentions, or whether the two cannot be distinguished. I will discuss whether it is possible to judge in the latter half of the chapter. See the chart below for Kagawa's rhetoric on the Asian invasion.

Chart 3.2: Kagawa's rhetoric for justifying the war against the US
Asian countries' invasion (colonization) by Western countries: British, the US, France, Netherlands, etc.
Japan was the only country in Asia to fight against Western countries to deliver Asian countries.

> The point of the Great East Asia Joint Constitution Declaration is whether it is granted as an inherent "right" of Asian countries and humans, or whether it is granted by the leadership country (the Japanese Empire).[11]

Before discussing 1936 Kagawa's American tour based on the political context, we need to review how Kuroda Shiro (b. 1896), who assisted Kagawa's KGM, summarized the movement's achievements and challenges after completing the KGM. Kuroda commented as follows:

---

11. Hatano, "Shigemitsu Mamoru," 39.

> Whether the nearly 800,000 people in the audience have taken a strong interest in Christianity since then, and how many of those who turned in their decision cards have become Christians, is a severe problem. It can also be said that this is a characteristic of the one-sided Kagawa evangelism. At that time, the audience who came to listen to ordinary evangelists was limited to a handful of intellectuals. All kinds of people who had no connection to traditional Christian churches gathered together. The churches of that time could not accept such people of the common class, so there was little possibility of welcoming those who made up their minds to follow Jesus. . . . However, as the Kingdom of God Movement progressed, the number of baptized people gradually increased for several years, and even if you look at the *Christian Years* magazine, the number of Christians increased sharply yearly. If things continued as they were, by 1937, the Japanese churches would surely have gained strength. *However, those expectations were miserably betrayed. It was met with a truly global horror event. Namely, World War II. In the latter half of the Kingdom of God Movement, the Manchurian incident occurred in 1931, shocking the world. In 1937, it changed to the Sino-Japanese incident, and finally, in 1941, the war was expanded to a world war, and Japan committed to fighting against Christian countries including the United States and Britain.*[12]

Kuroda's above statement in the last paragraph in italics expresses the reality of Japanese Christianity that the church at that time did not welcome citizens at the bottom of society and the harsh reality of the social situation facing the Japanese military's war against the United States. As the KGM progressed while Japan was headed toward war with the United States and other Western countries, and under the militaristic government policy that puts the national polity first, how did Christian leaders deal with the government's national policy?

Onomura Rinzo (小野村林蔵, 1883–1961),[13] a Presbyterian minister, in the *Kamino Kuni Sinbun* (神の国新聞, KGM's newspaper, hereafter *KKS*), June 1930, commented:

> I feel that the Christian faith is nothing but a great driving force for putting into practice the spirit of the national polity (imperial

---

12. Kuroda, *Research on Kagawa Toyohiko*, 192–93; emphasis added.
13. Church of Christ in Japan Editing Committee, "History."

rescript). Christianity should support the spirit of the national polity and should never do anything to hinder it.[14]

Considering that Onomura sent a message to the *KKS* in 1930, during the latter period of the KGM, it is clear that Japanese Christianity was in line with the spirit of the national polity (*kokutai*) even during the KGM period. This means that the Christian faith in Japan coexisted with the national polity without resisting state authorities even at the risk of martyrdom.

Kagawa's interview in the US in 1936 continued. Kagawa continued to respond to the questions as follows:

Q1. Do you think that the United States is a Christian nation?

A1. If you want a frank reply, I think you are half Christian and half pagan. You certainly do not apply your Christian principles to industry, and we can never have a truly Christian nation as long as our industrial relations remain un-Christian.

Q2. Do you think the international relations trend is Christian or un-Christian?

A2. Of course, there is plenty that is un-Christian in the relationship between nations, and yet the world is getting smaller, and people are drawing closer to one another in many ways. We almost feel that New York belongs as much as it much to us as it does to you. We buy more wool from Australia than England does. We are in close touch with you by radio.

Q3. What do you consider the worst evil in the world today from an international viewpoint?

A3. The failure of nations to inject Christianity into their economic problems and into their trade relations. Even the so-called Christian nations follow a "dog eat dog" policy concerning their foreign trade.[15]

Kagawa's remark of "dog eat dog" might be presumed to be based on the desperate competitive principle of "the law of the jungle" in the international market. Considering that Kagawa participated in the 1921 labor strike at Kawasaki Mitsubishi Shipbuilding as a labor union leader, we can be sure that he had a good grasp of the actual nature of Japanese conglomerate shipbuilders. Therefore, Kagawa should have recognized that

14. Kurokawa, "Kingdom of God Movement," 36.
15. Bradshaw et al., *Kagawa in Lincoln's Land*, 45.

Japanese enterprises were also considered *one of the worst evils in the world*. Finally, Kagawa was confronted with the most severe question that he did not want to receive from an American reporter:

> Q: Why did Japan withdraw *from the arms conference and from the League of Nations*?
>
> A: I am not sure we have fully withdrawn from either. We still send labor delegations to the labor conference in Geneva, and we are still *sympathetic toward reducing armaments*, but I want to make indisputably clear that unless we can inject Christianity into *the economic relations between nations, and into the industry, it is idle to talk about reducing armaments*. If we cannot agree on steel and cotton and oil and shipping, there is little use in trying to agree on the size of guns. It is my firm conviction that if the nations of the world can agree, as Christians should, on the vital problems of international trade and industrial relations, there will be no need for guns. On the contrary, if we continue to disagree with each other about steel and shipping and cotton and oil, how can we believe that an agreement as to the size of armaments will be anything more than superficial?[16]

Why did Kagawa refer to the issues of disarmament and world trade without replying to the question of the arms conference and withdrawal from the League of Nations? Needless to say, Kagawa's comment on both issues is based on the political context in the past:

> Japan had been conflicting with Western states, the US, Germany, France, and the U.K. on unequal treatment, especially treatment of restarting tariff autonomy.[17]

Kagawa linked the past unequal treaties against Japan by Western countries to the issue of disarmament and argued that Japan received unequal treatment from the West when it came to global trade and national security issues as well. This injustice was the same as the attitude of Christians who protested the anti-Japanese immigration law of the United States in 1924, and not only second-generation Japanese Christians but also first-generation Christians such as Nitobe protested this injustice. The attitude was the same. Kagawa's advocacy for rectifying colonial policies, unequal tariffs, and racial discrimination in the West is highly praised. This issue is

---

16. Bradshaw et al., *Kagawa in Lincoln's Land*, 45; emphasis added.
17. Asonuma, "Japan's Demand for Tariff Autonomy," 74.

not worth discussing theologically based on my theme of war responsibility at the book. *However, Kagawa should be criticized for not mentioning that Korea and Manchukuo were also subject to discriminatory treatment by Japan.*

Why did Kagawa refer to the issue of economic sanctions and disarmament, and why did he insist that the disarmament issue should be resolved if the countries that were imposing economic sanctions were exterminated? Notwithstanding Japan's military aggression against China in the Manchurian incident of 1931, it is speculated that he argued that if the United States did not impose an economic blockade on Japan, it would be a Christian way of avoiding a war between Japan and the United States. Nevertheless, Kagawa justified Japan's military aggression in China because of the Netherlands, France, and the United Kingdom, which had colonized Asian countries. Then Kagawa should have recognized that Japan's military aggression in China could not be justified even though the Netherlands, France, and the United Kingdom had colonized Asian countries.

Kagawa's Visits to Korea in 1938 and 1939

Kagawa's Visit in 1938

In 1912, even two years after the Korean annexation by Japan in 1910, Kagawa stated his supportive message for the independence of Korea. He said:

> If Japan were a vassal state to Russia today, we would stand for the independence movement of Japan. Based on this thought, Korean Christians had every reason to raise the protest movement. The state that had been suppressing colonized states would fall victim to a more severe calamity, and it falls on the imperial house.[18]

Kagawa's statement wished for Korea's independence because Japan had colonized Korea after the Russo-Japanese War (1904–5) to protect and aim for security in the northeast Asian region.

In 1919, Kagawa also stated:

> Both publishers in Japan, *Japan Advisers* and *The Kobe Chronicle*, do not report in detail on the Jeameri massacre in Mizuhara, Korea. Why have Japanese newspapers kept silent on this incident?

---

18. Takeuch, *Kagawa Toyohiko and Volunteers*, 177.

> *The loss of the world of spirit in Japan is the dissipation of humankind's conscience.*[19]

Kagawa criticized Japanese media for using a hyperbolized message by referring to the eschatological view of the end of the world.

The following year in 1920, Kagawa said,

> I came back to Japan from China, via Korea, where I recognized the culture spread from west to east, I had an inextinguishable depression. I was convinced the new intense light should shine on the dark Asia.[20]

Based on the sociopolitical context of the East Asian states of China, Korea, and Japan, Kagawa faced the reality of a disordered state situation. His statement "I recognized the culture spread from west to east" may reveal the Eastern power's involvement in the regions of East Asia.

In 1939, how did Korean Christians meet Kagawa?

Kagawa's Visit in 1939

An article of the *Keijo Nippo* (京城日報, *Kyongsong Ilbo*, "The First Time in 14 Years") dated June 19, 1938, indicates that Kagawa visited Korea in 1924. Unfortunately, Lee Sunhye (李善惠) claims that there exists no information on the period of absence.[21] Thus, we should examine the relationship between Kagawa and Korean Christians based on his visit in 1938.

Since *komin shinminka seisaku* (皇國臣民化政策, making Korean people to be the emperor's subjects based on such as worshiping at the shine, reciting the Vow of Japanese Subjects) was deployed in October 1937, Lee commented on the different perspectives from Kagawa's reflection on his Korean visit in 1938. On December 1, 1939, Kagawa commented:

> They [Korean Christians] are not only observing a worship service but also devoting themselves to practical missionary work. In Sonchon, I visited a person from the church who carries out social welfare work at home for the elderly and an orphanage by their contributions. After having seen their works, I recognized that, first, Christians in mainland Japan should start to change their traditional looking at Korean Christians so that both Christians

---

19. Kagawa, *Complete Set*, 10:23.
20. Lee, "Kagawa's Social Welfare Practices," 143.
21. Lee, "Kagawa's Social Welfare Practices," 147–48.

would be united into one. Then, Korean Christians would follow the same way.²²

Lee claims:

> Based on the viewpoints of Korean people, I, as a Korean, feel uneasy with Kagawa's thought that he believed Koreans had the minds to follow the same way as Japanese people.... I noticed that Kagawa looked down on Korean people.... However, I admit that thousands of people attended Kagawa's meetings.²³

What was Kagawa's reflection on the meetings? Lee claims that the Korean people might have had difficulty in attending Kagawa's meetings, as all attendees had to make the "Vow of Japanese Subjects (oath of the imperial subject). Kagawa didn't mention their hardness."²⁴

Kagawa commented:

> Traveling to Korea was hard because of taking trains three times at 3:30 AM, and skipping breakfast four times . . . , nonetheless, the Korean people lifted my spirit whenever I met the joy shown on their faces. . . . On reflection, Korean churches are excellent. Exceptionally good churches. Compared with a Korean church, a Japanese church is not sincere. They are "neither cold nor hot," and would be "spit out of God's mouth."²⁵

How did Korean attendees accept Kagawa's sermon in the meetings? Lee introduced Korean attendees' common understanding of Kagawa's sermon and lecture as follows:

> Korean attendants confessed that Kagawa had the power to read a person's mind and his words pierced their hearts. Above all, the story of Kagawa's life in the slum gave them a great sensation and reverence for him. Even though his lectures took two hours, after his lecture, they were filled with regret when it ended.²⁶

Kagawa was not welcomed by Korean people, including Christians and churches, because of the Japanese government's policy of *komin shinminka seisaku* (皇國臣民化政策, making Korean people the emperor's

---

22. Lee, "Kagawa's Social Welfare Practices," 173.
23. Lee, "Kagawa's Social Welfare Practices," 173.
24. Lee, "Kagawa's Social Welfare Practices," 176.
25. Lee, "Kagawa's Social Welfare Practices," 176.
26. Lee, "Kagawa's Social Welfare Practices," 181.

subjects). Thus, Kagawa was regarded as a Christian who stood alongside the oppressor. However, they might have recognized that Kagawa had justified regaining the state sovereignty of Korea. Nonetheless, Korean people might have never forgiven Kagawa as a Japanese because of the martyrs who died in the March 1 movement in 1919 by the Japanese government.

"The story of Kagawa's life in the slum gave them a great sensation and reverence for him."[27] It was not a story of the well-known Japanese Christians who could neither overcome the Japanese sociopolitical climate nor detach from it. However, Kagawa had cooperated with the Japanese government polity, including worshipping the emperor as not a religion, just the same as Tomita, who had been with him as they studied at Meiji Gakuin University STH, moved to Kobe Seminary School, and studied at Princeton Theological Seminary. Both were Presbyterians and had dedicated their lives to Nihon Kirisuto Kyokai (日本基督教会, the United Church of Christ). The Koreans never accepted a Japanese Christian Kagawa but accepted what they saw as the sacrificial love given to the socially and economically unprivileged.

Kagawa's Apology for Japanese Military Atrocity against the Chinese in the 1930s

In the early 1930s, Kagawa visited China, where he expressed an apology for the atrocities the Japanese military had committed against the Chinese people. *The World Tomorrow*, in an article entitled "Kagawa as a Pacifist," reported:

> Last winter Kagawa conducted a series of meetings in China, in which he lectured on his experience in applying the Gospel to social conditions. First of all, however, he sought to make his position clear regarding the situation between the two countries. The following sentence is from a sermon to Shanghai college students: "What we have to learn about Christ is the spirit of forgiveness. And in that spirit, I ask your pardon to me, to Japan. Many of you might think Japan is a terrible country, but I ask you to consider

---

27. Lee, "Kagawa's Social Welfare Practices," 181.

that the fault of Japan is the fault of the leaders of the military party. I am not a militarist nor are most of our people."[28]

At this period, Kagawa excused the attendees for atrocities by stressing that it was not most people but the military who did cruel acts. He defended Japan itself without taking full responsibility for the inhuman acts of the military. But, why did Kagawa preach to attendees on the spirit of forgiveness when he had no right to demand anything from the victims? He commented:

> Dear Brothers and Sisters: I want to ask your pardon for my nation. . . . Most of the Japanese people were against sending any kind of troops to your province of Shantung. And we Christians were bitterly opposed to it. Therefore, pardon us, pardon me especially, because our Christian forces were not strong enough to get victory over the militarists. But the day will come when we shall be harmonious and peaceful and strong enough to do so, and when both nations will be harmonious and peaceful in the Name of Christ.
>
> We Japanese love China. Do you know the origin of the city of Kyoto? There was a colony of Chinese farmers who possessed the villages on the site of modern Kyoto. And because they had the highest culture then known, the Japanese Imperial household moved to that section. As the city of Kyoto grew up, 80 percent of its many noble families came to be of Chinese descent. Among the immigration strains in Japan, from the Southern Seas, from Korea, from Siberia, from Mongolia, the one that has contributed the dominant factor to Japanese civilization is from China. Therefore, we love China.
>
> But unless we become more religious in both Japan and China, we shall never have permanent peace. . . . Sometimes we are very selfish and do not see the need of praying. . . . It is quite true, when you are contented, and have no holy ambition to build up the nation, you may have to desire to pray. . . . But can you forget the misery of the nation, and of the poor? If you are contented with the sort of world we have at present, there is no use in praying. But if we want real peace and real harmony, there are many problems for the solution of which we must pray. We must pray for world peace, for the uplifting of power, for the desert to be made green, for the

---

28. Takenaka, "Kagawa as a Pacifist," page no. unavailable.

New Age, and for the New Society. We must pray for science to be controlled by Conscience.

If you pray, world peace will be realized; the poor will be emancipated. Abraham Lincoln prayed through the night before he wrote his Emancipation Proclamation. Do you consider that kind of prayer superstitious? Nevertheless, I believe it was because he prayed that the four million poor slaves were emancipated.[29]

Nunokawa quoted the contribution of Stanley E. Jones (1884–1973) to *The Christian World*, from an article dated November 3, 1932, as follows:

I recognize that the government of Manchuria was bad. But two wrongs never did make one right. They do not do so in this case. I recognize that all Japanese do not agree with this policy of aggression against another nation. I could speak of Kagawa of Japan in China, and they responded with affection and respect.[30]

Preamble of the Greater East Asia Declaration

It is the fundamental principle of establishing world peace that all the countries of the world should mutually benefit from each other and enjoy the common prosperity of all countries. However, to maintain the prosperity of their own country, the United States and Great Britain suppressed other countries and peoples, and they carried out the invasion and exploitation of the Japanese people in Greater East Asia. The cause of the Great East Asia War, which has been overshadowed, is still there. The countries of Greater East Asia will work together to ensure the stability of Greater East Asia and build an order of coexistence and mutual prosperity based on moral principles.

1. Each country in Greater East Asia will respect each other's autonomy and independence, and work together to help each other achieve peace, thereby establishing an affinity for Greater East Asia.
2. Each country in Greater East Asia should respect each other's traditions, encourage the creativity of each ethnic group, and enhance the culture of Greater East Asia.

---

29. Nunokawa, "Concept of International Order," 24–25.
30. Nunokawa, "Concept of International Order," 47.

3. Each country in Greater East Asia will cooperate closely to promote Greater East Asia's economic development and prosperity.

4. Each Greater East Asian country should strive for international relations, eliminate racial discrimination, promote cultural exchange, open resources, and contribute to the world's progress.[31]

What is noteworthy about the preamble and the four articles in the above declaration is that in the preamble, Japan criticizes the British and the US for exploiting Asian states. In comparison, in the four articles, the *independence* and *freedom* of the Far East states can be achieved. The above two issues of *independence* and *freedom* can be divided into two categories: whether Japan grants *independence and freedom* as a leading nation or whether nations and people have them as *inherent rights*, rather than their being granted by a leading nation.

"China's Reconstruction and Japan": With Brotherly Love, without Seeking Profit

In China, Kagawa stated that he defended the Greater East Asia Joint Declaration and advocated the unity of Asian countries. Kagawa recognized the universal evil inherent in war, both in the West and in Japan. He also criticized the continued colonization of Asia by the West. When we read the previously unpublished manuscript for "China's Reconstruction and Japan," we can see that Kagawa criticizes not only the West but also the evils of both the West and Japan as "China's Reconstruction and Japan" was based *on the premise* that the world would share an international economic policy, international immigration policy, and international exchange policy based on brotherly love without seeking profit.[32]

The Greater East Asia Declaration, declared in November 1943, advocated the independence and freedom of the Asian countries in the Greater East Asia Co-prosperity Sphere. Japanese Foreign Minister Shigemitsu Mamoru (1887–1957) emphasized that independence and state freedom were inherent rights of Asian countries and ethnic groups.[33] Shigemitsu sought to organize the Greater East Asia Co-prosperity Sphere based on

---

31. Institute for Advanced Studies on Asia, "Greater East Asia Declaration."
32. See "China's Reconstruction and Japan," in Kagawa, *Complete Set*, 13:3–29.
33. Hatano, "Shigemitsu Mamoru," 39.

the "independent nations" of Greater East Asia in a spirit of mutual equality and mutual benefit because if the members of the Greater East Asia Co-prosperity Sphere institutionalized mutual independence, equality, and mutual benefit, it would have the effect of strongly curbing the territorial ambitions and economic monopoly of the Japanese Empire itself, as well as curbing "military omnipotence" and "control ideology."[34]

In other words, Kagawa defended the political stance of Foreign Minister Shigemitsu and went beyond Shigemitsu's political stance to promote a universal international brotherly economy, international exchange policy, international immigration policy, etc., based on redemptive love. Kagawa stated his thoughts on the everlasting peace of Asia as follows:

> If everlasting world peace is to come in any form, it must be based on international socioeconomic cooperation. First and foremost, consider the joint use of resources [(1) e.g., the Japanese military invasion of Asian countries in search of resources], the joint handling of immigration issues [(2) e.g., the anti-Japanese immigration law of 1924], and the thoroughness of international financial institutions [3]. If the Greater East Asia Declaration can be operated completely away from profit in the international economic process [(4) in a spirit of co-operation], peace in the East will be ensured forever [(5) i.e., eternal peace based on redemptive love].[35]

Kagawa raised three points (1–3) for solving the causes of the war of aggression and proposed a method of operating the cooperative free from profits (4). He was confident that if measures 1–4 were put into practice, lasting peace would be achieved in Asia; if not, peace would not be achieved. The basic premise of Kagawa's plea for China to support the Pacific War based on the Greater East Asia Declaration should be understood as relating to Kagawa's proposal above. Therefore, Kagawa never appealed to China to support the Pacific War without considering the above proposal.

Brief Summary of Kagawa's Message to China in 1944

Kagawa visited China at the end of 1944, praying for China's complete recovery, and preaching to the Chinese people a recovery plan based on redemptive love. However, this recovery effort went beyond the intention of the Greater East Asia Declaration. This is because Kagawa tried neither

---

34. Hatano, "Shigemitsu Mamoru," 44.
35. Kagawa, *Complete Set*, 13:28.

to control China by force nor to justify the Greater East Asia Declaration intended by the Japanese military, but in line with the expression "Japan has awakened," which Kagawa said in "China's Reconstruction and Japan."[36]

He hoped that Japan would repent and move forward with mutual brotherly love as equal nations. In other words, when Kagawa asked China for forgiveness for the crimes Japan had committed against China and presented a plan for China's reconstruction, Kagawa said:

> The sense of redemptive love was born in China. The day when a large number of those who bear the disadvantages of the weak and poor emerge, China will realize that it has been forever restored.[37]

This helps in understanding Kagawa's feelings of redemptive love for China.

How did Kagawa react to the Japanese invasion of China, which caused many civilian casualties? Kagawa apologized to Chinese Christians, saying that he was "sorry for that," but could he still justify the war of aggression? Using the excuse of the inhuman acts of the military authorities by citing Western colonial policy in Asia and his statement that Japanese Christians were carrying a cross is not justifiable. Considering that Kagawa's words and actions in China were directed not only toward China but also toward the countries of the Greater East Asia Co-prosperity Sphere, including South Korea and Taiwan, Kagawa's culpability is significant.

Kagawa's Evangelical Work after the War

Third Extraordinary General Assembly of the UCCJ[38]

Almost eleven years after the war, the UCCJ held the Third Extraordinary General Assembly (June 7–8, 1946) with Kagawa attending as one of UCCJ's leaders at Fujimicho Church, which was founded by Uemura Masahisa (Presbyterian). The UCCJ decided to promote evangelical work with the name New Japan Construction Christian Movement for three million people in Japan.

Based on the resolution of the Extraordinary General Assembly to develop the NJCCM, on the day after the general meeting (June 9, 1946), the opening conference of the NJCCM was held at Aoyama Gakuin University,

---

36. Kagawa, *Complete Set*, 13:29.
37. Kagawa, *Complete Set*, 13:27.
38. See UCCJ, *Reorganization of the UCC*, 78.

where the National Christian Conference to Celebrate the 2,600th Anniversary of the Imperial Reign was also held in 1940. The conference adopted the declaration as follows:

> We, the Japanese people, are keenly aware of our responsibility for this war. In particular, as a Christian who believes in the gospel of peace, I would like to confess my deep remorse and repentance. We are confident that our infinitely forgiving Heavenly Father, with His abundant grace, will open the path to rebirth and resurrection for us. However, when we face the reality of the indescribable devastation of war and see the deplorable suffering of our fellow citizens, we become aware that a new cross awaits us.
>
> Here, we resolve to build a new Japan based on the cross of Christ and thereby realize a truly moral world order. Taking this opportunity, deliberately held on the day of Pentecost, we pray for the Christian evangelization of all of Japan, the revival of faith in Christ, and the expansion and strengthening of Christ's church. This is why, in the unity of all Christians, we bear upon ourselves the afflictions of a nation, hunger, stupor, and want. In grief, I hope that I will devote myself to serving the people. Therefore, the New Japan Construction Christian Movement three-year plan is developed here.[39]

We notice that the declaration confessed to God responsibility for the war. However, regrettably, it did not have apology words for the countries Japan had invaded in Asia, especially Korea and China. The point is that Kagawa committed to this evangelical movement as a key leader; thus, we should recognize that also as a member of the UCCJ, Kagawa confessed to war responsibility at this moment.

New Japan Construction Christ Movement (NJCCM, 1946–49)[40]

Kagawa contributed to the NJCCM, as he was a well-known Christian in Japan, thanks to the KGM before the war.

In 1947, at the meetings of the NJCCM, Kagawa stated as follows:

1. The gospel of Christ cannot be spread to Japan simply by doctrine or dissemination. It must be a religion of life that can save people's lives.

---

39. UCCJ, *Reorganization of the UCC*, 194.
40. Kuroda, *Research on Kagawa Toyohiko*, 204–5.

KAGAWA'S EVANGELICAL WORK, PATRIOTISM, AND REPENTANCE

Since the religion of Christ is a religion of life, love, and blood, we must promote the religion of the cross as the gospel of society as well as of personal salvation.

2. This time, for the first time in recorded history, Japan suffered a crushing defeat in war. Now we are a full-fledged person. Until then, Japan had boasted that it was great and great. However, he kept repeating his foolishness of being like a frog in a well and not knowing the ocean, and in the end, he fell into an unavoidable catastrophe. We have to look at world history. I can't help but read about the great events of judgment and love, destruction, and salvation that are taking place before the absolute God.

3. Japan can't receive special treatment before the God of absolute fairness. God's judgment lies in the rise and fall of history. People with a heart can see God through history. We must become enlightened and know what God throughout human history has done.

4. Jesus is redemptive love, not to use people, but to serve and be used by people. Jesus's political consciousness lies in his desire to be a redeemer rather than a ruler, accepting people's weakest points, their shortcomings, and forgiving them for their mistakes. He comes down from above and lifts the fallen. . . . Herein lies the key to Jesus's love of neighbor.[41]

I am convinced that Kagawa's method was to preach a Christian message to Japanese people who came to the mass evangelism meeting for the first time without using Christian terminology, as almost all the attendees might have had a background in the Japanese religious spirituality of Buddhism, Shintoism, and Confucianism. Thus, Kagawa exhorted, "Japan had boasted that it was great and great," instead of saying, "All who exalt themselves will be humbled, and all who humble themselves will be exalted" (Matt 23:12 NRSV). He preached, "Japan can't receive special treatment before the God of absolute fairness," instead of preaching that "God shows no partiality, but in every nation, anyone who fears him and does what is right is acceptable to him" (Acts 10:34–35 NRSV) with eschatological perspective. For on the judgment of God, he talked about "the great events of judgment and love, destruction, and salvation that are taking place before the absolute God" instead of saying, "For God so loved the world that he

---

41. Kainou, *Immediately after the War*, 370–73.

gave his only Son so that everyone who believes in him may not perish but may have eternal life" (John 3:16 NRSV), as John 3:16 preaches punishment to those who do not believe in God's only Son.

Table 3.5: Results of the NJCCM (1946–48)	
A. Number of Christians	200,071
B. Number of attendees	745,428
C. Number of newcomers	200,987
D. Population of Japan	78,101,000

B/A x 100 = 377 percent increase

C/A x 100 = 100 percent

A/D x 100 = 0.26 percent

Kagawa's Statement for the NJCCM

Kagawa inscribed "The Year of Christ" at the conclusion of his prayer instead of "Showa," which was the name of the Japanese emperor's era. For the Japanese, it looked extraordinary, but Japanese Christians might have encouraged Kagawa's strong demonstration of delivering the Christian message to the Japanese. It is something like a declaration of commitment in the NJCM. See Kagawa's prayer below.

> [1] The Japanese people, who refused to accept the God of the creation of the universe as their god and loved myths and idols, were forced to fall into the depths of defeat, albeit fragile. [2] And it became clear that the only thing that could save Japan from its rotten destiny was God's great love and sacrifice, which is the driving force behind the re-creation of life.
>
> [3] There is no crisis as difficult as today for Japan and its people. If we do not now discover that the path to Japan's re-creation lies at the cross, Japan will forever be reduced to a barbarian tribe living on an island in the Pacific Ocean.
>
> The Year of Christ August 26, 1946, in Sapporo[42]

---

42. Kagawa, *Complete Set*, 4:4.

Kagawa began by sharply proclaiming God's judgment on Japan's past mistakes (1). In response to God's judgment against Japan, Kagawa confessed that God had provided salvation through the love of his only begotten Son on the cross (2). Finally, Kagawa preached to all Japanese people the response to God's judgment and the grace of redemptive love on the cross. Kagawa's statement expressed his hope that Japan could recover by believing in God, even in a situation where Japan had lost everything and was left with nothing. (3). After describing Kagawa's love for the Japanese people in response to the above introduction, Kagawa began his actual sermon, where he first preached repentance toward God for Japan's past mistakes.

Kagawa started his sermon at the NJCCM meeting by introducing the story of the prodigal son.

> God is our heavenly Father. I lost my parents when I was young, so I looked up to them and wanted to experience their love. The biggest reason why I believe in the religion of Jesus Christ is because it teaches that God is the father and parent.[43]

Kagawa first preached the love of God by introducing his upbringing. Considering that in the poor villages of Japan at the time, many people sent their daughters to become geishas or to work in factories, leaving their families to live their lives alone, Kagawa said, he began speaking in a way that would reach those people's hearts with the love of Christ.

Kagawa suddenly explained the love of God in an easy-to-understand manner by looking at the differences between Buddhism and Christianity in a story in which he preached the love of God. We must understand that most of his audience lived in a Buddhist climate. Kagawa said:

> Religion traditionally has two aspects. One is from heaven towards humans, and the other is from humans towards heaven. Buddhism belongs to the latter. Jesus's religion is based on the idea that God's grace will be discovered from heaven when humans become nothing.[44]

---

43. Kagawa, *Complete Set*, 4:5.
44. Kagawa, *Complete Set*, 4:6.

Kagawa Exhorted Attendees at NJCCM to Confess Repentance to God

Kagawa introduced David's confession in Ps 51 and exhorted each audience member to confess to God the sins committed in the war period and to pray for God's forgiveness. While preaching the love of God, Kagawa presented the theological differences between Buddhism and Christianity and preached the love of God in Christianity, considering his audience, who were in a Buddhist climate. Regarding repentant confession, after introducing that a certain scholar said that repentant confession is not suitable for Japanese people, Kagawa claimed that it is famous in Japan that Kumagai Naozane (1141–1207), who killed Taira no Kiyomori (1118–81), confessed repentance and entered Buddhism. He explains that repentant confession is universal when a human being sins.[45] Kagawa preached repentance for the crimes committed in the war, considering the spiritual context of Japan, but Kagawa also prayed as follows, taking into account the global context of the time, going beyond Japan and Asia.

> Hopefully, we will cleanse ourselves of our sins, the sins of the nation, and the sins of humanity, and each person will be reborn, Asia will be reborn, and the world will be reborn. We pray that Jesus Christ will cleanse us so that we can establish a world without police, without prisons, and without arms. Amen.[46]

Based on Kagawa's message in the above statements and prayer, it should be clearly understood through his statement below that Kagawa did not simply adhere to a Christian idealist theology, although it was being developed in other parts of the world besides Japan. Kagawa stated.

> [1] Religion cannot eliminate evil. However, by believing in God, who is life, we can fully overcome evil. All religious experience, from primitive religions to high religions, shows that it is possible to overcome evil through religion. Religion was a belief to overcome evil. However, [2] lower primitive religions prayed for victory over natural evils, natural disasters, earth disasters, and diseases, while [3] higher religions began to pray for the power to overcome character evils.[47]

---

45. Kagawa, *Complete Set*, 4:8.
46. Kagawa, *Complete Set*, 4:12.
47. Kagawa, *Complete Set*, 4:62.

It is clearly understandable that he could identify [1] with Christianity as [2] Shintoism and [3] Buddhism.

International Political Context around the Period of Pearl Harbor in 1941

As we need to analyze Kagawa's war responsibility, recognizing the international political context around the period of Pearl Harbor in 1941 is required. Hatakeyama Kenichi's helpful article is entitled "The U.S. Military's Strategic Debate on the USSR in the Last Half of WWII (1943–45)." See as follows:

> In August 1941, even President Franklin Roosevelt, who led the recognition of the Soviet Union in 1933, viewed the Soviet Union as an "ally" insofar as it remained an *enemy's enemy* fighting Nazi Germany, the enemy of the United States. Furthermore, after the outbreak of war between Japan and the United States on December 7, 1941 [the day of Pearl Harbor], *the United States increased pressure on the Soviet Union to get it to participate in the war against Japan*, but the Soviet Union refused to respond, making all kinds of excuses.
>
> On December 16, President Roosevelt proposed to Joseph Stalin, the supreme leader of the Soviet Union, that he would like to immediately hold *a conference in Chongqing [in China] with representatives from the Soviet Union, China, Great Britain, the Netherlands, and the United States*. He proposed a meeting between the British and Chinese ambassadors and the Soviet leader, but the Soviet Union did not respond to this idea.[48]

We notice in the first paragraph that the US viewed the Soviet Union (the USSR) as an ally after the Pearl Harbor attack in 1941, even though the USSR had been an enemy because of the communist ideology. In the second paragraph, the US also tried to persuade to join the Allied nations of Europe to destroy the Axis powers (Germany, Japan, and Italy) based on the military strategy for teaming up with the Soviet Union.

I am not focusing on the political context itself during the first stage of the Pacific War but want to discuss *how Kagawa perceived the universal social evils of Western countries, and of the Soviet Union and Japan, that were visible throughout the war*. If we can identify with Kagawa's recognition of

---

48. Hatakeyama, "U.S. Military's Strategic Debate," 148; emphasis added.

this issue, we can find out his intention in justifying the order of Greater East Asia based on the Declaration of Greater East Asia below for fighting against the US and Britain when he visited China in 1944.

I discussed how Kagawa's confession of responsibility for the war, which is the theme of the book, is related to and developed with the work of Kagawa's mass evangelism. Whether the time was bad or good, I appreciate that God called Kagawa to preach the gospel. Kagawa's faith remained unchanged throughout his life. However, what Kagawa consistently said was that he adhered to the personalism that he had learned at Boston University (as will be discussed later) for continuing his work in the war situation, by considering the political context of the times and by showing respect for the Japanese spiritual climate.

We must also remember that Kagawa treated the emperor and the imperial family with respect after the war. He had given lectures to His Majesty the emperor, encouraged His Imperial Highness Higashikuni to become a Christian, and had a close friendship with His Imperial Highness Mikasa. Kagawa proposed that Japan adopt a constitutional monarchy but insisted on including Communism as a political party. In addition, without deifying the emperor, in Hokkaido in 1946, Kagawa prayed, "Japan refused to accept the God of the creation of the universe as its god, and the Japanese people, who loved myths and idols, did fall into the abyss of defeat."[49]

49. Kagawa, *Complete Set*, 4:4.

4

Kagawa Resonated with First-Generation Christians' Heritage of Reverence for the Emperor and Patriotism

INTRODUCTION

As the title of this chapter implies, I review how second-generation Japanese Christians such as Kagawa, Yanaihara Tadao, and Yoshino Sakuzo inherited the faith of first-generation Christians, especially how both generations confronted the government—the issue of the emperor, whom subjects were demanded to worship—and how they recognized the West, which had been exploiting the Asian states. First, see table 4.1 below for an understanding of the sociopolitical context of both generations of Christians.

Table 4.1: Chronology of sociopolitical context	
1858	Treaty of Amity and Commerce between the US and Japan (unequal treaty)
1866	Niijima (Joseph Hardy Neesima) is baptized in the U. S. A.
1868	Meiji emperor is enthroned, Meiji government is established.
1873	Meiji government abolishes the ban on Christianity.
1873	Uemura Masahisa is baptized by John C. Ballagh
1875	Ganghwa Island incident

Feb. 1876	Japan-Korea Treaty of 1876 (unequal treaty for Korea)
June 1876	Ebina Danjo is baptized by Leroy L. Janes.
1878	Nitobe Inazo and Uchimura Kanzo are baptized by Merriman C. Harris.
1891	Lèse-majesté incident by Uchimura Kanzo
1894–95	First Sino-Japanese War
1898	Yoshino Sakuzo is baptized by Anny S. Buzzer.
1899	*Bushido*, by Nitobe Inazo, is published.
1904	Kagawa Toyohiko is baptized by Hayy W. Meyers.
1904–5	Russo-Japanese War
1909	Fiftieth anniversary of Protestant mission in Japan
1910	Japan-Korea annexation
1911	Yanaihara Tadao joins Uchimura's Bible study class.
1919	*Heimondo* (Japanese morality of commoners), by Nitobe Inazo, is published.
1920	League of Nations (LN) is organized.

The central topic of this chapter is how Protestantism, which was brought to Japan by American missionaries at the end of the Edo period and Meiji era, was accepted by the first generation of Japanese Christians, and how their Christian faith and theology were not only carried down to but also deepened in the next-generation Christians, including Kagawa.

We will focus on the emperor issue, the conflict with Western Christianity, the response of Christians to the national power that views Christianity as an enemy, and the national strategy to use Christians for the modernization and internationalization of Japan.

To achieve the goal of this chapter's title, I selected first-generation Christians leaders such as Ebina Danjo (海老名弾正, 1856–1937), Uemura Masahisa (植村正久, 1858–1925), Nitobe Inazo (新渡戸稲造, 1862–1933), Uchimura Kanzo (内村鑑三, 1861–1930) and Kagawa's contemporaries, second-generation Christians such as Yoshino Sakuzo (吉野作造, 1879–1933) and Yanaihara Tadao (矢内原忠雄, 1893–1961).

Though the above first-generation Christians belonged to different denominations (Ebina was a Congregationalist, Uemura was a Presbyterian, Nitobe was Quaker, and Uchimura was a founder of the non-church movement), both the first- and second-generation Christians stood under the anti-Christianity climate of Japan and conflicting relation with Western Christian countries, to which Japanese Christians had not necessarily had a close or subordinate relationship; on the contrary, they firmly believed that they were Christians on an equal footing with the Western church. Especially, non-church movement members Uchimura and Yanaihara cultivated their faith in a way that denied Western traditional theology.

Thus, through tracing back to works of Kagawa's trailblazers who trod thorny paths, I try to prove that Kagawa resonated with the first-generation Christians' heritage of reverence for the emperor and patriotism by transcending different sociopolitical contexts and generations.

I will discuss the above-mentioned subjects based on the contents below.

Table 4.2 Christians of first and second generations	
First generation	**Second generation**
Ebina Danjo (1856–1937)	Yoshino Sakuzo (1879–1933)
Uemura Masahisa (1858—1930)	Kagawa Toyohiko (1888–1960)
Uchimura Kanzo (1861–1939)	Yanaihara Tadao (1893–1961)
Respect for the emperor	
All three Christians	All three Christians
Patriotic spirit	
All three Christians	All three Christians
Tension with Western countries	
All three Christians	All three Christians
Attitude to state authorities	
Supported or forced to support by law theologically (Ebina and Uemura)	Protested theologically (Yoshino and Kagawa)
Theological protest	
Uchimura	Yanaihara
Attitude to military policy	
Supportive (Ebina)	Forced to support (Kagawa—end of Pacific War)
Criticism of military policy	
Uchimura and Uemura	Kagawa (end of Pacific War) and Yanaihara
Support of colonial policy	
Ebina	Yoshino (even though he criticized)

After the Treaty of Amity and Commerce between the United States and the Empire of Japan (hereafter TACUJ) was concluded in 1858, Protestant Christianity was introduced by American missionaries, due to article 8, which specified freedom of religion as follows, with subsections enumerated for reference:

Table 4.3: Treaty of Amity and Commerce between the United States and the Empire of Japan, article 8[1]
1. Americans in Japan shall be allowed the free exercise of their religion, and for this purpose shall have the right, to erect suitable places of worship. No injury shall be done to such buildings, nor any insult be offered to the religious worship of the Americans.
2. American citizens shall not injure any Japanese temple . . . , or offer any insult or injury to Japanese religious ceremonies, or the objects of their worship.
3a. The Americans and Japanese shall not do anything, that may be calculated to excite religious animosity.
3b. The government of Japan has already abolished the practice of trampling on religious emblems.

The content of article 8 was historical in that it enabled the introduction of Protestantism into Japan. Still, it was concluded with the United States at the end of the Edo period when the ban on Christianity was still legally valid and foreigners were not allowed to enter Japan. It not only allowed freedom of Christian religion in the settlements but also strictly adhered to the Japanese religion (see subsects. 2–3a). Furthermore, it is important to note that Japan included in the treaty the fact that Japan had ended its oppression of Christians (3b), to show the United States that it was a country capable of concluding international treaties. This is because Japan continued to recognize that Christianity was in opposition to Japan's national polity.

1. National Graduate Institute for Policy Studies and Institute for Advanced Studies on Asia, "Treaty of Amity and Commerce."

KAGAWA RESONATED WITH FIRST-GENERATION
REVERENT FEELING FOR THE EMPEROR.

Based on the statement of Nitobe at the Fiftieth Anniversary Japanese Protestant Mission Conference in 1909, we review how both first-generation Christians, Nitobe, and Uchimura, had a reverent feeling for the emperor. Both had studied at Sapporo Nogakko Agricultural College, founded by the Meiji government in 1875, now Hokkaido University, and had become Christians thanks to William Smith Clark (1826–86), president from 1876 to 1877.

Nitobe's Statement at the Fiftieth Anniversary Japanese Protestant Mission Conference in 1909

At the Fiftieth Anniversary Japanese Protestant Mission Conference, Nitobe delivered a long statement to the attendees of the conference, to which Katsura Taro (1848–1913), the prime minister, and Komatsubara Eitaro (1852–1919), the minister of education who was responsible for religious organizations, sent a message of congratulation. We notice that Japan concluded the Anglo-Japanese Alliance in 1902 and defeated Russia in 1905 in the Russo-Japanese War (1904–5); Prime Minister Taro wanted not only to keep a favorable relationship politically with Japanese Christians but to demonstrate that the Japanese government guaranteed freedom of religion. For Japanese Christians, it was an appropriate occasion to demonstrate how Japanese Christians had contributed to the development of Japan. Nitobe also did not miss referring to the lèse-majesté incident of Uchimura Kanzo, to eradicate Japanese people's perception of Uchimura as a traitor of the state. Nitobe stated as follows.

> As a Japanese citizen, the first thing that comes to mind is the safety of the imperial family and how well their Majesties are doing. I heard from Ebina [Danjo] earlier that the Japanese people's patriotism will never be compromised, but at the same time, the same goes for their loyalty to the imperial house. . . . For a time, Christians were suspected by the world of being disrespectful. The source of that suspicion was my friend. If you look at the feelings of your friend, you will find that he has no such feelings. He is a man with a stronger sense of loyalty to the imperial family than those who accused him [applause].[2]

2. Committee of the Fiftieth Anniversary Japanese Protestant Mission Conference, "Lecture Collection," 166–67.

CHRISTIANS' THEOLOGICAL PERSPECTIVES ON RELATING TO STATE AUTHORITIES

Uchimura Kanzo (内村鑑三, 1861–1930)

I was surprised and moved by Uchimura's interpretation of Rom 12–13 as he interpreted that both chapters are described as continuing the teachings based on love. Uchimura commented:

> Having preached morality among individuals in the twelfth chapter of Romans, Paul begins in chapter 13 to preach morality toward governments and nations. If you think about it, it may seem that chapter 13 contains a completely different commandment from chapter 12, but that is not the case. As a continuation of the teaching of love in chapter 12, Paul preached the way of dealing with nations in chapter 13. We should love people, we should love those who suffer from us, we should love our country, and we should also love the country that causes us suffering. This is a spiritual commentary that consistently flows through chapters 12 and 13.[3]
> Romans 1:1 says, to those who are above and have authority, all people should obey; for there is no authority that does not come from God, but the authority that there is the authority that God has established. It is an exhortation to submit to the political authority of this world. The reason for this was that he emphasized that even the powers of this world were all created by God. Paul admonishes those who insist that Christians should submit only to God and have no need to submit to the powers of this world. In verse 2, it says, for this reason, those who disobey shall themselves be subject to the judgment. If you go against the authority of this world, you go against the authority established by God, that is, you go against God's regulations. Therefore, it is only natural that he would be subject to such judgment.[4]

Uchimura's lèse-majesté incident occurred in 1891, but he was forced to leave Daiichi High School (currently the Faculty of Liberal Arts, University of Tokyo). His *Study of the Book Romans* was based on his lecture on Romans in 1921; when he delivered the commentary on Romans in public, it was thirty years after he had lost all worldly honor. Uchimura's Romans exhortation proceeds as follows:

---

3. Uchimura, *Book of Romans*, 424.
4. Uchimura, *Book of Romans*, 425.

> Even when political transgression reaches its peak and all the people suffer, Christians should resort only to peaceful means. He should pray for the accomplishment of his goals with an unyielding heart. However, even if the objective is not achieved, one should not resort to arms and start a rebellion. We should limit ourselves to peaceful means and leave the decision of success or failure entirely in the hands of God.[5]

Then how did Uchimura have a feeling of reverence for the emperor, as Nitobe said he did at the Fiftieth Anniversary Japanese Protestant Mission Conference in 1909? Uchimura expressed his feeling of great depression and fear of the incident, but he expressed his reverence for the emperor as follows:

> On this day, I could not help but pray for His Majesty the Emperor of Japan, looking at the Grand Castle nearby. After praying, I worried because I thought my words would be disrespectful. Ever since I was punished for the incident with lèse-majesté, I feel great fear every time I mention His Majesty's name. However, sometimes true feelings are hard to suppress. I have no choice but to pray for His Majesty, sometimes at great risk.[6]

Both Uchimura and Uemura Faced the State with Love

Uchimura and Uemura's understandings of Rom 13, which describes the relationship between Christians and the state, are similar. Uchimura explains the continuity between chapters 12 and 13 of the book of Romans, and Uemura argues that Christians should take Christ's Sermon on the Mount into consideration when dealing with the nation. Now, I will give an overview of the similarity of both sides on facing the nation with love, because Rom 12 is related to the Beatitudes in Matt 5:14 and 6: 1–3.

Uemura (植村) commented in a lecture with the title "The Kingdom of God" in 1902 that a Christian should have an eschatological hope while serving the lord of the state in this living world.

Uemura's faith in the nation can be clearly understood by reading the following from *God*, the first book in the Evangelism Series,

---

5. Uchimura, *Book of Romans*, 428.
6. Honda, "Interpretation of Romans 13:1–7," 7.

1. We should advocate the kingdom of God, which is harmonious with Japan's spirituality of Bushido, to the world.[7]

2. A state would not survive if the people did not trust their king and government.[8]

3. *What Jesus taught about the "kingdom of God" and in the Sermon on the Mount is the constitution for his followers. We should store this spirits in our hearts. . . . Though it is significant to serve a lord of the state, devoting our whole lives to God in heaven while holding the warm, great feelings that enter into the hearts of the populations of all the nations must be accomplished.*[9]

First, we notice that the name of the above book's series implies it is a book of evangelism or missiology. Thus, Uemura intended to introduce the doctrine of Christianity to both Christians and non-Christian native Japanese. And, Uemura might have used this book as one of the textbooks for the students of the Meiji Gakuen School of Theology for their mission work after graduation in Japan, where the anti-Christianity climate remained deeply entrenched. The worldwide well-known book *Bushido*, written by Nitobe Inazo in 1899, might have caused some confusion to readers because of how a Christian could kill himself for the lord of the local domain in the nineteenth century.

My Interpretation of Uemura's Statements Based on the Above

On point 1, Jesus died on the cross to redeem all God's created human beings; Jesus's followers could dedicate their entire lives to God in responding to God's love with the help of the Holy Spirit (redemptive love). The rhetoric of using Bushido is that as a Japanese samurai could die for his lord of the local domain, we Christians can die for God. Uemura intended to imply that only Jesus's followers could die for the lord, which he intended to be the emperor. Thus, the above content of point 1 represents a *covenant*.

Point 2 represents the content of Rom 13:1. Through Uemura's two words "king" and "government," we could think of "the emperor" and "the state authorities." The words "the state would not survive" should be followed by "if Christians did not follow the God-established state authorities."

7. Uemura, *God*, 45.
8. Uemura, *God*, 47.
9. Uemura, *God*, 47; emphasis added.

"What Jesus taught about the 'kingdom of God' and in the Sermon on the Mount is the constitution for his followers"—Uemura's interpretation of point 3 is that the premise of Paul's message in Rom 13 is that, in the Sermon on the Mount, Christ preached the building of the kingdom of God, and serving the weak and poor is just the same, as Uchimura echoes the continuity between chapters 12 and 13 of Romans.

The conclusion of Uemura's message on the mission of Japanese Christians for salvation is strongly identical to what Kitamori Kazo, who also wrote the book *The Theology of the Pain of God*, commented in his book *Commentary on the Confession of Faith of the United Church of Christ* that

> Faith does not allow for an attitude of feeling safe as long as only one person is saved. Faith seeks to be saved along with others. We ask that others join us in sharing the truth of the one gospel.[10]

HOW THE SECOND-GENERATION CHRISTIANS RESONATED WITH THE FIRST-GENERATION CHRISTIANS' ATTITUDE TOWARD THE STATE AND EMPEROR

I review how both Kagawa, a Presbyterian, the same as Uemura, and Yanaihara, Uchimura's disciple of the non-church movement, responded to the state authorities during the so-called Fifteen Years War period when Japan conflicted with the Western powers militarily for expanding its territories in Asia.

First, I examine how Kagawa respected the emperor and trusted the state authorities based on his theology of redemptive love. Second, I review how Yanaihara protested against the state during the Marco Polo Bridge incident in 1937. However, even though both had patriotic spirits, both Yanaihara and Kagawa were recognized by the government as traitors of the state.

Kagawa's Theology against the State Authorities

To review how Kagawa took over the first-generation Christian heritage of respecting the emperor with patriotic spirit, it is important to reflect on

---

10. Kitamori, *Commentary on the Confession*, 10.

Uemura's message, which was delivered publicly to Japanese people based on the political contexts of both within and without the country.

In the previous section, we were able to understand Uemura's theology through his book *Kami* (神, God). Taking into account the international political context in which Japan was at war with a Christian Western empire for the first time, I analyze what kind of message Uemura sent to the Japanese people.

Uemura's Statement at the First Stage of the Russo-Japanese War

Uemura stated:

> Russia arrogantly withstood the invasion. . . . The blood of the Caucasian patriots appeals to heaven against *the immorality of the Russian people*, and its mournful voice is heard vividly over history. Finns are the same as Polish. The people of Finland and the people of Poland alike raised their voices of lamentation. . . . Stundists had their freedom of Christian faith constrained and suffered from the unprecedented persecution of Protestantism. . . . Russia itself became a Christian country. However, Russia does not give Protestant Christianity the freedom that we have in Japan. . . . Russia's aristocratic despotism and its crimes of abusing its subjects have finally given birth to the nihilist party and the anarchist party, and the bones of patriots are piled up in the ice fields of Siberia in extreme misery. It is just because of the crimes they have committed in Manchuria since the return of Liaodong, just as Daniel repented before God for the sake of his beloved people of Israel, that Christians in Russia must repent deeply today.[11]

Considering that Uemura made the above statement public in April 1904, which was the time when the Russo-Japanese War broke out (Feb. 1904), he was criticizing the inhumanity of Russia, a Christian country. It was a statement that appealed to the Japanese people: that the Japanese Christians would never join forces with Russia, which was a fellow Christian nation, and that Uemura, as a Japanese citizen, declared Russia as an enemy. Though this was Japan's first war with a Christian nation, Uemura's rhetoric of the statement was quite similar to Kagawa's radio statements during the Pacific War.

---

11. Yoshinare, "Civilization, War and Christianity," 150.

1945: Kagawa's Radio Message to America

Woe to you, America.... You talk about equality, yet you oppress the minorities, manipulate freedom, and try to maintain superiority which the Almighty God would never permit you to do. Repent America. *The name of Jesus is smeared by the heavy bombing.... Alas, Japan would never experience Christianization due to America....* As the crusaders isolated Asia Minor from Jesus, this Pacific war removed the Far East from Christ forever.[12]

We acknowledge that Kagawa's rhetoric of the radio message during the Pacific War resembles Uemura's message during the Russo-Japanese War. This means that even though there were almost four decades of time difference between both wars, Uemura and Kagawa had to demonstrate that Japanese Christians had strong loyalty to the state, even though Japan had been engaging in war with Christian nations.

Yanaihara's Protest against the State Authorities

Yanaihara was forced to leave Tokyo University because he had proclaimed an anti-military policy in the article "Koka no Riso" (国家の理想) in *Chuo Koron* (中央公論) in September 1937, almost two months after the Marco Polo Bridge incident occurred.[13] On December 2, 1937, *Tokyo Asahi Shimbun* (東京朝日新聞) reported Yanaihara's departure Tokyo University, in which Yanaihara commented that "I love Japan with my whole heart," which represented Uchimura's spirit of two *j*'s, Jesus and Japan.

---

12. Schildgen, *Toyohiko Kagawa*, 230–31; emphasis added.
13. Yanaihara, "Ideal of the Nation."

Picture 4.1: Yanaihara states, "I love Japan with my whole heart" (*Tokyo Asahi Shimbun* [東京朝日新聞], Dec. 2, 1937).

On the theme of *koka no riso*, he criticized the Japanese military invasion, based on Isa 1:15–16; 5:18, 20; 11:1–9; 22:1–4; 30:10, 15–16, as he commented,

> Justice is to assert our own dignity while protecting *tasha no songen* [他者の尊厳, others' dignity] without damaging them. Though justice is based on the nation, it exists as an objective spirit beyond the nation.[14]

Based on Isaiah, Yanaihara claimed.

> Isaiah proclaimed that both justice and peace are the ideal of the state (Isa 11: 1–9). By their reaching out bloodied hands to the poor neighboring people, God does not accept their worshiping and prayers (Isa 1:15–16). . . .[15] The idea is *konpon teki genin* [根本的原理, the underlying reason] which makes the state and the race continue to exist. The state and race that have lost their ideal cannot exist but perish. . . .[16] We cannot despise the ideal of the nation. If one person in the state steadfastly maintains the ideal, he is *shin no aikokusha* [真の愛国者, a real patriot].[17]

---

14. Yanaihara, "Ideal of the Nation," 7.
15. Yanaihara, "Ideal of the Nation," 18–19.
16. Yanaihara, "Ideal of the Nation," 21.
17. Yanaihara, "Ideal of the Nation," 22.

As Yanaihara published his article just after the Marco Pole Bridge incident in 1937, it was clear that he criticized the imperial military of Japan that deployed the military invasion operation in China. Yanaihara intended to proclaim both God's love and his judgment through the book of Isaiah because he used words from 11:1–11. In his commentary on the book of Isaiah, he said:

> Even if the worst happens, to those people who believe in God, he gives them hope, and at the time of his judgment, he lets them know the meaning of his judgment and clarifies the spirit of his *keirin* [経綸, governing the universe] and *mokuhyo* [目標, purpose of judgment].[18]

Despite Yanaihara's intention, the Tokyo University of the Department of Economics forced him to leave the university on the charge of his disloyalty to *kokuta* (国体: national polity). We notice that both Kagawa and Yanaihara had been genuine *shin no aikokusha* (愛国者, nationalists) as had Uchimura, the first-generation Christian. Though Uchimura had to cope with the state in the Meiji period, and Yanaihara in the Showa period, both delivered the Christian message by transcending the governments' policies in those days.

In 1946, one year after the war, Yanaihara published the book entitled *Nihon Seisinn to Heiwa Kokka* (日本精神と平和国家, The Japanese spirit and a peaceful nation). As we have identified that Yanaihara was a pacifist, we can reaffirm that he was *shin no aikokusha* (真の愛国者, a real patriot), just as Kagawa's commitment to helping the poor coexisted with his nature of patriotism. Yanaihara commented:

> Not like a Western state's *sensi kunshu* [専制君主, an absolute monarchy], the emperor is at the center of the state, and he treats the people with a sense of familiarity as *minzoku no kashu* [民族の宗家, a paterfamilias of the Japanese race]. Japanese people have been respecting the emperor with loyalty to him with a spirit of patriotism. . . . In any state in the world, the relationship between a king and his subjects has existed for a brief period because their kingdom was based on a suzerain-vassal [king and slave] relationship.[19]

---

18. Yanaihara, *Bible Commentary on Isaiah*, 135–36.
19. Yanaihara, *Japanese Spirit*, 92–93.

Yanaihara's statement represents a spirit of ardent patriotism by positioning the emperor as familiarly as *minzoku no souke* (民族の宗家, a paterfamilias of the Japanese race). Thus, we cannot conclude that Kagawa had an exceptional view of the emperor.

Ebina Danjo's Concepts of Patriotism, *Minpon Shugi* (Democracy), and Colonialism Were Carried Down to Yoshino Sakuzo

Given that the subject of this book is a confession of responsibility for the war, we will examine how Ebina Danjo religiously understood patriotism, *minpon shugi*, and colonialism, as these three issues are related to the war issue.

Ebina Danjo's Concept of Patriotism

Ebina, in the magazine *Shinjin* (Born again; Ebina defined *shinjin* as a person in the kingdom of God who was born again as a Christian), in an article entitled "Patriotism at Its Peak," commented:

> Patriotism at its peak cannot be achieved unless it is rooted in the spiritual and moral belief in the God of all things. Those who recognize God's majesty in their hearts and are conscious of their dignity will extend their ideals to the nation, bear the fate of the nation upon themselves, and form a relationship of inseparable love.
>
> Christian faith gives birth to our patriotism, and only through Christian faith can our patriotism be forever purified and pulsate the eternal honor of our nation. We also aim to build a kingdom of God in the eternal glory of the nation. The self-confidence of the power that reveals the will of God is also the revelation of God to us.[20]

Ebina's theology states that the Christian faith creates patriotism and purifies the nation and its polity; and God gives Christians the determination to take responsibility for the nation's destiny. It is positioned as the foundation of their faith and can be understood as something common to first-generation Christians.

20. Hong, "Ebina Danjo's Interpretation," 17.

Although there are differences in the expressions used to testify to their faith, patriotism is common to Nitobe, Ebina, Uemura, and Uchimura, all of whom were first-generation Christians who came from samurai families.

However, what should be noted is that in Japan, where there is a climate of anti-Christianity, Christians should confirm that they are the testifiers who have received God's call, saying that they have been sent by God to Japan.

Considering that Ebina's above comment was made public in June 1904, under the title "Patriotism at Its Peak," during the first stage of the Russo-Japanese War (Jan. 1904—May 1905), we must not forget that Japanese state authorities had judged Christians as traitors to the nation. In other words, Ebina expressed more than that Christians were not with Western Christian states but were always with Japan, as the Japanese imperial government was demanding an increasing fighting spirit of the war.

Ebina's Minpon Shugi (Democracy), Which Related to National Polity

Ebina visited the US and Great Britain four times from 1908 to 1923. During this period, Ebina commented in *Shinjin* magazine, dated 1918 and 1919, as follows,

> In the kingdom of God, each person is a king....[21] This message is where true democracy arises for the first time. A great and noble spirit has arisen within each individual....[22] This is an element that is in common with the gospel of the kingdom of God and *minpon shugi* [democracy].[23]

Based on the above comment, we should not consider Ebina's *minpon shigu* the same as that of the principle established in the West, because it was ultimately based on loyalty to Japan's national polity. It can be concluded that Ebina's logic remained unchanged throughout his life. Ebina's *minpon shigu* (democracy) was advocated through his experience in the tour to America as follows. Miyagawa, Congregationlist, after criticizing the inhuman treatment of the colonized countries of the Western countries, stated:

21. Hong, "Ebina Danjo's Interpretation," 18.
22. Hong, "Ebina Danjo's Interpretation," 16.
23. Hong, "Ebina Danjo's Interpretation," 18.

The Meiji government abolished the feudal class system based on the contents of the emperor's Five Public Notices (1868) and enacted the Constitution in 1889, which specifies religious freedom and provides education to all citizens.[24]

Ebina, in his book *Awakening with the World* (published in 1917), commented:

> Democracy has been inspiring Europe and the United States, and they began to seek sympathy for Japan. *The democratic principle is no longer a principle limited to one country or one region.* The democratic principle has already swept through and dominated the Americas. . . . As long as democracy has deepened its foundations in Europe, it not only dominates Russia but is also going even further and gaining momentum, to dominate Germany as well. This democratic principle is now dominating China as well.[25]

Though Ebina defined democracy without referring to it as *minpon shugi*, he emphasized democracy as a universal concept by commenting, "The democratic principle is no longer a principle limited to one country or one region." However, he specified that Japan introduced democracy at the first stage of the Meiji Restoration period. He might have demonstrated that Japan became a state that governed based on democracy.

> *Isn't Japan's Meiji Restoration that of royalism, and, at the same time, the rise of democracy?* It must be said that such a decisive action for ethnic equality was an unprecedented feat comparable to that of the monarchy. Many classes that had been abandoned as people for more than a thousand years were broken down and joined in the equality of the four peoples. Significantly, we have now produced officers from that rank who command the military. Because of this great accomplishment, Japan achieved a victory in the Sino-Japanese War and gained national prestige in the Russo-Japanese War. It must be noted that much of the nation's colonial development is due to the rise of democracy [*minpon shugi*].[26]

---

24. Miyagawa, "National Morality and Christianity," 73–74.
25. Ebina, *Awakening with the World*, 130; emphasis in original.
26. Ebina, *Awakening with the World*, 130–31; emphasis in original.

KAGAWA RESONATED WITH FIRST-GENERATION
Congregationalists' Colonialism

Ebina criticized Western supremacy and denounced the colonial policies of Western countries with sharp anger. However, it should not be overlooked that he praised the ability of Western countries to govern the colonial regions and their achievements in bringing civilization to their colonies. This is because his assessment quickly turned into an apologia defending the colonialism of Japanese imperialism.

Miyagawa, during this period, also commented in the *Jiji Sagen* (1916) as follows.

> When I attended a Congregational world conference held in Boston, Lyman Abbott, a chief editor of *Outlook* magazine, said in a speech, "White people have been given the power to rule over people who are incapable of governing themselves." Just after the speech, I saw three thousand attendees greet him with great applause, and I felt deeply indignant. This mistaken idea is based on the thought of white people's superiority in the world. It is a fact that Americans expelled Indians and stole their land. Others colonized states, for example, Spanish people in the Philippines, Hollanders in Java, British people in India, Egypt, and Australia, France in Madagascar and Vietnam, Germans occupied Jiaozhou Bay and the Pacific Island nations, and Russia in the northern part of Manchuria.[27]

Miyagawa also described the achievements of Western colonial policy as follows:

> However, in the area where they captured the land, they certainly managed to govern it better than when they were in the hands of the natives, and in some areas, they have tried to establish civilizational facilities and improve their nation, so there is no lack of compensation for their merits and demerits.[28]

Yoshino thoroughly criticized Ebina's evaluation of the colonial policies of Western countries mentioned above through his own essay "Inspection of Manchuria and Korea," and ultimately published suggestions for improvements to Japan's occupation policy of Korea. The historical impact of what he did is significant.

---

27. Miyagawa, *Current Events*, 13–14.
28. Miyagawa, *Current Events*, 14–15.

Yoshino's *Minpon Shugi*: Position of the Emperor and Criticism of Colonial Policy

Yoshino Sakuzo, one of Ebina Danjo's disciples, discussed the democracy advocated by Ebina and the colonial policy based on the Meiji Constitution, which stipulated national sovereignty by the emperor. This article provides an overview of the interpretation that the basic political goal of activities should be the people. In addition, we will discuss how that democratic principle confronted colonial policy, especially assimilation policy. In the end, Yoshino, like Ebina, took up constitutional democracy within Japan and confirmed that Japan had no choice but to take up imperialism in the colonies. Takada Sanae, a lawyer, claimed:

> While Japan has no choice but to adopt imperialism outward, it cannot forget that internally it is necessary to maintain the peace and happiness of the nation through constitutionalism.[29]

Definition of Minpon Shugi (Specified in "Shinjin" Date in Oct. 1914)

> In today's academic fields of political law, it has at least two different meanings. The first means "the sovereignty of the state resides in the people in legal terms," and the second term represents the sense that "the fundamental goal of the sovereign activities of the state should reside in the people politically." When used in this second sense, we sometimes translate it as *minpon shugi* (民本主義, democracy). Since the first meaning is a separate concept, it is acceptable to apply a different translation. Therefore, I think that the conventionally accepted translation of "democracy" is appropriate to express this first meaning.[30]

Yoshino defined *minpon shugi* as "the fundamental goal of the sovereign activities of the state should reside in the people politically" by separating from the so-called democracy–based legal terms, especially from the Meiji Constitution, which species that "the Empire of Japan shall be reigned over and governed by a line of Emperors unbroken for ages eternal."[31]

---

29. Hirano, "Political Thought on Reconstruction," 5.
30. Yoshino, *Yoshino Sakuzo Omnibus*, 3:100.
31. National Diet Library, "Constitution of the Empire," 1.1.

Then, how did Yoshino cope with not damaging the emperor's sovereignty? Yoshino justified the emperor's status as a ruler of the state. He stated, "The sovereignty of a country like ours, which has His Majesty as the overall ruler of national power, rests with the people."[32]

How did Yoshino relate *minpon shugi* to Christianity? Yoshino, using not *minpon shugi* but democracy, explained the relationship between democracy and Christianity based on legal interpretation to prove the relationship is universal as follows:

> When we say that the essence of democracy is personalism, we cannot help but immediately think of the close relationship between democracy and Christianity. The rationale reason behind democracy is personalism. Therefore, to thoroughly realize democracy, it must be closely grounded in the theory of personalism. However, the thoroughness of the theory does not directly translate into the active force for realization. For democracy to be realized in all areas of society, individualism must function as a living belief among humankind. Theory must assist in the activity of such beliefs. However, the source of active power must be found in religious faith.
>
> Isn't Christian personalism even more active as a content of its faith? As all human beings are children of God, we recognize the one sacredness of all human beings is tied to Christ. Has there ever been a belief in personalism that is so certain? Therefore, the Christian faith has no choice but to manifest itself in all aspects of society and directly contribute to democracy.[33]

However, Yoshino had to cope with both ultranationalists and leftists, as Takeda Kiyoko commented, "Yoshino was criticized by the nationalists and the extreme leftists."[34] He defended the constitutional government framework as follows:

> We call constitutional government the administration of the Constitution and the management of national affairs in accordance with political principles. Even if such a principle had been established in politics, this political principle should be used as a shield under the legal theory that the monarch could appoint or dismiss a minister whatever he wants. When there is a movement

---

32. Yoshino, "Meaning of Constitutional Government," 24–25.
33. Yoshino, *Yoshino Selections*, 1:163–64.
34. Takeda, "'Man' in Taisho Democracy," 71.

to defend the constitutional government, the movement to justify the constitutional government arises for the first time. Therefore, the work of people who shared in supporting the Constitution is a kind of political movement within the scope of the Constitution and does not seek to destroy the legal principles of the Constitution. Rebellion against the legal aspects of the Constitution is a revolution. Revolutions should not be confused with movements to defend the constitutional government.[35]

Yoshino was attacked by both ultranationalists and left-wing forces, but the state thoroughly suppressed the left-wing forces using the Peace Preservation Act (1925, 1928, and 1941), and Yoshino played a central role in establishing the so-called Taisho democracy. However, the movement became powerless once the war began, and Japan proceeded down the path of imperialism through armed aggression. Finally, we will examine how Yoshino confronted the country's colonial policies in Korea, Manchuria, and Taiwan, focusing on the Korean colonial issue.

Korea and Manchuria Inspection Tour (Presented in June 1916)[36]

In 1914, Yoshino made public the definition of democratic people's principles mentioned earlier and visited Manchuria and Korea from March to April 1916. It is necessary to examine how Japan, which ruled Korea, and the people of Korea themselves viewed Japanese rule. When the Korean independence movement broke out in March 1919, Yoshino made public his statement titled "Minimum Demands Regarding the Reform of Korean Governance" in August 1919 based on his inspection.[37] Furthermore, in the same month of the same year, he published a paper titled "China and Korea's Exclusion of Japan and the Reflections of Our People."[38] In other words, what was the minority view when the ruling policies of the Japanese Empire encountered resistance from colonial nationalism? Let's look at this problem from Yoshino's colonial theory.

---

35. Yoshino, *Yoshino Sakuzo Omnibus*, 3:100.
36. Yoshino, "Inspection of Manchuria and Korea," 145–47.
37. Yoshino, *Yoshino Sakuzo Omnibus*, 9:69–104.
38. Yoshino, *Yoshino Sakuzo Omnibus*, 9:105–13.

Unfairness towards Korean People

The first thing that travelers notice upon entering Korea is that the power of the Japanese state is extremely assertive through the Korean government. It is reminiscent of the relationship between government officials and ordinary people in Japan during the feudal era. However, governing a foreign nation is coercive and not successful.[39]

Lack of Compassion for Koreans as Weak

However, just because the Japanese are one step above does not mean that they can look down on or oppress Koreans. In this regard, the views of most Japanese residents in Korea, with almost no exceptions, seem to be missing the point. There are very few people who behave in such a way as to console Koreans even though they are in a socially weak position.[40]

Hopelessness of Koreans employed in the Governor-General's Office of Korea

Most Koreans who are assigned to the governor-general's office see no light in their future and have reached the height of disappointment. High-ranking officials on the Japanese side boast that they have positioned many Koreans as administrative and judicial officials, with the fundamental principle of universal brotherhood in politics in Korea. I think that Koreans have never been grateful for their efforts. There seems to be no one who appreciates the current situation as a blessing to Japan.[41]

Recognition and Dignity of Koreans as Civilized People

It is only natural that Koreans do not appreciate Japanese rule as much as the Japanese side thinks. Of course, if it becomes a problem of magnitude, the responsibility should be placed on the Japanese people. Koreans had remained independent for a long time. They were an independent nation that had a civilization.

---

39. Yoshino Sakuzo, *Yoshino Sakuzo Omnibus*, 9:4–5.
40. Yoshino Sakuzo, *Yoshino Sakuzo Omnibus*, 9:7.
41. Yoshino Sakuzo, *Yoshino Sakuzo Omnibus*, 9:10.

They recognize that they had once encountered the pioneers of civilization in our country.⁴²...

Fine railroads, ports, schools, and courts are all thanks to the Japanese, but I don't think Koreans are particularly grateful for these things.⁴³

Necessity of Freedom of Speech

In Korea, the government severely restricts freedom of speech not only for Koreans and Japanese residents. Nonetheless, it is essential to clarify what Koreans who are dissatisfied with Japan are claiming, and how powerful these dissidents are, as a reference for the governance of Korea.

Abolition of Military Politics (Specifically Military Police Politics)

Korea's public security would not have been maintained as well as it was without the military police system. However, because the military police system is an all-powerful ruler, the happiness of Korean residents is being violated because of this system. Military police were not originally trained as administrative officers. Their actions, especially their attitude towards the residents, and their reports to the central government, especially their reports on personnel affairs, are biased toward self-centeredness and cannot be justified.⁴⁴

Criticism against Assimilation Policy

Assimilation is by no means a government-only project but a national project. This project can be achieved only through tremendous joint efforts between the public and private sectors. First of all, seeing the heartless attitude of the Japanese residents in Korea, I am extremely concerned about the future of our country's assimilation policy.⁴⁵

---

42. Yoshino, *Yoshino Sakuzo Omnibus*, 9:13.
43. Yoshino, *Yoshino Sakuzo Omnibus*, 9:16.
44. Yoshino, *Yoshino Sakuzo Omnibus*, 9:19.
45. Yoshino, *Yoshino Sakuzo Omnibus*, 9:29.

After completing his field trip, Yoshino appealed to Japan to improve its governance of Korea. In April 1919, he appealed to the people through the nationwide magazine *Chuokoron* for ways to improve Korean governance under the title "Exercising Conscience in Foreign Affairs" as follows.

Anti-Japanese Attitude in China and Korea and Reflection on the Japanese People[46]

Yoshino organized his contents as below:

1. Riots in Korea and China
2. Reasons for Koreans' Anti-Japanese Attitude
3. Reasons for Chinese's Anti-Japanese Attitude
4. Causes of Recent Riots in China and Korea
5. Who Is Responsible for the Riots?
6. So, are the Japanese People Inherently Aggressive?
7. Moral Responsibility as a Leader of the East[47]

The above article was published by *Chuokoron* (中央公論), a nationwide magazine, in August 1919. See the contents of "Moral Responsibility as a Leader of the East":

> Japan itself is indeed responsible for being criticized in China and Korea. Although I believe that most of the blame we are facing lies with the warlords, the people are not completely blameless either.
>
> Reflecting on this point, we must respect and sympathize with both the Koreans and the Chinese, hold ourselves accountable for all our faults, and we Japanese will be able to make amends. Unless you proceed with an honest attitude, no amount of excuses for Korean and Chinese misunderstandings will have any merit.
>
> The cause of the riots in China and Korea is, of course, misunderstandings among their people, but it cannot be said that the bulk of the blame should be placed on the bureaucrats, and there is also no shortage of people who should urge the people as a whole to reflect. Unless the Japanese people of the future do not deal with this issue and become capable of making mistakes,

---

46. See Yoshino, *Yoshino Sakuzo Omnibus*, 9:55–66.
47. Yoshino, *Yoshino Sakuzo Omnibus*, 9:112–13.

we will never be able to advance our aspirations in the East. The current situation and Japan's current attitude are generally viewed with suspicion by Western countries as well.[48]

To understand Yoshino's statement, it is important to consider international political contexts such as the Russo-Japanese War (1904–5), Japan's annexation of Korea (1904), and the conclusion of the Anglo-Japanese Alliance to prevent Russian expansion (1902).

When Yoshino advised Japanese people through *Chuokoron* magazine, published in August 1919, it was just before Japan entered World War I (1914–18), and Japan had invaded northeast China at the expense of colonized Korea. Based on this historical background, Yoshino was calling on the Japanese military, government officials, and Japanese citizens to urgently strengthen their moral obligation to the outside world, especially to China and Korea.

However, while some scholars argue that Yoshino's defense is a thesis that justifies Japanese imperialism, Yoshino argued that even though the West had colonized Asia, he had a strong desire to adopt an international democratic structure in the world.[49] For this reason, Yoshino argued that Japan needs to learn from the West and understand the need to build an international democratic framework.

Ebina Danjo was a Christian who defended the Russo-Japanese War, but how did Yoshino respond to Ebina's religious stance? It can be judged from his statement above that Yoshino tried to improve the political framework of the colonial powers in Northeast Asia, including Japan, in a democratic and humanitarian manner.

How did Yanaihara (1893), who was of the same generation as Yoshino (1878) and Kagawa (1888), view the political framework of the time? In 1937, he criticized the Marco Polo Bridge incident and the invasion of weak countries by strong countries through his article "The Ideal of the Nation."[50] In 1946, after the war, he published his book, *The Japanese Spirit and a Peaceful Nation*, and never relaxed his criticism of the nation. Yanaihara's appeal to the Japanese people to avert God's judgment to bury Japan for the atrocities Japan committed during the war is in keeping with the apocalyptic theology that Uchimura held.

---

48. Yoshino, *Yoshino Sakuzo Omnibus*, 9:112–13.
49. Yoshino, *Yoshino Sakuzo Omnibus*, 9:55–66.
50. Yanaihara, "Ideal of the Nation," 7.

Like Hirano Yukikazu, in his article "Political Thought on Reconstruction of Imperial Japan Yoshino Sakuzo in World War I," though Yoshino applied Ebina's concept of democracy to the international context, based on his understanding of the postwar period, Yoshino could not admit the stage of the colonial autonomy theory to the political independent, as Hirano recognized below, while Yanaihara tried to correct the colonial rule in an international context with a prophetic attitude that had an inherent eschatology. This was someone who followed Uchimura's religious stance. Hirano commented:

> Yoshino's theory of criticism of colonial rule, derived from his theory of international democracy, cannot be understood in terms of the progressive liberation of colonies through the stages of assimilationism → colonial autonomy theory → political independence.[51]

CONCLUSION

In this chapter, we learned that Kagawa's reverence for the emperor and his patriotism, which is love of country, were common to first-generation and second-generation Christians like Kagawa. However, Kagawa's uniqueness was that he practiced mass evangelism and social transformation through service to the socially disadvantaged, based on his Christian brotherhood economics theory of redemptive love and individualism. Kagawa's work was carried out not in urban areas with large Christian populations and churches, but in Japan's periphery, rural areas, such as fishing villages and mountain villages. The missionary work there was aimed at people who were excluded from Christianity and who had never encountered the Christian gospel. In the following chapters, we will examine in detail how Kagawa faced the issue of the emperor and the nation during the war period.

---

51. Hirano, "Political Thought on Reconstruction," 4.

5

The Emperor

INTRODUCTION: KAGAWA'S REVERENT FEELING FOR THE EMPEROR

The tension between the emperor system and Christianity is illustrated in that the government authorities enacted both the Peace Preservation Law (PPL) in 1925 and the Religious Organization Law (ROL) in 1939, as the government regarded Christianity as against the emperor system. The PPL was completely revised in March of 1941, and the Religious Organization Law made all Protestant churches merge into the UCCJ in 1941.

The PPL was first enacted in April 1925 to eliminate communists in Japan, because of the influence of the Russian Revolution in 1917. The state authorities, even immediately before the end of the Pacific War, had strong suspicions about Christians and the church because the military government had never accepted the Christian doctrine of God's judgment on human beings, including the emperor, and because of the close parent-child relationship with Western countries, mainly Britain and the United States. Kagawa is an example: the SHP secretly reported Kagawa's sermons, lectures, etc., both domestically and internationally, fifty-eight times, by far the most compared to other Christian leaders. Kagawa was interrogated by the SHP four times after the Pacific War before the end of the war. In this political context, we will look at how Japanese Christians, including Kagawa and the UCCJ, responded to the government and how they accepted the emperor in consideration of their faith.

Table 5.1: Chronology related to the emperor	
1868	FPN (anti-Christianity)
1868	Charter of Oath in Five Articles (deleted anti-Christianity article)
1889	The Constitution of the Empire of Japan is established: article 28 specifies freedom of religion
1925	PPL is established.
1939	Religious Organization Law (ROL) is established.
Mar. 1941	PPL is completely revised.
Apr. 1941	RJACLC is held.
June 1941	UCCJ is established.
Dec. 1941	Pacific War breaks out.

On June 27, 1943, at Kobe Church, Kagawa said"

> Though we Christians have groaned under persecution and oppression, we do not need to worry because we have gained official authorization from the emperor.[1]

However, despite Kagawa's reverence for the emperor, on November 20, 1943, the SHP stated:

> The Kobe Prefecture brought Kagawa to the military police office for interrogation as he denounced our State Shintoism [Shrine Shinto]. As the authority recognized that Kagawa had not intended to denounce Shinto and he exhibited remorse for his criticism, the authority of the prosecutor's office released Kagawa after receiving his submissions of written oath in which he pledged to refrain from critical statements in public.[2]

We notice Kagawa's statement at the Kobe Church, where he described the emperor's treatment of Christianity. As we recognized in the earlier chapter of "Japan against Christianity," religious freedom was guaranteed by the Constitution by the name of the emperor in 1889, and the government authorized the mission work of Christianity in 1899. Thus, it was

1. Institute for the Study of Humans and Society, *Movement of Christianity*, 3:22.
2. Institute for the Study of Humans and Society, *Movement of Christianity*, 3:23.

not surprising that the SHP released Kagawa from its office after finishing the interrogation. The SHP recognized that Kagawa had not denounced Shintoism because Kagawa appreciated the emperor's favorable treatment of Christianity. The above story makes us understand Kagawa's attitude toward the state authorities of the military government and the emperor.

Though there had been an anti-Christianity climate in Japan, Kagawa had a reverent feeling for the emperor up to his death in 1960. Kagawa's respecting the emperor was strongly related to his patriotism for Japan, just the same as for Japanese Christians before the war.

TENSION BETWEEN THE EMPEROR SYSTEM AND CHRISTIANITY

After Protestant foreign missionaries introduced Christianity during the Meiji Restoration period in the middle of the nineteenth century, respecting the emperor and the imperial house was important for Japanese Christians because the emperor was the state's sovereign.

The Constitution of the Empire of Japan, the so-called Meiji Constitution, which was established in 1889, specified that:

- The Empire of Japan shall be reigned over and governed by a line of emperors unbroken for ages eternal (art. 1).
- The emperor is sacred and inviolable (art. 3).
- The emperor has the supreme command of the army and navy (art. 11).[3]

See the below chart for an understanding of the political structure. Note that the elder who was a former senior statesman could give advice to the emperor and that only the military had the right to send the minister of both the army and the navy to the cabinet.

---

3. National Diet Library, "Constitution of the Empire."

THE EMPEROR

Chart 5.1 The emperor as the state's sovereign

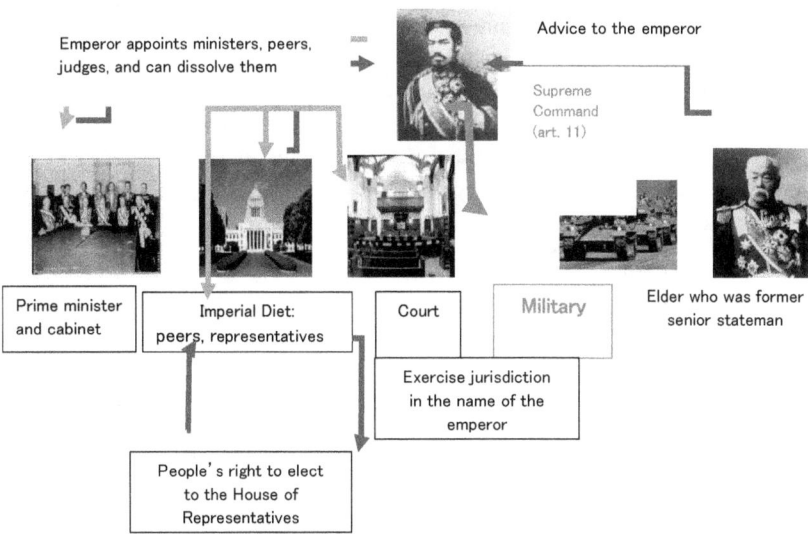

As the Constitution of the Empire of Japan, the so-called Meiji Constitution declared that the emperor ruled Japan politically and religiously:

Article 3: The emperor is sacred and inviolable.

Japanese Christians had difficulty in worshiping the emperor as a god. Though they believed the emperor was placed under God's judgment at the end of the world when the UCCJ was established in 1941, based on the ROL of 1939, it could not enact both its constitution and the Confession of Faith (信仰告白), which could specify God's judgment at the end-times on the living and the dead, including on an emperor, but only the constitution (教会規則). It was only in 1953, nine years after the war, that the UCCJ enacted the Confession of Faith. See article 5 of the constitution below, authorized by the Ministry of Education in 1941.

Article 5 of the Constitution Authorized by the Ministry of Education in 1941: Outline of the Doctrine of the UCCJ (教団規則)

The Ministry of Education of the Japanese government (MEJG), based on the ROL of 1939, applied to establish the United Church of Christ in Japan (UCCJ) and authorized the UCCJ's constitution (教会規則, literally, rules of the church), in which article 5 specified the below complete Confession of Faith.

> The Father, the Son, and the Holy Spirit revealed in Jesus Christ and testified in the Bible, are the Trinity of God, for the sin of the world and its salvation, through the redemption of his Son who became man and rose from the dead. He forgives the sins of believing, makes them righteous, purifies them, and gives them eternal life. The church is the body of Christ, called by grace, who awaits the coming of the Lord to keep the worship service, perform the sacraments, and preach the gospel.[4]

We notice that the UCCJ's Confession of enacted after the war in October 1953 further specifies:

> He ascended into heaven, and sitteth on the right hand of God the Father Almighty; from thence He shall come to judge the quick and dead.[5]

This confession testifies that the Japanese emperor is, like one of God's created human beings, placed under God's judgment and needs the redemptive love of the cross of Christ.

Based on the previously mentioned sociopolitical context of Japan, this book aims to review Kagawa's viewpoint of the emperor before, during, and after the so-called Fifteen Years War (starting with the Manchuria incident in 1931 and ending with the Japanese surrender in 1945).

To achieve the goal, first, I describe the sociopolitical context of the emperor's emergence as a sovereign of the state during the Meiji Restoration period after Japan opened the country to the world due to the agreement with the US in 1858. Second, I try to claim that Kagawa had feelings of gratitude to the emperor before, during, and after the periods of the Fifteen Years War, and even after the war until his death. Third, I review why Christians recognized an emperor of high moral character. Fourth, I examine the theological perspective about the relationship between the emperor and the people based on Rom 13, as Kagawa used both words (emperor, people) when he was asked about his justification of the war.

---

4. UCCJ, *UCCJ during the War*, 22.
5. UCCJ, "What We Believe."

THE EMPEROR

SOCIOPOLITICAL CONTEXT OF THE EMPEROR'S EMERGENCE AS A SOVEREIGN OF THE STATE

The Meiji Era (1868–1912) began with the Meiji emperor's proclamation of the Charter Oath in Five Articles (COFA) in March 1868,[6] before the establishment of the Constitution of the Empire of Japan in 1890.

In 2003, the House of Representatives, based on the Basic Materials of the Meiji Constitution and the Constitution of Japan, recognized that

> the COFA was also emphasized by the Meiji government and the Freedom and People's Rights faction as a starting point when advocating the realization of constitutional government and a parliamentary system.[7]

The newly-organized Meiji government (organized in January 1868) established revolutionary social reforms such as abolishing the traditional class system by classing clan retainers as "the descendant samurai" (士族; see chart below) and farmers, craftsmen, and merchants as "commoners" (平民); establishing the democratic parliamentary system (the House of Peers and the House of Representatives), a new court system (the Supreme Court, the Court of Appeal, and District Courts), and a compulsory education system; expanding the suffrage (a male over twenty-five years old for the House of Representatives), etc.

Chart 5.2 Social reformation: Percentage of population by status at the beginning of the Meiji era (thanks to the social reformation of the Charter Oath in the Five Articles of 1868)[8]

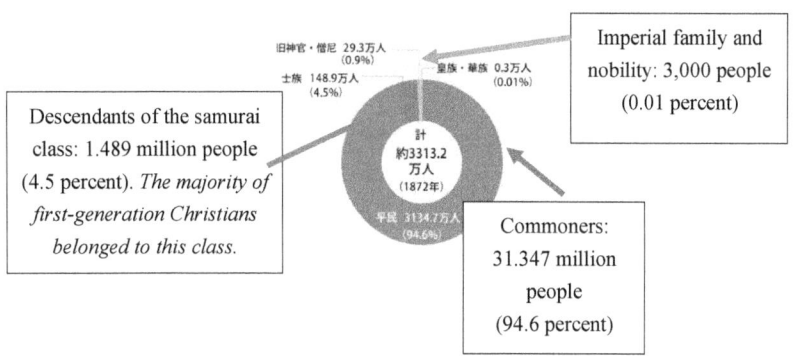

6. "The Charter Oath in Five Articles," in Meiji Jingu Shrine, "Enshrined Kami."
7. House of Representatives, "Basic Materials," 3–4.
8. National Diet Library, "Population by Status."

Weakness of the Cabinet System Due to the Imperial Prerogative Supreme Command of the Military[9]

> The Meiji Constitution was promulgated in 1980 after being drafted by Ito Hirobumi (伊藤博文, 1841–1909) and his committee, which took the Prussia Constitution as a model.[10]

The Imperial Prerogative Supreme Command of the Military existed in the domain where the principle of political responsibility was unsuitable. Prussian scholars claimed that war is outside domestic law and order, and that armed forces act in line with the movements of foreign enemies. The Meiji Constitution had article 12 ("The Emperor determines the organization and peace standing of the Army and Navy"), which belonged to the domain of domestic law and order, and article 11 ("the Emperor has the supreme command of the Army and Navy"), which existed outside of the domestic law and order.[11]

Then, how did the military authorities use political means to control even the prime minister and his cabinet? In 1900, *gunbu daijin geneki bunkan sei* (軍部大臣現役文官制) was established, which was a regulation to limit military ministers' appointing authority only to active *taisho* (generals) and *chusho* (lieutenant generals); it limited this regulation to military officers, such as *taisho* and *chusho*, exclusively, without appointing a civilian to narrow down the candidates to the government cabinet.

> In December 1912, as the second Saionji (西園寺公望) Cabinet (1911–1912) rejected the demand from the Japanese Army to increase two army divisions in Korea, Uehara Yusuke, a minister of the army of his cabinet, resigned suddenly from the Saionji Cabinet. Then, the Saionji Cabinet was forced to resign because the cabinet could not install a successor.[12]

In addition to the above incident, the arbitrary actions of the military, armed with the power of the Imperial Prerogative Supreme Command bestowed by the emperor, had continued using this means even up to the period of the Manchurian incident in 1931. Mori Yasuo claims:

---

9. National Diet Library, "Population by Status."

10. National Archives of Japan, "Promulgation of the Constitution"; see also House of Representatives, "Basic Materials."

11. Arakuni, *Minister of State*, 3–4.

12. Mori, "Civilian Minister System," 243.

They [Japanese politicians] failed to establish political supremacy over the Army for eight years from 1924, when a political party government was developed, leading to militarism afterward.[13]

Let's examine a historical example that shows Saionji's anguish during his time as a *genro* (元老, adviser to the emperor; Saionji lived 1849–1940).

Saionji the Elder's Conviction: Maintaining the Emperor's Neutrality

Sadako N. Ogata commented in her book *Defiance in Manchuria: The Making of Japanese Foreign Policy, 1931–1932*:

> It is important to note at this point that a strong force at the highest level of Japanese politics constantly endeavored to neutralize the political influence of the emperor. It was the unswerving conviction of Saionji, the last and the only existing elder statesman, that a constitutional monarch's function was to act according to the advice of those in responsible posts, and not to override their decisions nor to take the initiative in formulating policy. For the prevention of imperial despotism, and the proper development of constitutional government, Saionji's concept was theoretically beyond reproach. However, in the context of the existing Japanese political structure, the military could defy the civil government under the mantle of the "independence of the Supreme Command," especially when the settlement of the Manchurian Affair depended upon the successful control of the army, the lack of imperial intervention, meant the abrogation of the only available consistently opposed the resort to imperial admonition, for he judged, for example, that "even if the emperor spoke, the army would not possibly obey," and "should the emperor express himself and the army disobey, it would seriously damage the imperial character."[14]

At the time of the Manchurian incident, it turns out that the military had ignored the warnings of the emperor and the government, thus the system of constitutional monarchy had collapsed. Also, although there are still doubts about his work as an elder (元老, *genro*), we should not forget that Saionji himself had no choice but to resign from his cabinet.

Ogata's above comment in which she quoted Saionji's conviction that "even if the emperor spoke, the army would not possibly obey" exposed not

---

13. Mori, "Civilian Minister System," 241.
14. Ogata, *Defiance in Manchuria*, 151–52.

his weakness but the weakened cabinet system of Japan at the period of the first stage of the Fifteen Years War (1931–45). In addition to the cabinet's weakness of political power, the military had weakened the political power of any government political organization through a coup d'état in the form of the young imperial Japanese Army, such as the May 15 incident in 1932 and the February 26 incident in 1936 as detailed below.

KAGAWA'S OBSESSION WITH THE EMPEROR SYSTEM

See the list of ministers who were killed by the ultranationalistic army youth officers. In addition to the weakening political system, Japanese ultranationalists assassinated or attempted to kill politicians in the name of the emperor. How did Kagawa react to these historical barbarous incidents?

Table 5.2: Ministers who were killed or suffered assassination attempts by the ultranationalistic army youth officers[15]		
Name	Year Killed or Resigned	Remarks
Takahashi Korekiyo	1936 by 2.26 incident	Killed, prime minister
Tanaka Giichi	1929 by Zhang Zuolin incident	Resigned, prime minister
Inukai Tsuyoshi	1932 by 5.15 incident	Killed, prime minster
Saito Makoto	1936 by 2.26 incident	Killed, prime minister
Okada Keisuke	1936 by 2.26 incident	Verge of being assassinated, prime minister

The National Diet Library recorded the 2.26 incident under the title "Rise of the Military: The 2.26 Incident of 1936":

> A document to suppress the uprising] was passed along to the rebellious officers, but instead created confusion, as some changes were made in the wording of the text on the way. At one point, events seemed to be unfolding in the rebellious officers' favor, but when the Emperor made his will clear shortly thereafter, by firmly

---

15. Sasaki, "Reexamination of Prime Minister," 254.

declaring that the revolt should be suppressed, the rebellion was quelled some three days later, in February 1936.[16]

The emperor's resolute intention to subdue the February 26 incident supports Kagawa's admiration for the emperor's actions, which led him to defend the emperor after the war. In the immediate aftermath of the war, through an interview with Mark Gayn and an open letter to MacArthur, Kagawa revealed that the emperor took a firm stance on critical political issues in Japan. The discussion on the open letter to MacArthur will be discussed in a later chapter. Mark Gayn (1902–81), a Canadian journalist and the author of the book *Japan Diary*, had a two-hour interview with Kagawa in Tokyo on January 22, 1946, a half year after the end of the Pacific War. Gayn reported"

> He [Kagawa] said he stood for control of wealth, redistribution of land, and the abolition of feudalism. But though he was against feudalism, Kagawa was for the emperor. "We need him," he said strongly. "In recent years, five premiers have been assassinated. The parties keep quarreling with each other. What we need is an arbiter. Hirohito is a man of tragedy. I sympathize with him. The nation and the Diet are responsible for the war. He is not."[17]

Kagawa recognized the emperor as the only "arbiter" who could deal with the critical political situation in Japan.

Though we recognize that Kagawa respected the emperor as the moral leader of the state based on the political context we already reviewed, we should examine Kagawa's theological understanding by focusing on Rom 13, by which Kagawa referred to Paul's words for justifying the war. Kagawa interpreted Rom 13 in his book *Social Movement of the Bible*, which was published in 1928, as follows:

> In this way, Paul's Letter to the Romans, who had a well-established social order and law, is from the Romans. He said, "Let all submit to the authorities above." This shows that the Christians never included subversive elements and acted according to the social order of the time.[18]

Kagawa's interpretation of the Bible is orthodox. However, the problem is that when a ruler established by God observes the human rights of

---

16. National Diet Library, "2.26 Incident of 1936."
17. Gayn, *Japan Diary*, 99.
18. Kagawa, *Social Movement of Bible*, 229–30.

the people and governs them with redemptive love, which is synonymous with Kagawa's theology, Kagawa's interpretation of the Bible is acceptable; but when Kagawa realized that Japanese military authorities were committing atrocities against their Asian neighbors, it is no surprise that Kagawa's understanding of the Bible was perceived as superficial and contradictory.

In 1937, the year the Sino-Japanese War broke out, Yanaihara Tadao (1893–1961), Kagawa's contemporary, criticized Japan's aggression against China through the book of Isaiah. The Japanese government recognized his criticisms as anti-national and forced him to leave the Faculty of Economics at the University of Tokyo. Based on the relationship between the state and Christians, I discuss these issues in another chapter.

Based on the previously mentioned sociopolitical context of Japan, this book aims to review Kagawa's viewpoint of the emperor before, during, and after the so-called Fifteen Years War (starting with the Manchuria incident in 1931 and ending with the Japanese surrender in 1945).

Why Kagawa Recognized the Emperor as a Moral Leader for Non-Christians in Japan

The Imperial Rescript of Education (IRE) was issued with the signature of the Meiji emperor in October 1890. The IRE was used as the moral standard not only for students in a school but for all Japanese citizens. The Meiji Constitution, promulgated in February 1889, stipulates freedom of religion in article 28 because the West requested the abolishment of the ban on Christianity, as mentioned previously. To discuss the relationship between the Meiji Constitution and the IRE, we should understand the content of the IRE below. Nonetheless, we should recognize that Kagawa as a Christian never adopted the IRE as his moral standard; Kagawa commented there is no redemptive love in Oriental thought,[19] although he recognized and valued Meiji Japan's established moral standards by the emperor for the Japanese population.

The Imperial Rescript on Education

Know ye, Our subjects:
Our Imperial Ancestors have founded Our Empire on a basis broad and everlasting and have deeply and firmly implanted

---
19. Kagawa, *Complete Set*, 13:83.

virtue. Our subjects ever united in loyalty and filial piety have from generation to generation illustrated the beauty thereof. This is the glory of the fundamental character of Our Empire, and herein also lies the source of Our education. Ye, Our subjects, be filial to your parents, affectionate to your brothers and sisters: as husbands and wives be harmonious, as friends true; bear yourselves in modesty and moderation; extend your benevolence to all; pursue learning and cultivate arts, and thereby develop intellectual faculties and perfect moral powers; furthermore advance the public good and promote common interests; always respect the Constitution and observe the laws; should an emergency arise, offer yourselves courageously to the State; and thus guard and maintain the prosperity of Our Imperial Throne coeval with heaven and earth.

So shall ye not only be Our good and faithful subjects but render illustrious the best traditions of your forefathers.

The Way here set forth is indeed the teaching bequeathed by Our Imperial Ancestors, to be observed alike by Their Descendants and the subjects, infallible for all ages and true in all places. It is Our wish to lay it to heart in all reverence, in common with you, Our subjects, that we may all thus attain the same virtue.[20]

The COFA in 1868, the Meiji Constitution (issued in February 1889), and the IRE (issued in October 1890) were the fundamental contracts between the emperor and his subjects, which built up Japanese political polity. Ajima Hisashi (安嶋彌) states:

> Ito Hirobumi [伊藤博文, 1841–1909], who was a crucial figure in the drafting of the Meiji Constitution, contributed to establishing the Meiji Constitution by clearly understanding that the basis of the modern constitution was to limit the power of the monarch and guarantee the rights of the people.[21]

This means the Meiji Constitution has a monarchical emperor-centered nature that demands sacrificial loyalty from the subjects. Fukushima Kiyonori (福島清紀) recognizes similarities between articles 1 and 3 of the Meiji Constitution and the Imperial Rescript on Education, which requires the subjects to show their absolute sacrificial loyalty to the emperor. Thus, he understands the ultranationalist state system as having been constructed by the state's unification of secular power and spiritual authority.[22] Then

---

20. Ministry of Education of the Meiji Government, "Imperial Rescript on Education."
21. Yasujima, "Imperial Rescript on Education."
22. Fukushima, "Politics, Religion, and Education," 21.

how did Kagawa respect the emperor? To examine Kagawa's remarks on the emperor, I refer to his statements during and after the war. This is because, if the government put pressure for propaganda purposes on Kagawa to speak during the war, it is necessary to ascertain whether his statement was true or not.

Kagawa's Public Statements of Reverence for the Emperor

At the 2600th anniversary celebration of the Japan Empire, which was held in October 1940, Kagawa stated.

> When we think back, the Almighty has directed an unthinking providence toward Japan and has endowed Japan with a ruler who loves his subjects and is unparalleled in the world. . . . In our country, there is no savagery of slavery, no caste system, and the spirit of moderation and mutual assistance arises on its own. . . . When love and justice perish in the West, we should spread the gospel of restructuring human society through the help of Japan to save the world.[23]

Based on the COFA, the Meiji Constitution, and the IRE, Kagawa's comments on "a ruler who loves his subjects" could be understood that as the emperor abolished the social hierarchical system with the samurai at the top, which was the basis of the samurai class political system, and the emperor's subjects were given education, land ownership, appointment to the government and military bureaucrat and officers, economic equality by abolishing the samurai's family stipend,[24] and men's election to the House of Representatives, Kagawa might have interpreted the emperor's having transformed the ultra-feudal state as a first step to achieving freedom of religion.

On "there is no savagery of slavery, no caste system," there is no doubt that Christians, including Kagawa, were grateful for the emperor's reforms by abolishing the ban on Christianity during the Toyotomi and Tokugawa

---

23. Kagawa, *Complete Set*, 24:398–99.

24. The *chitsuroku shobun* (秩禄処分), the family stipend (hereditary stipend) of peers and samurai in the Meiji era. It was achieved by promulgating the *kinroku* public bond certificate issuance regulations (Grand Council of State Proclamation 108) in August 1876. *Karoku* is the stipend (salary) given by the feudal lord to the feudal retainers (vassals) under the Tokugawa shogunate government.

eras. In June 1943, in the middle of the war, the SHP reported that Kagawa said at Kobe Church as follows:

> Though we Christians have groaned under persecution and oppression, we do not need to worry because we have gained official authorization from the emperor.[25]

Kagawa's statement represents his real gratitude for the emperor's authorization given to Christians.

Nonetheless, as Fukushima Kiyonori recognizes that the Meiji Constitution and the IRE formed an ultranationalist state system, as they were constructed by the state's unification of secular power and spiritual authority, we should clarify why Kagawa justified the emperor during and after the war. Even if it can be judged that Kagawa's commitment to serving the socially poor can be appreciated as having something to do with the social change that the emperor performed in making the social class system equal, we acknowledge that his nationalistic ideas built a wall to keep other countries out.

Based on the discussion of the postwar Japanese Christians' movement to abolish the imperial system, I will discuss the emperor system issue again in the concluding chapter of this book.

HOW DID THE WORLD VIEW THE JAPANESE EMPEROR AFTER THE WAR?

Before concluding this chapter, we should recognize how the people in America, which Japan engaged in war; in China, which Japan invaded; and the Japanese themselves positioned the emperor concerning the war criminality, based on both political context and theological understanding, especially the interpretation of Rom 13.

Takeda Kiyoko (武田清子, 1917–2018), professor of history at International Christian University at Mitaka Tokyo, in her book, *The Dual-Image of the Japanese*, commented.

> The *New York Herald Tribune* commented that "There can never be peace so long as the medieval Mikado system is maintained,"[26] and in the *Nation* "Hirohito is directly responsible for Japan's

---

25. Institute for the Study of Humans and Society, *Movement of Christianity*, 3:22.
26. *New York Herald Tribune*, "Public Opinion Poll on the Emperor," Feb. 29, 1944.

military adventures."²⁷ According to a Gallup poll reported by the *Washington Post* in June 1945, 70 percent of the American public wanted some kind of punishment for Emperor Hirohito.²⁸ The *New York Times* also reported Chinese opinion that the emperor should be given the death sentence of life imprisonment with hard labor to show that he was a mere man and not an omnipotent divinity.²⁹ . . .

One way to approach the question of popular views of the emperor and the emperor system during the immediate postwar period is to look at several polls that were conducted during this period. One of them was reported in the 9 December 1945 issue of the *Yomiuri Hochi Shimbun*. The report was based on public opinion polls carried out by three private institutes. Entitled "Support of the Emperor System is the General Feeling of the *Nation*," the article emphasized that 95 percent of the population polled supported the emperor system.³⁰

We understand that there was a huge gap between the US and China's perception of the emperor as a war criminal and the attitude of the Japanese to defend the emperor and the imperial system during the period immediately before and after the end of the war. How did Kagawa position the emperor during this period? Quoting the *Chicago Daily News* of September 11, 1945, Schildgen commented:

> He [Kagawa] admitted that he had not protested the war after Pearl Harbor because the government had cautioned him to keep quiet. He defended his lack of action by offering a fundamentalist interpretation of the Bible that nationalized the emperor system as the divine right of kings. The following sequence of questions and answers is illustrative of his waffling:
>
> Q: In view of your faith as a Christian, as absolute above Japan, would you be willing to say that the emperor could be wrong?
> A: No, I can't say that.
> Q: Does that mean that the emperor is always right?

---

27. *Nation*, "Public Opinion Poll on the Emperor," Mar. 4, 1944.
28. *Washington Post*, "Gallup Poll," June 29, 1945.
29. *New York Times*, "Public Opinion Poll on the Emperor," Aug. 12, 1945.
30. Takeda, *Dual-Image of Japanese Emperor*, 10, 122.

> A: I refer you to the 13th chapter of Romans, which says, in effect, "Obey the authority who is endowed with power from above," and the emperor is.[31]

Kagawa replied based on Rom 13, on how he interpreted the Pauline letters concerning the relationship between the state authority and people.

Kagawa commented in his book, *Seisho no Shakai Undo* (聖書の社会運動, The social movement of the Bible), as follows.

> In any case, Paul does not preach blind and absolute obedience to state authority based on the Pauline letters: First Corinthians 4:8, "You are already satisfied; you have already grown rich; you have become kings without us! Indeed, I wish that you had become kings so that we also might become kings with you"; Romans 5:17, "For if by the one man's offense death reigned through the one, much more those who receive abundance of grace and of the gift of righteousness will reign in life through the One, Jesus Christ"; Second Timothy 2:12, "If we endure, We shall also reign with Him. If we deny Him, He also will deny us." As an emancipated man, Paul, of course, exhorted submission to authority, but he does not say to be content with a life of slavery. So, each one demanded through Jesus, "I wish that you had become kings."[32]

As Kagawa interpreted based on the above Pauline Letters, he claimed that Christians should not be blindly obedient to authority. This meant Kagawa did not regard the emperor as a living god but as a person who needed to be saved by God. Then, how should we explain the difference between the fact that 95 percent of the Japanese people still supported the emperor even after the war, and Kagawa's understanding of the Bible, which denied blind obedience to the emperor? In a December 9, 1945, report, the *Yomiuri Hochi Shimbun* confirmed that 95 percent of the Japanese supported the emperor system in a postwar poll. Were Christians included in that 95 percent? Unfortunately, the *Yomiuri Hochi Shimbun* did not report on the percentages by religion in its postwar polls, so it is impossible to speculate whether Christians were included in the 95 percent.

As Takeda Kiyoko conducted a survey of Christians on the relationship between their faith and loyal sentiment based on the Japanese political context in and around 1955, I will examine how Takeda's analysis should be interpreted.

---

31. Thorp, "No Early Rebirth."
32. Kagawa, *Social Movement of Bible*, 230.

Table 5.4: Relationship between Christian faith and patriotic sentiment

Table 5.3	Relationship between Christian faith and patriotic sentiment[33]						
Age group relationship	(A)	(B)	(C)	(D)	(F)	(G)	Average
(X) Harmonious	81.51	67.7	45	35.7	26.3	0	49.3
(Y) Easy to be antagonistic	11.1	19.4	20	28.6	31.6	63.4	22.8
(Z) Contradictory	7.4	12.9	35	35.7	42.1	63.6	27.7
(Y) + (Z)	18.5	32.3	55	64.3	73.7	100	50.5
Age group relationship	(1)	(2)	(3)	(4)	(5)	(6)	(7) Average
(A) Harmonious	81.51	67.7	45	35.7	26.3	0	49.3
(B) Easy to be antagonistic	11.1	19.4	20	28.6	31.6	36.4	22.8
(C) Contradictory	7.4	12.9	35	35.7	42.1	63.6	27.7
(B) + (C) =	18.5	32.3	55	64.3	73.7	100	50.5

(A) Before the Russo-Japanese War (before 1905): Those who were born before 1887
(B) Before the Taisho democracy era (1906–16): Those who were born between 1888 and 1897
(C) Taisho democracy era (1916–26): Those who were born between 1898 and 1907
(D) Surging-up period of the left-wing movement (1926–36): Those who were born between 1908 and 1916
(F) A period from the China incident to the end of WWII (1937–45): Those who were born between 1917 and 1936
(G) The postwar period (after 1945): Those who were born in 1927

It is a great surprise that Takeda's table shows that nearly 40 percent of Christians immediately after the end of the war believed that the imperial system was easily antagonistic to their own beliefs.

According to Takeda's analysis, Christians after the war (group G) found nothing in the relationship between their beliefs and the emperor

---

33. Furuya, *Japan and Christianity*, 145. Furuya stated that the survey was carried out by Takeda Kiyoko around 1955.

system that harmonized with their beliefs. As Kagawa was born in 1888, he belongs to group B, those who were born between 1888 and 1897. Kagawa might have been in the group of those Christians who had found the emperor system harmonious with their faith.

But, how I can prove that Kagawa had faith that "harmonized with the loyal and patriotic sentiment" based on his theology of redemptive love? Kagawa loved the Japanese people regardless of their social status based on his theology of redemptive love. There is no need to testify that Kagawa loved all Japanese people, including royal family members personally, going beyond social human rights. The story is that when Kagawa received an invitation from Prince Higashikuninomiya, just immediately after the war, Kagawa asked the prince to become a Christian. It is one of the historical pieces of evidence of Kagawa's love.

How did Yanaihara, a contemporary (1893–1961) of Kagawa who belonged to the same group B as Kagawa consider harmonizing with the loyal and patriotic sentiment? In 1934, Yanaihara, on the subject of the Japanized Christianity, stated as follows:

> Japanized Christianity is a conversion of Japanese sentiments into Christianity, not a conversion of Christianity into the Japanese spirit. Therefore, Christianity should not only demonstrate the virtues of the Japanese spirit but also compensate for its inadequacies and purify what it lacks.
>
> The touchstones of Japanized Christianity are the problems of the Shinto shrine and the national polity or nationalism. Not making good decisions towards these problems is negative for the progress of Japanese Christianity. An important matter lies in how the national polity is interpreted, as a Christianity that is always able to go along with the idea of the national polity of extremely self-centered exclusive nationalism cannot be said to be a genuine Christianity. Christianity is to purify the concept of our national polity, and the concept of the national polity is not to control the truth of Christianity.[34]

Yanaihara's comment resembles the words of Rom 12: 1–2, "I appeal to you therefore, brothers, by the mercies of God, to present your bodies as a living sacrifice, holy and acceptable to God, which is your spiritual worship. Do not be conformed to this world, but be transformed by the renewal of your mind, that by testing you may discern what is the will of God, what is good and acceptable and perfect" (NRSV). As Paul exhorted

---

34. Yanaihara, *Complete Works*, 18:222–23.

Christians not to be "conformed to this world," Yanaihara criticized both Japanized Christianity and the state itself. As we learned when the Second Sino-Japanese War broke out in July 1937, Yanaihara criticized the state authorities by claiming, "It is against justice for a strong country to invade the rights and interests of a weak country in the name of its national interests." He never conformed to this world his whole life. But, how was Kagawa confronted by the state?

Kagawa's sacrificial love for the socially poor is not "the idea of the national polity of extremely self-centered exclusive nationalism," but Kagawa's justifying the Japanese military invasion of Asian countries and colonization of Manchukuo, Taiwan, and Korea in the name of liberating Asian countries exploited by Western powers was the wrong decision to take "towards these problems" and was absolutely against the "progress of Japanese Christianity" during the war period. Thus, I recognize that these contradictory dualities of Kagawa were a significant factor in his responsibility for the war. Now let's examine how Kagawa confessed his responsibility after Japan was defeated in the war.

Both Kagawa and Yanaihara regarded the emperor as the father of the family—"a paterfamilias of the Japanese race"[35]—in the relationship between the emperor and his subjects. In a situation of defeat in which everything has been lost, we are made to stand before God as one human being of the same defeated nation. This portends that the emperor and his subjects will be placed before the judgment of God when they are in a place where all security of life is gone.

How did Kagawa confess his war responsibility to the Japanese-invaded countries, especially Asia during the Fifteen Years War, based on his statement of apology before and after the Fifteen Years War?

CONCLUSION

This chapter illustrated that regardless of the generation, whether the first generation or the second generation, Japanese Christians had reverence toward the emperor and patriotism for Japan. They adhered to a Christianity that was embedded in the Japanese spiritual climate, while the government authorities regarded Christians as traitors to the state.

35. Yanaihara, *Japanese Spirit*, 92.

Kagawa claimed to bow down to the emperor by insisting doing so was a duty of the subjects. However, regardless of Kagawa's paying the highest respect to the emperor, the SHP reported what he said in 1942 as follows:

> Those of us who believe in Christianity never worship idols, and of course, we do not do so even now. However, the Japanese nation bows down to shrines and temples. While this may formally amount to idolatry, the ministry of the Minister of Home Affairs has said that the shrines and temples worshiped by our ancestors are worshiped by the Minister of Home Affairs. It is argued that the people must worship in the sense of ancestor worship. The Bible clearly states that they should obey their superiors, and there is no difference between them and ordinary people, but in short, it is a matter of belief.
>
> It is a well-known fact that Christians are generally pacifists, especially as individuals, my pacifism remains unchanged from beginning to end. The reason for this goes without saying: war is a grave sin.[36]

Kagawa's statement represents what Christians, including Kagawa, believed in rejecting the worship of idols and their theological justification for following the state authorities of the non-Christian state. In the following chapters, we will review how Kagawa survived, especially during the period of the Pacific War from 1941 to 1945.

---

36. Institute for the Study of Humans and Society, *Movement of Christianity*, 2:151.

6

Theological Perspective on a Response to the State

INTRODUCTION

For an understanding of the sociopolitical context, see table 6.1. below.

Table 6.1: Kagawa's theological perspective on a response to the state	
1897	Boston University STH personalism[1]
1928	*The Social Movement of the Bible*[2]
1928–41	KGM[3]
1933	Japan withdraws from the LN (Matsuoka Yosuke speaks at the LN)
1936	*Brotherhood Economics*: Kagawa attends Walter Rauschenbusch conference
1940	Kagawa is detained by SHP as an anti-war movement suspect (Matsuoka orders release of Kagawa).

1. Amemiya, *Kagawa Toyohiko in Youth*, 19, 199.
2. Kagawa, *Bible on Social Movement*, 240–41.
3. Kurokawa, "Kingdom of God Movement."

Mar. 1941	PPL is completely revised on March 2.
May 1943	Kagawa is detained by SHP in Tokyo as an anti-war movement suspect.
June 1943	Kagawa is detained by SHP in Kobe as an anti-war movement suspect.
Oct. 1943	Kagawa publishes in the *Pillar of Light*: "Dying as a Martyr in the National Crisis."
July 1944	Kagawa is detained for nine days at SHP headquarters.
July 1944	Radio message against the US[4]
1945	Kagawa escapes to Tochigi due to the rumor of an assassination plan by the ultranationalists.
1946–49	NJCCM
1949	*A Reexamination of Oriental Thought*

This chapter aims to testify how Kagawa loved his homeland by loving Japanese people. Loving Japanese people was based on his theology of redemptive love. Kagawa, in the book *Brotherhood Economics*, which was published in 1936, confessed:

> Nestorian Christianity preached the only doctrine and did not try to teach the love of Christ. Seventy-five years ago, the first missionary came to Japan from America. In those days Christianity was forbidden by the government. The reason for this was that four centuries earlier when the Jesuit missionaries came to Japan, pirates from the same countries of the West were plundering many islands in the seas south of Japan. On account of this, the Japanese government became suspicious of the growth of Christianity and feared it would bring political invasion in its wake.[5]

Kagawa's doctrine of brotherhood focused on loving the Japanese people rather more than on teaching theology, by stressing the importance

---

4. Kuroda, *Research on Kagawa Toyohiko*, 204–5.
5. Kagawa, *Brotherhood Economics*, 6–7.

of economic perspective. Kagawa said that the love of Jesus is more important than understanding theology (doctrine). However, he by no means neglected theology itself. As Kagawa claimed to love Japanese people without focusing significantly on theology, based on the Japanese anti-Christianity sociopolitical context by going back to the period when Jesuit missionaries came to Japan, the redemptive love theology was created as a means of coping with the state authorities' persecutions against Catholic Christians during both Toyotomi and Tokugawa periods, in which edicts were issued for expelling Christians. Kagawa's redemptive love was carried down to the modern era of the Meiji to Showa periods, which saw Shinto established by the Japanese imperial government and in which Japanese people were forced to worship the emperor during the Pacific War.

To achieve the goal of this chapter, I should demonstrate how Kagawa loved both his homeland and the Japanese people based on the Japanese sociopolitical context. First, we should review the Boston University School of Theology's personalism, which gave Kagawa the unshakable conviction his whole life to respect non-Christian spiritualities.

BOSTON UNIVERSITY SCHOOL OF THEOLOGY: PERSONALISM

Amemiya Eiichi (1927–2019) in *Seisyun no Kagawa Toyohiko* (Kagawa Toyohiko in youth) related Kagawa's narrative:

> Meiji Gakuin had an excellent library.... I read Bowne's religious philosophy when I was seventeen years old, and to this day, I have been able to move forward with a focus on personalist religious philosophy without getting too swayed ideologically, because I came across such good books when I was young.[6]

As Kagawa said, he was seventeen years old in 1897 when he read Bowne's book, *Personalism*. How did Borden Parker Bowne's theology of personalism influence Kagawa? We need Kagawa's theological understanding of Boston University personalism from the Japanese sociopolitical context. Bowne commented on his book *Personalism*:

> Christian attitude also toward the non-Christian religions has greatly changed in recent years. Christians themselves have been slow in understanding the truth and glory of the Gospel, the good

6. Amemiya, *Kagawa Toyohiko in Youth*, 199.

news of God. For a long time, it was held that God was good only to those to whom the Christian revelation had come and that all others were unconditionally lost. But at last, we have learned that God is not made good by the Christians's revelation, but only declared and shown to be good; he has always been good; he has always been the Father Almighty and has always had purposes of grace concerning his children, *whether they knew him or not*. The insufferable blasphemy that condemned the whole non-Christian world indiscriminately has utterly disappeared among intelligent Christians. The God who has been dealing with all past generations is the God of grace whom our Lord has revealed, and they are still in his hands, whether in this world or in any other.

Similarly, Christian thought has changed concerning the great outlying non-Christian systems. These also were thought at one time to be evil and only evil, and without any value whatsoever for their adherents. Accordingly, it was the fashion to deride and decry these religions, to emphasize their shortcomings and failures, and to oppose Christianity in its ideal form.

But further study has revealed how unjust all this was, and now we have come to believe that the great non-Christian systems also had their place in God's providential plan for men. We find it possible to think of Confucius (孔子), Mencius (孟子), Buddha, and many others as veritable prophets of the Most High, and as having done an important work among the people for whom they wrought; not indeed making anything perfect, but preparing the way and contributing much to the organization and development of the people. And this, too, should not surprise, still less offend, any Christian, for we are told that *a portion of the Spirit is given to every man*, that *there is a light which lighteth every man that cometh into the world;* that *God is no respecter of persons, but that in every nation he that feareth God and worketh righteousness is accepted of him.*[7]

How did Kagawa apply the Boston University personalism to the anti-Christian spiritual climate? Kagawa applied it to the Japanese spiritual climate rooted in Buddhism, Confucianism, and Shintoism. Though Bowne's thought of personalism for understanding Oriental thought seems abstract, Kagawa had to apply it in Japan, an actual non-Christian world. Before reviewing Kagawa's comment on Oriental thought, it is helpful to note how a Buddhist regards Christianity, as it brings Christian love into sharper focus.

---

7. Bowne, *Personalism*, 288–90; emphasis in original.

A Reexamination of Oriental Thought

Kagawa, in his book *A Reexamination of Oriental Thought*, which was published in 1949 when he finished the mass evangelism work of the NJCCM, commented:

> After reading the Eastern sacred books, I recognized that redemption would not be fulfilled by a civilization of mankind. A caterpillar does not become a butterfly by itself. The power in heaven has made a butterfly from a caterpillar. Even if we lost the heaven, the heaven peers at our heart and it reveals the holy of holies for lifting us to the heave. The heavenly power does not belong to us. It, of course, does not neglect us; it is a transcendent and fundamental existence that exalts a human being from the inside. The existence is love itself. As the Highest, it is responsible for the universe. It warms our soul from the inside, and it indemnifies finite beings' evils we committed in the past. We believe that it holds a respectable will for filling us with hope of resurrection by using a historical revelation.
>
> After observing the Eastern thoughts, though the Chinese started thinking from the universe, they didn't experience that the universe gave a redemptive love. In India, though Indians started from Rigveda in which they found divinity immanent in human nature, though they saw a vision of salvation, they could not reach the life of redemptive love after seeking the way of Moksha.
>
> After the war, the defeated Japan had to head up to a new road in which we had to throw ourselves on the love of the Highest, we should not be spoiled by love. To be connected to the Highest, we should throw away the rotten part. There is enough sap [樹液] to go around the rotting part for restoration. The sap should be the principle of life. The love of the cross is conceivable to be the principle of life and the principle of the redemptive love for Japan. The consciousness of universality that Christ had would be expanded to Japan by accompanying a togetherness based on redemptive love.[1]

The above writings tell Kagawa's thoughts as a Japanese Christian on his respecting Japanese spirituality without wavering in his theology of redemptive love. Nevertheless, we must admit that Kagawa's theology of redemptive love had lowered the hurdle for keeping the Christian faith, especially when the state authority regally forced Christians to follow

---

1. Kagawa, *Complete Set*, 13:83.

the national polity of worshiping the emperor and cooperating with the military operation in Japan's neighboring countries in Asia in the name of delivering Asia from Western powers.

In response to the threat of the Russian Revolution in 1917, the Japanese government enacted the PPL in 1925 to severely crack down on left-wing subversive elements. Christians and churches, with Kagawa as their leader, developed the KGM nationwide, but the government, which had doubts about Christianity, conducted strict surveillance of the KGM and Kagawa's words and actions.

Kagawa's Way of Life as a Christian in Japan

Then how did Kagawa survive as a Christian in Japan amid an anti-Christian climate? His book, *Christ and Japan* (published in 1934), seven years before the Pacific War, gives us an understanding clearly through reading how Kagawa kept his form of existence his whole life up to his death in 1960. See what he commented.

> Whenever I visit the Great Shrine of Ise I do not worship Ama-Terasu-O-Mikami as a goddess. I do, however, remove my hat and bow reverently. The guard on duty finds no fault with this. The educational authorities ask nothing more. Some missionaries, however, look upon this as idol worship and clashes occur. These missionaries may find satisfaction in ignoring Japan's whole history and in destroying the memorials of the nation's builders.
>
> The people of Japan, however, always keen on preserving things of value, will discover that Japanese Christians take second place to none in their eagerness to conserve the nation's historical traditions. For instance, it was Christians who promoted the movement to preserve the traditional relics of Ninigi-no-Mikoto, the grandson of Ama-Terasu-O-Mikami. If Christians give evidence that they also have a high appreciation of Japan's past and its culture, it will help non-Christians to understand the true spirit of the Christian faith. It is most unfortunate that Protestants carry with them a sort of spirit of antagonism, and that the Roman Catholics take an attitude of intolerance.
>
> When these attitudes of Christians are compared with the tolerance of the Zen sect the disparity is great. This question of Shinto shrines will probably be made an issue again and again. I find myself in agreement with the attitude of the educational authorities that the shrines of State Shinto should be treated as

monuments to the builders of the nation and not be looked upon as religious institutions. There is no need respect for shrines of doubtful and unworthy origin. But our hats should come off in respect for the nation's builders. In Japan both Shinto and Buddhist believers frequent Christian churches and attend weddings and funerals held under Christian auspices. Thus, when Christians refuse to reciprocate by attending Shinto and Buddhist functions of this character it creates a most unfortunate impression. On such occasions, it is necessary for us to omit the religious implication but fulfill our social obligation.[2]

Kagawa's above comment represents how a Christian should behave in a Japanese community. However, he admits it is hard for a Christian to observe a Japanese traditional religious rite. Some Christians might believe that we should extend heartfelt condolence to the bereaved at a temple or a shrine without observing Buddhist or Shintoism manners of funeral service.

In 1942, during the war, at Kochi Church of the UCCJ, Kagawa said,

Those of us who believe in Christianity never worship idols, and of course, we do not do so even now. However, the Japanese nation bows down to shrines and temples. While this may formally amount to idolatry, the ministry of the Minister of Home Affairs has said that the shrines and temples worshiped by our ancestors are worshiped by the Minister of Home Affairs. It is argued that the people must worship in the sense of ancestor worship. The Bible clearly states that they should obey their superiors, and there is no difference between them and ordinary people, but in short, it is a matter of belief.

It is a well-known fact that Christians are generally pacifists, especially as individuals; my pacifism remains unchanged from beginning to end. The reason for this goes without saying: war is a grave sin.[3]

Kagawa's comment corresponds with what Kagawa said in his book *Christ and Japan* in 1934; his faith was consistent even though he was being observed by a military police officer. Especially on views on war, in the second paragraph, Kagawa confessed he was against the war because of its sin. As a Christian leader, Kagawa had been pursued strictly by the SHP. In

---

2. Kagawa, *Christ and Japan*, 88–90.
3. Institute for the Study of Humans and Society, *Movement of Christianity*, 2:151.

the 1940s, Kagawa had been detained four times by the SHP. Finally, the SHP ordered Kagawa not to criticize national polity in public as follows:

> The Kobe Prefecture brought Kagawa to the military police office for interrogation as he denounced our State Shintoism [Shrine Shinto]. As the authority recognized that Kagawa had not intended to denounce Shinto and he exhibited remorse for his criticism, the authority of the prosecutor's office released Kagawa after receiving his submissions of written oath in which he pledged to refrain from critical statements in public.[4]

Despite Kagawa's respectful attitude toward Japanese traditional spirituality, the local government authority did not trust Kagawa, as they had been inquiring secretly about Christians during the war.

ROMANS 9:3: KAGAWA'S JUSTIFICATION FOR COOPERATION WITH THE MILITARY

In 1952, when Yokoyama Haruichi had almost completed the writing of the *Rinjinai no Toshi Kagawa Toyohiko* (隣人愛の闘士賀川豊彦先生, A warrior of love for his neighbors: Kagawa Toyohiko) and was alone with Kagawa, he asked Kagawa about his thoughts and deeds during the war. Yokoyama said.

> Kagawa said only one word, "For I could wish that I were accursed and cut off from Christ for the sake of my own people, my kindred according to the flesh." It was the word of Romans 9.[5]

As Kagawa didn't explain why he referred to this biblical quote for expressing how he justified war to Yokoyama, we must interpret that Kagawa, like Paul and Moses, asked God to forgive what Japanese people sinned during the war. Does this mean that Kagawa claimed he was not responsible for war? To prove my interpretation that Kagawa might not have committed any immoral deeds during the war—I claim that he did not confess war responsibility on an individual basis—I need to clarify the words of Rom 9:3.

The words of Rom 9:3 are incomprehensible, specifically, the words of being "cut off from Christ." How does a Christian love his neighbors without having Jesus's help? Jesus commanded in John 15:

---

4. Institute for the Study of Humans and Society, *Movement of Christianity*, 3:23.
5. Yokoyama Haruichi, in Muto, *Biography of Kagawa*, 67–68.

> This is my commandment, that you love one another as I have loved you. No one has greater love than this, to lay down one's life for one's friends.... You did not choose me, but I chose you. And I appointed you to go and bear fruit, fruit that will last so that the Father will give you whatever you ask him in my name. (John 15:12–13, 16 NRSV)

What Jesus said is understandable by most Christians as these words encourage that God will be with us when we ask him in the name of Jesus Christ to "lay down our life for our friends."

But to understand the words of Romans, we should first examine Calvin's book, *Commentary on Romans*, as Kagawa was a pastor in the Presbyterian Church. Calvin commented on Rom 9:3:

> *For I could wish, etc.* He could not have expressed a greater ardour of love than by what he testifies here; for that is surely perfect love which refuses not to die for the salvation of a friend.[6]

Though Calvin said that that is "perfect love which refuses not to die for the salvation of a friend," did Kagawa die for the people of Japan, including Christians and churches? He did not. More precisely, Kagawa denied dying as a martyr for Japan when he met Gandhi in 1939.[7] Calvin supplemented his view:

> But there is another word added, *anathema*, which proves that he speaks not only of temporal but of eternal death; and he explains its meaning when he says, *from Christ*, for it signifies a separation. And what is to be separated from Christ, but to be excluded from the hope of salvation? It was then a proof of the most ardent love, that Paul hesitated not to wish for himself that condemnation which he saw impending over the Jews, so that he might deliver them. It is no objection that he knew that his salvation was based on the election of God, which could by no means fail; for as those ardent feelings hurry us on impetuously, so they see and regard nothing but the object in view. So, Paul did not connect God's election with his wish, but the remembrance of that being passed by, he was wholly intent on the salvation of the Jews.[8]

As Kagawa was a Presbyterian, he might have accepted the theology of the election of God and might have understood Calvin's commentary.

---

6. Calvin, *Commentary on Romans*, 291; emphasis in original.
7. Gandhi, *Collected Works*, 68:296.
8. Calvin, *Commentary on Romans*, 291.

THEOLOGICAL PERSPECTIVE ON A RESPONSE TO THE STATE

Nevertheless, we must examine to what extent Kagawa agreed with or understood the Calvinistic theology of the doctrine of election, as Kagawa confessed that he was influenced by John Wesley, the theologian of Arminianism. Kagawa commented:

> At the age of a little more than twenty years old, John Wesley's *Diary of Faith* was one of the great influential books. . . . Wesley's mission movement has the power of individual salvation and a transformation of social structure. . . . If a person does not have a spiritual awakening, he cannot transform a community.[9]

How did Wesley interpret Rom 9:3? In Exodus 32:32, which is the parallel passage of Rom 9:3, Wesley commented:

> This expression may be illustrated by Romans 9:3. For I could wish myself to be an anathema from Christ, for my brethren's sake. Does this imply no more than not enjoying Canaan? Not that Moses absolutely desired this, but only comparatively expresses his vehement zeal for God's glory, and love to his people, signifying, that the very thought of their destruction, and the dishonor of God, was so intolerable to him, that he rather wishes, if it were possible, that God would accept of him, as a sacrifice in their stead, and by his utter (complete) destruction, prevent so great a mischief.[10]

Mosses said to God, "Alas, this people sinned a great sin. they have made themselves gods of gold. But now, if you will only forgive their sin—but if not, blot me out of the book that you have written."

Based on the commentaries of both Calvin and Wesley, we could interpret Rom 9:3 as follows:

Chart 6.1: Romans 9:3: Interpretation of Moses and Paul	
God's Punishment	
Moses prayed to God for the salvation of Israelites who sinned and worshiped false gods.	Paul prayed to God for the salvation of Jews who rejected the gospel of Jesus Christ.

---

9. Kagawa Toyohiko, in Wesley, *Diary of Faith*, 1.
10. Wesley, "Notes on Exodus," ch. 32.

Chart 6.2: Romans 9:3: Interpretation of Kagawa
Kagawa prayed to God for salvation for Japanese military authorities who invaded Asian countries and committed atrocities against Asian people.

As Kagawa was neither Moses nor Paul but one of the ministers of the Japanese church, how did he dare claim that he was the same as both, the first prophet and one of Jesus's, spotless? Based on the biblical interpretation of Rom 9:3, Kagawa might have distorted its theological message by emphasizing what Calvin said in his *Commentary on Romans*: "It was then a proof of the most ardent love." As we have learned previously, Kagawa empathized with love more than with theologies. So, based on the biblical interpretation of both Calvin and Wesley on Rom 9:3, the chart should be revised as follows:

Chart 6.3: Romans 9:3: My First Interpretation
God's Punishment
Kagawa decided to receive God's punishment along with the Japanese people—thus, God's punishment for Kagawa, the UCCJ, the Japanese military, and the people who cooperated with the military invasion of Asian countries.

For considering Kagawa's interpretation of Rom 9:3, we should consider the alternative. Kagawa selected a way to accept God's punishment together with the Japanese people, including the Japanese militarists who were judged by the Tokyo Trials, without hoping to not be killed. It was almost ten years after the war when Yokoyama asked the reason for Kagawa's commitment to the war in 1950, and it was also three years after the Tokyo Trial had sentenced Japanese military leaders, government officials, and political leaders who had initiated the war and committed atrocities against Asian people and prisoners of war; commanders like Shirabe Masaji had been hanged.[11] Just immediately before the publication of his autobiography, Kagawa might have decided to introduce his witness in public. On this occasion, he might have had to reinterpret Paul's message as a new message, as in the following statement in his periodical *Hino Hashira* (Pillar of light, Kagawa's personal periodical, issued from June 1924 to May 1944) in 1943:

---

11. Shirabe Masaji (1914–2004) was baptized by Kagawa Toyohiko in 1930. During the Pacific War, Shirabe was a POW camp commander. As he observed the Geneva Convention Agreement, the Tokyo Trial did not judge him. He became a pastor of the Japan Baptist Convention and Okinawa Baptist Convention.

Paul, the apostle of Jesus, cried, "For I could wish that I myself were cursed and cut off from Christ for the sake of my people, those of my race," for the monarchy; we, the subject, should be prepared to die a martyr even were we cut off from Christ. To die for the state is the spirit of Christianity. Bearing suffering gives further glory. Death is the victorious remark. The cross is the crown of pride. . . . Christ who taught us to attain the truth would never deny but bless those who would shed blood to liberate Asia. We shall never make Churchill nor Roosevelt, who illegally plunder ethnic minorities by hiding the truth, win a victory.[12]

Chart 6.4: Romans 9:3: My Second Interpretation
God's Punishment

Kagawa decided to receive God's punishment along with the Japanese people—thus, God's punishment for Kagawa, the UCCJ, the Japanese military, and people who cooperated with the military and justified war.

Kagawa did not preach abstract theological teachings but engaged with each person with love on a personal level. Based on his faith, the above interpretation of Rom 9:3 could reasonably be correct.

For the supposition that Kagawa wanted to die for the Japanese people, there are two pieces of evidence. The first one, in 1928, appears in Kagawa's *Seishono Shakai Undo* (聖書の社会運動, Social movement of the Bible), in a comment on Rom 9:3 with the subtitle "Nationalism [民族主義, *mizokushugi*] and Democracy" as follows:

> Paul was an advocate of nationalism. Paul exclaimed that he wished to be accursed and cut off from Christ for the sake of the salvation of his race of Jews. We are not the people who do not know the importance of internationalism. However, we understand well that *the state is one of the kinds of existence*. We, like Paul, should be a real Japanese nationalist.[13]

When Kagawa published the above book in 1928, the Huanggutun incident occurred. The military had invaded the North China territory to defend against the Western powers' colonization of this territory, especially Russia and Britain, as Ishihara, the military strategy official, planned the military operation in this territory.

---

12. Kagawa, "Dying as a Martyr," 1.
13. Kagawa, *Social Movement of Bible*, 240–41; emphasis added.

Immediately after the war in 1945, we recognize the second piece of evidence as follows:

> Less than a month after the surrender, when asked by an American whether he [Kagawa] was grateful to the United States for conquering Japan and creating the possibility for him to assume a position of influence in the government, *his blunt and sorrowful reply was, I would rather be dead.*[14]

Kagawa's comment was related to the story of his hiding in Tochigi Prefecture when the ultranationalists were planning to assassinate him. He wanted neither to be assassinated by an ultranationalist nor to be a puppet of the American authority. Kagawa might have thought that if he became an agent of the United States, it would be regarded as a betrayal of the country, and it would be impossible to dispel the anti-Christian spiritual climate in Japan. What is the theological meaning of the story? Kagawa's mission of pointing out the hope in God's love allowed the postwar Japanese people, who had been completely exhausted by defeat, to embark on a new path even amid the impoverishment of the land. Kagawa wanted to live with the people. This means as Calvin interpreted that Paul did not connect God's election with his wish but wholly intended the salvation of the Jews. Remember that during the Pacific War in 1943, Kagawa commented:

> Paul, the apostle of Jesus, cried, "For I could wish that I were cursed and cut off from Christ for the sake of my people, those of my own race," for the monarchy; we, the subject, should be prepared to die a martyr even were we cut off from Christ. To die for the state is the spirit of Christianity. Bearing suffering gives further glory. Death is the victorious remark. The cross is the crown of pride. . . . Christ who taught us to attain the truth would never deny but bless those who would shed blood for liberating Asia. We shall never make Churchill nor Roosevelt, who illegally plunder ethnic minorities by hiding the truth, win a victory.[15]

Kagawa's justifying the invasion of Asian countries in the name of his theology could never be forgiven by Asian people, even though he insisted on dying for "the sake of my people, those of my race, for the monarchy," to bring deliverance from the bondage of the Western powers as Japan sacrificed civilian people in Asia. I think that God punished Kagawa because

---

14. Schildgen, *Toyohiko Kagawa*, 243; emphasis added.
15. Kagawa, "Dying as a Martyr," 1.

he and the UCCJ to which he belonged had committed to justifying the military propaganda, just the same as the majority of the Japanese people.

Chart 6.5: Romans 9:3: My Final Interpretation

God's Punishment

Kagawa decided to receive God's punishment along with the Japanese people—thus, God's punishment for Kagawa, the UCCJ, the Japanese military, and people who justified war crimes.

We have focused on Rom 9:3 and examined whether Kagawa put the words of Rom 9:3 into practice for the sake of Japan, even at the risk of death. However, we must recognize that Kagawa made his testimony after the war in 1952. This means that from a theological perspective, Kagawa, as a Presbyterian minister, considered, first, whether he was faithful to God during the war by words and deeds, and second, whether he admitted what he did by confessing unfaithful words and deeds after the war to God.

As the final judgment for Kagawa's deeds and works will be done at the end, I, as a Christian, am not allowed to declare such a final theological judgment on Kagawa but offer readers what Kagawa did confess as war responsibility after the war, and how Kagawa committed to serving and delivering God's message to the Japanese people with the conviction that God had forgiven his sins.

CONCLUSION

In this chapter, after Kagawa encountered the Boston University School of Theology's personalism, Kagawa did not look down on Japan's anti-Christian spiritual climate but was convinced that the gospel of Christianity could take root with redemptive love in Japan. After the war, Kagawa published his book *A Reexamination of Oriental Thought*, in which he publicly confirmed the absence of redemptive love in all Oriental thought. What this meant was that he did not deny the Japanese spiritual climate and serve the weak by evangelizing, but by focusing on redemptive love, which was absent from the Japanese spiritual climate, and preaching and serving the weak.

Also, although Kagawa's interpretation of the Bible is not confirmed by the words of Rom 9:3, I am convinced that Rom 9:3 shows the theological meaning of Kagawa's confession of responsibility for the war. I am also convinced that Rom 9:3 is God's word telling today's Christians how they can serve the nation to which God has sent them with redemptive love.

7

Kagawa's War Responsibility

INTRODUCTION

To verify Kagawa's confession of responsibility for the war, it is necessary to confirm how Japanese Christian leaders, including Kagawa, reconciled the emperor's issue with the Christian faith and the plan for establishing the UCCJ at the time of the ROL, which demanded all Protestant churches be united into one church of the UCCJ for detaching the UCCJ from Western churches (the ROL came into effect in 1940). This is because, during the period of the Pacific War (1941–45), Christians and the church were under military government oppression to follow the emperor-centered national polity. On the other hand, Kagawa delivered a radio message to the US entitled "Prophecy of America's Demise" in August 1944. Kagawa also justified military propaganda in China as a pacification unit member in October 1944.

However, as we have learned, Kagawa was detained by the military police in Tokyo just a month before the end of the Pacific War on August 15, 1945. Kagawa commented:

> During a nine-day interrogation at the military police headquarters, I was acutely aware of Japan's defeat in the war and the anguish he [Japan] felt was Japan's sins and the sins of other countries that rebelled against God's will and recognized that all human beings needed to repent.[1]

As Kagawa strengthened his awareness of Japan's sins and the sins of other countries, he asked God for repentance while the military police

---

1. Kagawa, *Complete Set*, 24:534.

interrogated him. Thus, I try to conclude that Kagawa confessed war responsibility by examining Kagawa's words and actions after the war. To achieve this goal, I examine, first, Kagawa's thoughts before the war based on the Riverside Japanese American Christian Leaders Conference (RJACLC) in April 1941; second, the anti-Christian spirit in Japan; third, Kagawa's confession of war responsibility itself, his message to Japanese people devastated by war defeat; and last, what Kagawa accepted as state authorities, including the emperor, MacArthur, the Korean president, and the American people.

Before discussing the above objectives, let us recognize the steps toward Kagawa's confession of faith. One month before the end of the war, Kagawa transcended his anti-Western criticism in justifying the Japanese military invasion of Asia countries, to humankind's sin, which was against the will of God. This means Kagawa repented of atrocities done in war by both the West and Japan. See table 7.1 and chart 7.1.

Table 7.1: Chronology of war responsibility confession

Aug. 1940	Kagawa is detained at the prison by Shibuya SHP due to anti-war acts (P1).
Apr. 1941	RJACLC
June 1941	UCCJ is established.
Dec. 1941	Pacific War breaks out.
1943–44	Kagawa is devoted to writing *Cosmic Purpose*.
May 1943	Kagawa is interrogated by Tokyo SHP for anti-war acts (P2).
Nov. 1943	Kagawa is interrogated by Tokyo SHP for anti-war acts (P3).
Aug. 1944	Kagawa sends a radio message entitled "Prophecy of America's Demise" through NHK (Japan broadcasting corporation).
Oct. 1944	Kagawa writes a manuscript entitled "China's Reconstruction and Japan" (A1).
Oct 1944–Feb 1945	Kagawa visits China as a member of the religious envoy (A2).
	Kagawa records his advice confessing war responsibility and adopting redemptive love with brotherhood economics in China.

July 1945	Kagawa is detained at the SHP for nine days. He prays war repentance of humankind's sin of war to God (P4, C1).
Aug. 1945	The emperor declares the IEEW.
Aug. 1946	Kagawa confesses war repentance at Hokkaido. He criticizes Japan for trusting not God but the gods of myth and idolatry (C2).
1950	Lecture tour of the US: American people accept Kagawa.
1955	Kagawa sends an open letter to Syngman Rhee, the president of Korea, who accepts Kagawa's statement of war responsibility.

Remarks:

1. P1–4 represent Kagawa having been detained by the SHP four times during the 1940s.

2. A1–2 represent Kagawa's message that promoted the recovery of China through brotherhood economics in the Asian world, based on the Declaration of Great East Asia.

3. C1–2 represents Kagawa's exorting repentance to God for Japan's having committed atrocities in Asia.

Chart 7.1 Kagawa's apology and criticism of US during and after war

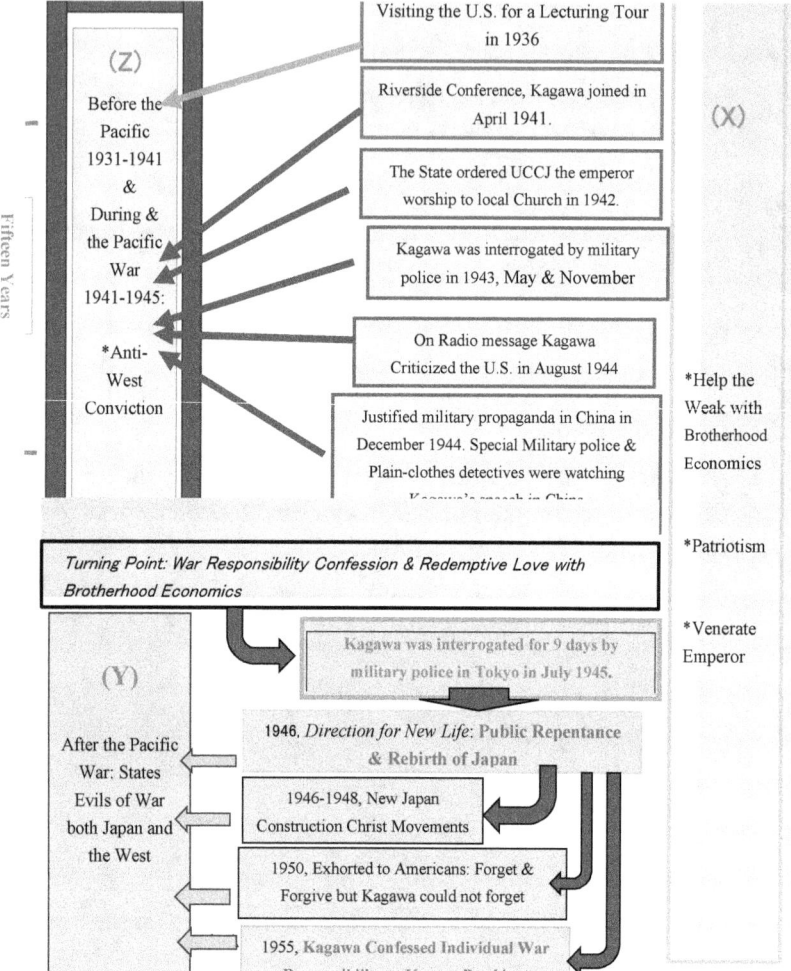

Relating Kagawa's confession of war responsibility to the pillars (Z, X, and Y) gives us significant theological and historical meaning, because pillar X coexisted with both pillars Z and Y. One month before Japan was defeated in the war, Kagawa in the military police station recognized the sin of both Japan and the West. At this moment, we can judge that Kagawa's eyes were opened to recognize, from God's perspective, the sins of both Western colonial aggression in Asia and the fact that Japan had similarly colonized Asia. At this moment, pillar Z disappeared from Kagawa's recognition. Nonetheless, we should not fail to understand Kagawa's recognition of humankind's evils such as the military-powered nations even after the war and his shift to eradicate those universal sins by brotherhood economics theory with redemptive love, as we have learned Kagawa criticized the economic theories of both capitalism, which concentrates wealth in the hands of the ultrarich, and communism, which uses violent evolution based on a materialistic view of history.

I presume that Kagawa's statement could be Kagawa's confession of sin. Nonetheless, I am required to offer theological commentary for Kagawa's confession as his individual one, even though he made his statement in the first-person plural. Based on Kitamori's following commentary on the UCCJ, I believe that Kagawa addressed his confession to both himself and to all Japanese people, including the emperor:

> A confession of faith is binding on those of us who confess it, for it is a heartfelt and voluntary confession that places responsibility on the confessor. This is because if someone voluntarily confesses something without being forced by someone else, they cannot easily deny what has been confessed. The more spontaneous and heartfelt the confession, the more responsible one must be for it.[2]
> ... Faith does not allow us to have the attitude that we feel safe as long as we are the only ones saved. Faith seeks to be saved along with others. We seek that others may share with us the truth of the one gospel.[3]

RIVERSIDE JAPANESE AMERICAN CHRISTIAN CONFERENCE (APRIL 20–25, 1941)

As the conference name implied, both Japanese and American Christian leaders participated in the meeting to discuss the emperor issue and the new all-Protestant church unification plan, to confirm whether both were developed by military government order or by Japanese Christians' intention.

As we have learned previously, at the RJACLC in 1941, Abe Yoshimura (阿部義宗, 1886–1980, the bishop of the Japan Methodist Church) justified the important issues of both the UCCJ's establishment and the Japanese

2. Kitamori, *Commentary on the Confession*, 8.
3. Kitamori, *Commentary on the Confession*, 10.

Christians' worship of the State Shinto shrine, in order to receive American members' understanding. How did Kagawa comment on these issues? At the conference, Abe Yoshimura played a significant role, as he was selected as the co-moderator of the Japanese leaders, with Dr. Douglas Houston for the American leaders.

> Abe justified the Japanese Christians' approval of the non-religious patriotic shrine, which differs from the religious Shinto shrines. Japanese Christians never participate in the rites of the religious Shinto shrines. At the conference, regarding the shrine issue, the American leaders concluded that it is up to Japanese Christians to decide what kind of behavior is appropriate for Christians. Abe also defended the establishment of the Unified Church in Japan because the Japanese Constitution specified the freedom of religious belief, and the government had neither interfered in the Christian creed nor intended to be involved in the matter.[4]

Abe stated the two most troublesome and controversial issues at stake, which the US participants wanted to know clearly through the words of Japanese leaders. These issues were the Japanese Christians' worship of the emperor and the establishment of the unified Protestant church by the government's strong involvement in the forceful means of *Syukyo Dantai Ho* (宗教団体法, ROL) and *Chian Iji Ho* (治安維持法, PPL), in which article 1 specifies:

> Anyone who forms, or knowingly participates in, groups whose goal is to deny the system of private property or to change our national essence shall be sentenced to prison or penal servitude of up to ten years. Anyone who attempts to commit this crime also will be punished.[5]

Abe's statement not only relieved American leaders' anxiety, as he did not expose any real story at the time of discussing the unified church's forming by the government officials but also obtained the American leaders' decision that was most convenient for Japanese leaders. American leaders "concluded that Japanese Christians should decide by themselves whether they should be faithful acts or not on this issue."[6]

Harold E. Fey of *The Christian Century* was not satisfied with the contents of the RJACLC and speculated that he tried to find out the truth on

---

4. UCCJ, *Formation Process of UCCJ*, 193.
5. Huffman, "Peace Preservation Law."
6. UCCJ, *Formation Process of UCCJ*, 193.

the Japanese side through a personal interview with Kagawa. In particular, he understood that the following interview was conducted without taking notes, because the meeting included issues such as the emperor and the establishment of the UCCJ, which would be problematic if leaked to the Japanese government.

Exclusive Interview with Kagawa by Harold E. Fey

Harold E. Fey, in *The Christian Century* of May 21, 1941, made commentary after he had interviewed Kagawa alone without taking notes by heading sections of his article "Survival at Stake" (referring to the UCCJ establishment plan), "Amaterasu Omikami [天照大神] and the Shrine" (referring to worshipping through Shintoism), and "Christians and Emperor" (referring to worship and the relationship with the emperor).

Though we could not prove whether American leaders might have noticed that they could not receive the true story from the Japanese members, after the conference, Harold E. Fey (1898–1990, a correspondent, field editor, and executive editor of the journal until 1956) had his personal interview with Kagawa, and he reported the interview content by putting those headings over the delicate and significant issues that American Christians desperately wanted to know such as the relationship between Japanese Christians and the emperor, more precisely, the Japanese Christians' worship of the emperor. Before reporting on these issues, Fey delivered words by way of preface:

> While Kagawa knew that I would make some kind of report, *so much of our interview was specifically "off the record" that I will confine myself entirely to the impression which is distinctly my own.*[7]

Kagawa's comment to Fey continued as follows under the heading "Survival at Stake":

> The new united church in Japan, to Kagawa, *is an effort on the part of Japanese Christians to prepare Christianity in that country to survive, no matter what happens. This it could not hope to do under foreign control, especially if relationships between Japan and America further deteriorate.* Accordingly, longtime trends in the direction of Christian unity were brought to a culmination last fall when Christian leaders, noting the movement of international

---

7. Fey, "Kagawa Revisits America," 684; emphasis added.

affairs, anticipated measures of compulsion that the force at work in their own government might have been disposed to use and *on their own initiative set up the Japan Christian Church.*[8]

Though it was Fey's memory of the exclusive interview, Kagawa talked about the true story of Japanese Christians who survived, under Fey's heading "Survival at Stake." He confessed the history of Protestant Japanese Christians' unified church establishment from the early period of their history. The Japanese government used the legal rhetoric of unification of all Protestant churches so that it could control the religious organizations that had a strong relationship with Western countries, especially with the US. No doubt Fey confirmed that unification was accomplished by the military, which told them there was no alternative for achieving their goal.

Kagawa proceeded to the issue of the emperor. Under "Amaterasu Omikami and the Shrine [神社]," Fey commented:

> Japanese consider that Amaterasu Omikami, the sun goddess, is not the mythological figure foreigners believe her to be. The earliest records, he [Kagawa] says, show that the special organization of ancient Japan was matriarchal in character. Amaterasu Omikami was the living person who was the first ruler of Japan. . . . Kagawa shrewdly pointed out that President Roosevelt recently set aside the birthplace of President Wilson for the nation, and that the newspapers almost universally referred to it as a new "national shrine." The temple of State Shinto is to Japanese, he said, what the tomb of the unknown soldiers or the resting place of Lincoln or Washington is to America.[9]

Kagawa justified the Japanese Christians' paying respect to the emperor's ancestor, Amaterasu Omikami by referring to "Roosevelt who set aside the birthplace of President Wilson for the nation," as he tried to categorize it as the same nationwide memorial ceremony of both countries. Kagawa also tried to persuade Fey that "the emperor is revered as the head of the family of Japanese people" and representative of Japan as follows:

> According to this interpretation, when Christians worship at the shrines of Amaterasu Omikami they are simply paying respect to a revered ancestor. The attitude toward the imperial family is similarly one of reverence, not worship in the Christian sense. The emperor of Japan is a man of noble character, broad sympathy, and

8. Fey, "Kagawa Revisits America," 685; emphasis added.
9. Fey, "Kagawa Revisits America," 685.

penetrating intelligence, Kagawa said. Unlike certain pretenders and men obsessed with delusions of grandeur, he is not a man to "play God." ... The emperor is revered as the head of the family of Japanese people as well as the living representative of an unbroken line of ancestors going back to Amaterasu Omikami.[10]

Kagawa claimed that Japanese Christians, including himself, regarded the emperor not as a living god but as a human being for whom they had a profound reverence as the king of the nation. Kagawa's rhetoric on the emperor is in sympathy with that of Uemura Masahisa in his book *Kami* (神, God), in which Uemura (植村正久, 1858–1925) commented:

> Though it is significant to serve a lord of the state, devoting our whole lives to God in heaven while holding the warm, great feelings that enter into the hearts of the populations of all the nations must be accomplished.[11]

Though American leaders concluded not to judge the Japanese Christians' worship of the emperor as worship of an idol, if American leaders *had* suggested to Japanese leaders not to worship the emperor, the Japanese government would have had a good chance to destroy Christians based on legal means, by insisting that Japanese Christians were obeying a foreign organization's order. See the record reported by the Tokko (特高, SHP) in 1943 below.

> It is reported that the current state of Christianity in our country has recently begun to show a so-called Japanese tendency in some quarters, but the anti-Japanese thoughts and beliefs that have been permeated by foreign states, especially Britain and the United States, over many years have been hard to eradicate. Their anti-national character is being exposed in various places, and the number of anti-national acts by Christians is increasing every month.[12]

The SHP reported:

> The incidents of the suppression of Christianity were a nationwide phenomenon, and the criticism of Christianity by nationalists was that Christianity denied both the nation and the imperial family,

---

10. Fey, "Kagawa Revisits America," 685.
11. Uemura, *God*, 46–47.
12. Institute for the Study of Humans and Society, *Movement of Christianity*, 3:49–50.

and it also recognized that though Buddhism tended to be Japanized, Christianity was a strong enemy to the state.[13]

See the SHP report on the anti-Christianity of the nationalists:

> Since the Great Asia War started, the government unified Christian churches in Japan to make them restart Japanese Christianity. We oppressed and arrested those Christian churches that opposed being unified with the UCCJ. We recognized that the Bible teaches Christianity to be rebellious to the state and the national polity. Without denying the Bible, it is hard to eradicate Christianity in Japan. Thus, in times of war, the time is ripe for destroying Christianity.[14]

IMPERIAL EDICT OF THE END OF THE WAR (IEEW) AND OPEN LETTER TO MACARTHUR FROM KAGAWA

Although the Potsdam Declaration (hereafter the PD) was made by the United States, Britain, and the Republic of China on July 26, 1945 (the Soviet Union joined the declaration on August 8, 1945), Japan delayed accepting the PD because the Japanese government was "concerned about the survival of the Japanese Emperor by proclaiming that the sovereignty of the Emperor of Japan would not be touched."[15] In response to the Japanese government's claims, the Truman government's ultimatum was as follows:

> From the moment of surrender the authority of the Emperor and the Japanese Government to rule the state shall be subject to the Supreme Commander of the Allied powers who will take such steps as he deems proper to effectuate the surrender terms.
>
> The Emperor and the Japanese High Command will be required to sign the surrender terms necessary to carry out the provisions of the Potsdam Declaration, to issue orders to all the armed forces of Japan to cease hostilities and to surrender their arms, and to issue such other orders as the Supreme Commander may require giving effect to the surrender terms.[16]

---

13. Institute for the Study of Humans and Society, *Movement of Christianity*, 3:53.
14. Institute for the Study of Humans and Society, *Movement of Christianity*, 3:52.
15. Totani, *Tokyo War Crimes Trial*, 45.
16. Office of the Historian, "740.00119 P.W./8-1045: Telegram."

Based on the above statement, which clarified that the emperor's survival depended on the Allied powers, we recognize seriously the emperor's IEEW, which was broadcast to the entire world in Japanese and English on August 15, 1945, Japanese time. This means that as the emperor declared Japan's surrender in the war to Japan and the world, history has proven that he was prepared to receive the worst judgment, including the death penalty by the International Military Tribunal for the Far East, the so-called Tokyo Trial.

I remind us of Kagawa's speech celebrating the 2600th anniversary of the emperor on October 17, 1940, at Aoyama Gavin University. He stated, "We Japanese Christians believe that by God's providence, he gave Japan the unbroken lines of emperors who have been showing his subjects great compassion and mercy."[17] Kagawa states that Japan was given an emperor by God's providence. There is no doubt that it was God's providence that the emperor, Hirohito, declared the surrender of the war, as nobody could accept this responsibility but the emperor.

Kagawa's above confession described strong, profound respect for the emperor, whom Kagawa believed only represented Japan. Was Kagawa an exceptional Christian who was attached to Japanese feudalistic spirituality as the general headquarters recognized? We need to review Kagawa's contemporary, the academic Christian Yanaihara, who was installed as president of Tokyo University by succeeding Nambara Shigeru in 1951. Yanaihara, in his book *Nihon Seisinn to Heiwa Kokka* (日本精神と平和国家, The Japanese Spirit and a Peaceful nation), stated:

> Not like a Western state's *sensi kunshu* [専制君主, an absolute monarchy], the emperor is in the center of the state and he treats the people with a sense of familiarity as *minzoku no souke* [民族の宗家, a paterfamilias of the Japanese race]. Japanese people have been respecting the emperor with loyalty to him with a spirit of patriotism. . . . In any state in the world, the relationship between a king and his subjects has existed for a brief period because their kingdom was based on a suzerain-vassal [king and slave] relationship.[18]

Both Kagawa and Yanaihara regarded the emperor as the father (sovereign) of the family (state) in that everything had been lost because of the war in which Japan deprived Asian states of their sovereignties. Thus, they

17. Kagawa, *Complete Set*, 24:398.
18. Yanaihara, *Japanese Spirit*, 92–93.

had been made to stand before God as one human being (a defeated people) of the same defeated nation. This portends that they, the emperor and both Kagawa and Yanaihara, will be placed before the judgment of God when they are in a place where all security of life is gone, as Japan was defeated.

Yanaihara's statement clearly represents a spirit of ardent patriotism by positioning the emperors as familiarly as *minzoku no souke* (民族の宗家, a paterfamilias of the Japanese race). Thus, we cannot conclude that Kagawa had an exceptional view of the emperor. We should interpret Kagawa's intention in the open letter to MacArthur as based on this sociopolitical context immediately after the war, indicated by the IEEW below.

Imperial Edict of the End of the War (IEEW)

After pondering deeply, the general trends of the world and the actual conditions obtaining in Our Empire today, we have decided to effect a settlement of the present situation by resorting to an extraordinary measure. We have ordered Our Government to communicate to the Governments of the United States, Great Britain, China, and the Soviet Union that Our Empire accepts the provisions of their Joint Declaration.

To strive for the common prosperity and happiness of all nations as well as the security and well-being of Our subjects is the solemn obligation which has been handed down by Our Imperial Ancestors, and which We lay close to heart. *Indeed, We declared war on America and Britain out of Our sincere desire to secure Japan's self-preservation and the stabilization of East Asia, it being far from Our thought either to infringe upon the sovereignty of other nations or to embark upon territorial aggrandizement.* But now the war has lasted for nearly four years. Despite the best that has been done by everyone—the gallant fighting of military and naval forces, the diligence and assiduity of Our servants of the State, and the devoted service of Our one hundred million people, the war situation has developed not necessarily to Japan's advantage, while the general trends of the world have all turned against her interest. Moreover, the enemy has begun to employ a new and most cruel bomb, the power of which to do damage is indeed incalculable, taking the toll of many innocent lives. Should we continue to fight, *it would not only result in an ultimate collapse and obliteration of the Japanese nation, but also it would lead to the total extinction of human civilization.* Such being the case, how are We to save the millions of Our subjects; or to atone Ourselves before the hallowed spirits of Our Imperial Ancestors? This is the reason why We have ordered the acceptance of the provisions of the Joint Declaration of the Powers. We cannot but express the deepest sense of regret to Our Allied nations of East Asia, who have consistently cooperated with the Empire towards the emancipation of East Asia. The thought of those officers and men as well as others who have fallen in the fields of battle, those who died at their posts of duty, or those who met with untimely death and all their bereaved families, pains Our heart night and day. The welfare of the wounded and the war sufferers, and of those who have lost their homes and livelihood, are the objects of Our profound solicitude. The hardships and sufferings to which Our nation is to be subjected hereafter will be certainly great. We are keenly aware of the inmost feelings of all ye, Our subjects. However, it is according to the dictate of time and fate that *We have resolved to pave the way for a grand peace for all the generations to come by enduring the unendurable and suffering that is insufferable.* Having been able to safeguard and maintain the structure of the Imperial State, We are always with ye, Our good and loyal subjects, relying upon your sincerity and integrity. Beware most strictly of any outbursts of emotion which may endanger needless complications or any fraternal contention and strife which may create confusion, lead ye astray, and cause ye to lose the confidence of the world. Let the entire nation continue as one family from generation to generation, ever firm in its faith in the imperishableness of its divine land and mindful of its heavy burden of responsibilities, and the long road before it. Unite your total strength to be devoted to the construction for the future. *Cultivate the ways of rectitude; foster nobility of spirit; and work with resolution so as ye may enhance the innate glory of the Imperial State and keep place which the progress of the world.*

The 14th day of the 8th month of the 20th year of Showa [Aug. 14, 1945][19]

The IEEW is in harmony with the intent of the Greater East Asia Declaration. However, by deciding to end the war, the emperor is appealing to the people of Japan to carry out the feelings expressed in the Greater East Asia Declaration and to share with the people the hardships faced after the

---

19. National Graduate Institute for Policy Studies and Institute for Advanced Studies on Asia, "Imperial Rescript [of Surrender]"; emphasis added.

defeat of the war. Countries worldwide recognize that the emperor decided not to be defeated but to end the war:

> After deep consideration of the current situation, we have decided to seek a solution to the current situation through unprecedented means.

The emperor's feelings were expressed in this statement; what needs to be confirmed is that the emperor made Japan's decision to end the war. To be precise, the emperor is the only one who decides defeat. In 1946, after the war, Yanaihara echoed the emperor's decision by saying,

> The emperor is positioned as a paterfamilias of the nation.[20]

At the end of the war, Yanaihara expressed the following words in the poem.

Lamentation

> The people wept before His Majesty, and they cried together.
> Bow down before the Creator of heaven and earth.
> God, we have sinned, and we have transgressed, and You have not forgiven us . . .
> Defeat in war does not necessarily mean exile.
> We will stop relying on force and financial power,
> Rather, learn faith through suffering.
> So, Jehovah will judge the world on the day of judgment,
> Let us sing with joy of eternal peace and freedom.[21]

How did Kagawa respond to the IEEW? By reviewing the open letter to General MacArthur from Kagawa below, we can identify with his understanding of the IEEW.

The Open Letter Sent to General Douglas MacArthur on August 30, 1945

> Your Excellency: On August 15, Japan was labeled as a defeated country. That is a grim fact, and everybody has to admit it. Till one minute before the proclamation of the Imperial Rescript

---

20. Yanaihara, *Japanese Spirit*, 92–93.
21. Yanaihara, *Japanese Spirit*, 59–61.

terminating the war, the Imperial Forces including the Army, Navy, and Air Forces were burning with unflinching fighting spirit. *However, with the issuance of the Imperial Rescript, Japan immediately stopped all her military action and began to tread on a new road.*

Your Excellency: You must have already received news as to the peaceful landing of the vanguards of the allied occupation forces amid a friendly atmosphere due to the thorough preparation made by the Japanese side. You must have by now met many Japanese people and noticed that their mouths were set firmly. All Japanese were determined to fight to the last. Everybody was aware of the power of the atomic bomb attacks. None of them doubted that the war would have to be continued even though he or she might be blasted to bits or burned to ashes, while His Majesty the Emperor willed so. Following the proclamation of the Imperial Rescript, however, Japan made a quick turn from war to peace. The determination and efforts of all the Japanese to start out on a new path are shown in their tightly set mouths. Can you find any other people like the Japanese?

Your Excellency: [3.1] The Japanese people are always ready to conduct themselves in compliance with Imperial Wishes. [3.2] By proclaiming the Imperial Rescript, His Majesty took over the suffering and privations brought about by the war, on His own shoulders. [3.3] Every one of His subjects wept upon receiving the Imperial Rescript and expressed his sincere regret for not having done as much as he ought to have. You know that [3.4] many military men and patriots killed themselves to apologize for their inability to perform their duties. [3.5] Others who also regretted that they could not serve His Imperial Majesty as expected have become resolved to exert their utmost to contribute toward the development of the world civilization and realization of world peace in compliance with Imperial Wishes.

The outcome of the San Francisco Conference in establishing the world organization is similar to Well's idea. However, studying Well's ideal and his wide historical knowledge, I point out here that the San Francisco Conference lacked one thing, and to this one thing, I must honestly draw Your Excellency's attention. In 1936, I was invited by the then US President as a State guest to study the unemployment problem. Just then America had 16,000,000 jobless men and women. One evening, at the house of Summer Welles, former Undersecretary of State, I met Harry Truman and others and had intimate talks with them. On the occasion, I remember,

> I suggested the setting up of an international cooperative system and they all seemed to agree with me.[22]

In the above words, we can recognize two significant contents. First, the emperor's decision to terminate the war and his wishes for his subjects. Second, the subjects' confession of regret for not having done as much as they ought to have and resolution to achieve the emperor's wish. Based on the structure of Kagawa's understanding, we should not fail to point out what Kagawa, as a Christian, wanted the Japanese people to know. First, Kagawa claimed that Christians, including Kagawa, selected the way to contribute to develop world civilization and realize world peace. Second, Kagawa declared that he did not belong to any group of patriots.

In conclusion, we should understand clearly why Kagawa exposed his reverent feelings toward the emperor in public, and how Kagawa positioned theologically the emperor who had been regarded as a living god of the *Kokka Shintosim* (State Shinto). A little less than a month after the war, Gerald Thorp questioned Kagawa. He said,

> Given your faith as a Christian, as absolute above Japan, would you be willing to say that the emperor could be wrong? Kagawa answered, no, I can't say that.[23]

Kagawa's testimony confessed the emperor was neither sacred nor God. More precisely to say, the emperor is under the judgment of God at the end of time.

We should recognize paragraph 3 as representing the close relationship between the emperor and his subjects:

Table 7.2: The structure of paragraph 3 and its explanatory diagram
3.2: The emperor's wishes for the Japanese people
3.1: The Japanese people's response to the emperor's wishes
3.3: All Japanese people regretted not having done enough to serve the emperor's wish to establish stabilization by libertine Asia from Western colonization and exploitation.
3.4: Military men killed themselves (切腹, *seppuku*) for not achieving the emperor's wish to liberate Asia from Western colonization and exploitation.
3.5: Others regretted and became resolved to exert their utmost to contribute toward the development of world civilization and realization of world peace.

22. Kagawa, "Plea for Sympathetic Treatment"; emphasis added.
23. Thorp, "No Early Rebirth."

KAGAWA'S WAR RESPONSIBILITY

Chart 7.2 Kagawa's understanding of the IEEW (Aug. 15, 1945) and subjects' response to emperor's demands (through the open letter to MacArthur)

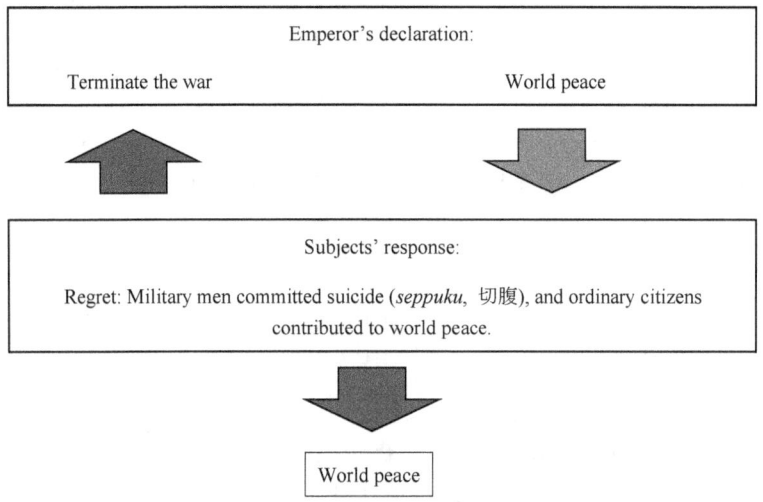

We also should not forget that at this moment when Japan stood still at the appalling calamity of the war, Kagawa asked General MacArthur, the commander of the Allied authorities, to assist Japan economically by demanding to ease the heavy reparation against Japan. Kagawa's requirement transcended the relationship between the authority and one of the citizens of the defeated country as he exhorted MacArthur to fulfill the spirit of the Charter of the United Nations by the San Francisco Conference in June 1945. It was surprising that Kagawa knew details of the Charter of the United Nations, which had been resolved during the time Japan had been attacked by the US forces, which had thrown Japan into chaos. In the open letter to MacArthur, Kagawa never forgets to claim the installation of an international cooperative system in the world.

I believe Kagawa's statement in the open letter to General MacArthur could be recognized as his Christian testimony to the Japanese people because he used the Japanese nationwide media *Yomiuri Hochi Shimbun* (読売報知新聞), dated August 30, 1945 (and printed in the English-language newspaper on September 2). He delivered a message to the Japanese people through the letter sent to General MacArthur, who landed on August 30, 1945, the same day Kagawa sent him the open letter at Atsugi Airport in Kanagawa Prefecture.

KAGAWA'S WAR RESPONSIBILITY

I review Kagawa's confession of responsibility for the war based on the contents of his statements related to his actual responsibility for the war within and without Japan, especially the lecture tour in the United States after the war in 1950 when he was invited by American Christians, and Kagawa's 1955 open letter to South Korean president Syngman Rhee, in which Kagawa apologized for the exploitation and inhumane acts during the colonial rule brought about by Japan's annexation.

Kagawa's Confession of War Responsibility in July 1945 and after the War

As we recognize, Kagawa made his confession of war responsibility in July 1945 when he was interrogated at the SHP headquarters. After the war, Kagawa commented on war responsibility four times. His second comment, then (the first one after the war), appeared in an article in the *Chicago Daily News* on September 11, 1945:

> We were too proud, lacked self-examination, love, and intelligence, and were too much misled by the militaries and shallow judges of America.... Everyone must repent, including me.[24]

Third, on September 24, 1945, on an NHK (Japan broadcasting corporation) program, Kagawa said:

> We realized that we, as an individual and as a Japanese citizen, should repent of sins committed in the past because we knew acts of atrocious cruelty committed by Japanese soldiers in Philippines during the war.[25]

Fourth, in 1950, on the lecture tour to the US, Kagawa stated:

> American Christians should forgive and forget as all Japan is doing.[26]

Fifth, in 1955, in an open letter to Syngman Rhee, the first South Korean president, Kagawa commented:

---

24. Thorp, "No Early Rebirth."
25. Kagawa, *Complete Set*, 24:416.
26. Bradshaw, *Unconquerable Kagawa*, 32.

> I, in the name of Jesus Christ, apologize for how Japan maltreated, Mr. President, your people.[27]

So, Kagawa made a war responsibility confession a fifth time after that first confession one month before the end of the war.

The first war responsibility was confessed from the military police jail as a repentant prayer to God one month before the end of the war in 1945. The second was addressed to all people worldwide, especially Americans, as Kagawa confessed to American media reporters. The third confession was addressed to Japanese people through the public broadcasting station. The fourth was addressed to Americans during the US lecture tour in 1950. The fifth and last confession was addressed to Korean president Syngman Rhee in 1955.

I believe that in visiting the US in 1950, just five years after the war, Kagawa might have hesitated, considering his criticism of the United States during the war. In July 1945, Kagawa confessed his responsibility for the war to God in prison, but this was a relationship between only God and Kagawa, and I don't think that Kagawa was actively trying to make this war responsibility confession in public in the United States.

I selected Kagawa's confession of war responsibility to the Korean president, Syngman Rhee, in 1955 because Kagawa sent the message through an open letter to a Japanese nationwide newspaper in Japanese. This means Kagawa wanted Japanese people to know the Christian relationship between the president and Kagawa, one of the Japanese local pastors who apologized with words that showed respect to the Korean president.

But, let us first review what Kagawa commented on in the US in 1950.

Kagawa in the US in 1950

As for the interpretation of the book of Romans, Kagawa commented:

> The book of Romans, written by St. Paul, was addressed to Christians in Rome who were governed strictly by laws, and social order was maintained. This means that Christians in Rome lived according to social order without including socially destructive elements.[28]

---

27. Kagawa, *Complete Set*, 24:440.
28. Kagawa, *Social Movement of Bible*, 229.

His understanding of the Romans shows a fear of authority and an appreciation of community. Thus, for Christians to survive in Japan, there had been no alternative but to display loyalty to the state. Thus, it is hard to believe that Kagawa's nationalism was only temporal, during the war. How about his attitude after the war? Did Kagawa express a nationalistic attitude or statement during his stay in the US when he visited in 1950? Yes, he did. Emerson O. Bradshaw, in his book *Unconquerable Kagawa*, said:

> There were few of his followers who disagreed with this stand of Kagawa just as there were few in his audiences who seemed to retain any doubt about his moral integrity during the war. On a few occasions, he was asked about his wartime views on America, but such questioning was rarely antagonistic. One such instance occurred in Rochester, New York, where Kagawa humbly replied, Of course, I became indignant when American bombs took the lives of two million citizens, drove ten million people from the cities to the rural areas, and destroyed five hundred Christian churches. But I never doubted the loyalty of American Christians. I recalled that when nations engage in a war, they become brutal. . . . American Christians should forgive and forget as all Japan is doing.

Thanks to Kagawa's confession, Bradshaw commented:

> All fears about his reception by the American public now proved groundless. Though his popularity may have wavered during the war, it now seemed greater than ever.[29]

Did Americans feel released by Kagawa's answer, because it was war that makes people brutal; did they feel satisfied that he trusted American Christians? I have another perspective on Bradshaw's observation, as Bradshaw was trying to persuade the American public. So, we are required to examine Kagawa's response by comparing his answer with the radio speech in 1944, to seek similarities in some excusing phrases in Kagawa's reply in 1950.

This phrase stands out:

> But I never doubted the loyalty of American Christians. I recalled that when nations engage in war, they became brutal.[30]

---

29. Bradshaw, *Unconquerable Kagawa*, 32.
30. Bradshaw, *Unconquerable Kagawa*, 32.

It seems Kagawa had a sense of what would help American Christians accept him. However, Kagawa stated the opposite idea in both 1944 and 1950 to the American public. See the comparison below.

Comparison of Kagawa's Speech between 1944 and 1950

As Kagawa made war repentance in July 1945 when he was interrogated by the military police, there was a difference in his speech between 1944 and 1950. Kagawa unilaterally criticized the United States in the message in 1944, while he pointed out the evils of war in both countries, Japan and the US, and prayed the American people to accept God's reconciliation in the message of 1950.

1950: Message against America during Lecture Tour to America

> Of course I became indignant when American bombs took the lives of two million citizens, drove ten million people from the cities to the rural areas, and destroyed five hundred Christian churches. But I never doubted the loyalty of American Christians. I recalled that when nations engage in war, they become brutal. ... American Christians should forgive and forget as all Japan is doing.[31]

In the reflection on war from prison, one month before the end of the war, Kagawa stated:

> I thought it was a mistake to go to war with the Allies, but I also thought that the foreign countries occupying the East were at fault.[32]

He pointed out the evils of both Japan and the US by criticizing that the American bombs took the lives of two million citizens, drove ten million people from the cities to the rural areas, and destroyed five hundred Christian churches, and he exhorted American Christians to forgive and forget as all Japan was doing. Forgetting represents the ultimate forgiveness. ("[Love] does not insist on its way; it is not irritable; it keeps no record of wrongs" [1 Cor 13:5 NRSVUE].)

---

31. Bradshaw, *Unconquerable Kagawa*, 32.
32. Kagawa, *Complete Set*, 24:534.

Nonetheless, God does not forget the sin. The UCCJ, to which Kagawa belonged, confesses the Apostles' Creed, which states:

> He shall come to judge the quick [the living] and dead.[33]

All guilty people are in a place where "the quick and dead" will be judged by God. Though Kagawa exhorted American Christians to forgive and forget as all Japan was doing, why did Kagawa criticize without forgetting America's evil in the war? Not irony, but I recognize Kagawa was one of the typical Japanese Christians who also needed the redemptive love of Jesus, as Kagawa had been not a saint but a sinful pastor, devoted to serving the poor.

1944: Radio Statement

> Woe to you, America. . . . You talk about equality, yet you oppress the minorities, manipulate freedom, and try to maintain superiority which the Almighty God would never permit you to do. Repent America. *The name of Jesus is smeared by the heavy bombing.* . . . Alas, Japan would never experience Christianization due to America. . . . As the crusaders isolated Asia Minor from Jesus, this Pacific war removed the Far East from Christ forever.[34]

By comparing Kagawa's statement in 1944 on the radio with his statement in 1950 during the lecture tour in the US, we acknowledge Kagawa's rhetoric of criticizing the US and demanding repentance. Kagawa claimed that while Japan committed atrocities during the war, the United States also bore responsibility for destroying Japanese citizens and churches, and he was preaching reconciliation between the two countries.

Americans Recaptured Kagawa; Not Kagawa Recaptured America

Americans welcomed Kagawa. Bradshaw expressed, "Kagawa Recaptures America." On the other hand, the postwar-born generation of Japanese Christians tends to criticize Kagawa as a war criminal and a forgotten Christian leader and denies that prewar Japanese Christians, including

---

33. UCCJ, "What We Believe." This confession was enacted Oct. 26, 1954.
34. Schildgen, *Toyohiko Kagawa*, 230–31; emphasis added.

Kagawa, made concessions to the state authority during the war. Bradshaw entitled the second chapter of his book "Kagawa Recaptures America":

> As we left the meeting place, whether with head held high in resolution determination or bowed low in humility, we knew we had been in the presence of a man who dared to follow Christ, though physically frail and human, a man whom we could understand love; a man whose faith serve as inspiration to us all.[35]

I understand that Bradshaw left the concluding message of the American people accepting Kagawa. But Kagawa did not recapture America, because of his patriotic nature. As Bradshaw stated, Kagawa was "physically frail and human" and failed to recapture America in the tour whenever he responded to reporters' vicious questions on his propagandistic statement during the war, without confessing his war responsibility.

Let's proceed to the next subject of war responsibility for Korea. See the full text of Kagawa's open letter to Korean president Rhee Syngman below:

The Open Letter Sent to President Rhee on December 13, 1955

> Your Excellency President Syngman Rhee, I appeal to the conscience of Your Excellency. Please lead the relations between Great Korea and Japan toward peace. Japan was defeated ten years ago, and thirteen new states have become independent in Asia since. If those countries should quarrel among themselves, and if unfortunately, they should repeat the catastrophe of fighting, they would become the world's laughingstock. But if on the contrary the newly independent states with only small armaments should cooperate and unite in a federation, I believe they would enjoy a heretofore unknown happiness. Here in Japan, we are about to greet Christmas 1955. On this occasion, I appeal to the conscience of Your Excellency whom I know to be a disciple of Christ and an apostle of peace. Please establish permanent peace between Great Korea and Japan. There was a time when the United States of America was a colony of Great Britain. Angered by Britain's oppression of the colonies, George Washington stood up and fought against England to achieve today's independence. However, as Your Excellency well knows, at present old hatreds are forgotten and the United States and Great Britain stand closely

---

35. Bradshaw, *Unconquerable Kagawa*, 36.

together linked in alliance, and between the United States and Canada there exists not a fortress, not a single soldier guarding the frontier. I wish the relationship between Great Korea and Japan would be like this. There are many old historical books in Japan. Among these, *Nippon Shoki* [the chronicle of Japan] was written in *Kanbun* [Old Chinese] and deals with the history of immigration to Japan. I particularly wish that Your Excellency carefully read the middle and latter parts of *Nippon Shoki*, recording the immigration of the Korean people to Japan. What is revealed is the true history of the Korean people who immigrated and settled in Japan. Touring many of the areas described in *Nippon Shoki* I was impressed that some 60 percent of present-day Japanese are in fact descendants of the Korean nation. Tokyo was developed by North Koreans while South Koreans settled in Osaka. There are no historians in Japan who doubt this fact. Therefore, I cannot find any reason why the Japanese people and Great Korea must quarrel over a matter of maritime resources. Did not David take the son of King Saul, who tried to kill him, to his palace and give him a fine treatment? I beseech Your Excellency as a Christian to have King David's magnanimity. As Saul tried to kill David, *the Japanese tortured Your Excellency and oppressed your people. In the name of Christ, I apologize to Your Excellency and appealing to your Christian conscience beg for your forgiveness.* As Your Excellency may remember, I opposed the annexation of Korea to Japan and have waited sincerely for the day of Korean independence. Those Korean intellectuals who knew something about the activities of Japan's Christian socialists know very well how I have waited for Korea's independence. Now that Korea has obtained its independence, I have a new prayer: that relations of friendship be established between Great Korea and Japan similar to the relationship between the United States, which fought its mother country to win independence, and Canada, with no need for a single fortress or soldier on their border. As you know, Japan has promulgated a peace Constitution and has abandoned war forever. However, this high ideal cannot be realized without the help of our neighboring people and states. If Japan and Great Korea can guarantee a true peace in Far East, like there is no need of armament between the US and Great Britain, it would brighten up greatly our world. I believe that the twenty-five countries of Europe would follow the example of these two Asian nations and abandon war and follow a course of civilization.

Japan's population is now nearing the ninety-million mark. Some three-million fishermen seeking food for these people are going out to sea looking for protein resources. Particularly the fishermen on the Japan seaside who are near Great Korea have been fishing in the Tsushima Strait currents. In recent years these fishermen have fallen into unbearable misery. When Japan surrendered on August 15, 1945, Generalissimo Chiang Kai-shek forgave Japan, declaring courageously: "Don't mistreat the Japanese in China." I listened to the broadcast. As King David forgave his old enemy and cherished his son, even if the Japanese cut fingers off from both Your Excellency's hands, forgive like the Lord who forgave his enemies on the cross, and bring about peace not only in the Far East but also in the world, through permanent peace between Great Korea and Japan. I have heard that the Assembly of the Republic of Korea was opened with a prayer to the Creator. I therefore appeal to the conscience of Your Excellency now that we are facing Christmas, as an appeal for peace.[36]

Kagawa did not confess his level of war responsibility in the open letter to Korean President Rhee when he stated:

The Japanese tortured Your Excellency and oppressed your people. In the name of Christ, I apologize to Your Excellency and appealing to your Christian conscience beg for your forgiveness.[37]

It was Japan who tortured and oppressed Korea but not Kagawa himself. Before discussing this subject, we need to take full consideration of the relationship between the president and Kagawa.

As Kagawa said, Japan was a defeated country, in which Kagawa was one of the common citizens; President Rhee was the head of an independent nation, which had regained state sovereignty by the Declaration of Independence on August 15, 1948. Though Korea had been annexed by Japan, the political relationship between both countries was on equal standing in sovereignty, guaranteed by international law, when Kagawa sent the letter to President Rhee. Both countries had a responsibility to promote their own national interests. Thus, President Rhee based his reply on protecting Korean interests, with a declaration of forgiving and forgetting for the past period in which Japan had ruled Korea. After receiving President Rhee's reply on December 19, 1955, *Mainichi Shimbun* reported on December 21, 1955, as follows:

---

36. Kagawa, "Open Letter to President Rhee"; emphasis added.
37. Kagawa, "Open Letter to President Rhee."

> The Korean President Rhee, who is well known as an anti-Japanese president, accepted by believing in Kagawa's petition in which Kagawa admitted injustice as injustice [*Hi wa hi to mitome*, 非は非と認め] and referred to the straitened situation of three million unemployed Japanese fishermen. Then, the president asserted Korea's justification.[38]

I noticed that the nationwide newspaper *Mainichi Shimbun* reported that Kagawa's "War Responsibility Message" in his letter was accepted by the president sincerely. The *Mainichi Shimbun*, filled with amazement, reported on the fellowship of both Christians who had not met each other.

In the *Mainichi Shimbun* of December 22, 1955, Suma Yakichiro (1892–1970), the vice-chairperson of the Research Commission Foreign Affairs of the LDP, commented:

> President Rhee stated that he did not have animosity against Japan based on the spirit of Christianity. If his feelings are true, we will find a light.[39]

As *Mainichi Shimbun* reported on Japanese statements arguing back against President Rhee's statement, Kagawa stated:

> Without having this feeling arising from both government and private individuals it is hard to establish permanent peace.[40]

Tae-Ryong Yoon, Korean Political Science Scholar, Valued Kagawa's Confession of War Responsibility

How did Kagawa, one of the common citizens of Japan, dare to send a letter to the foreign president? We need to review how Kagawa's letter was evaluated from a Korean perspective. Tae-Ryong Yoon, a Korean political science scholar, in an article on the Korea-Japan political relationship, states:

> This article starts with the idea that we need inter-paradigmatic inquiry as well as an interdisciplinary approach in studying state behaviors *due to the complexity of human nature complicated by*

---

38. *Mainichi Shimbun*, "For Japan-Korea Friendship."
39. *Mainichi Shimbun*, "Government Cautious."
40. *Mainichi Shimbun*, "For Japan-Korea Friendship."

rationality, morality, emotions, and even religion, all at the same time.[41]

Tae-Ryong, in the introduction, provides a crucial perspective of the complicated human nature, which transcends conflicting elements such as rationality, emotion, morality, and even religion at the same time. Based on his theory, he introduces and analyzes the relationship between President Rhee and Kagawa. Tae-Ryong states:

> Kagawa Toyohiko and President Rhee exchanged open letters in December 1955. This exchange suggests not only that Korea's *Realpolitik* fears of losing autonomy regarding Japan impedes Korea-Japan cooperation, but also that moral/normative aspects are very important in promoting cooperative relations in actual international relations; and both are inseparable. As Kagawa wrote,
>
>> The Japanese tortured Your Excellency and oppressed your people . . . I apologize to Your Excellency, and . . . beg for your forgiveness. Forgive like the Lord who forgave His enemies on the Cross and bring . . . permanent peace between Great Korea and Japan.[42]

Tae-Ryong referred to Kagawa's letter, which contributed to what Tae-Ryong valued as two significant matters: "Korea's *Realpolitik* fears of losing autonomy regarding Japan" and "moral/normative aspects . . . in promoting cooperative relations in actual international relations." Tae-Ryong, as a scholar of political science, never missed Kagawa's confession of war responsibility in achieving a permanent peace based on God's redemptive love. Tae-Ryong also cited the statement of Kanzaki Yoshio, who belonged to the Japan Communist Party:

> Kanzaki Yoshio, one of three councilmen of the Japan Communist Party (JCP)[,] said in August 1957, "Before the Tokyo government starts blaming Korea, it should improve its treatment of Korean residents and repent more of Japan's oppression of Korea," adding that Japan should stop looking down on Koreans.[43]

Kanzaki demanded Japanese repentance for Japan's oppression of Korea before blaming Korea and urged stopping looking down on Koreans.

---

41. Tae-Ryong, "Historical Animosity," 2; emphasis added.
42. Tae-Ryong, "Historical Animosity," 20.
43. Tae-Ryong, "Historical Animosity," 21.

As Kanzaki might have stood on the materialistic interpretation of history, needless to say, he spoke against the violation of Korean human rights and dignity in the name of protecting the communist regimes. No doubt that Kanzaki stood on the side of the socially unprivileged in the world. On the other hand, Kagawa, based on his theology of redemptive love sent an open letter to President Rhee addressing not only Rhee but also the people of the world, including Korean and Japanese people. Kagawa apologized for Japan's atrocities against the Korean people and God. God accepted his confession and showed his love, and gave his strength to love the Korean people. Kagawa's statement was made through his prayer, so it never was a perfect letter. Based on the theme of this chapter, "War Responsibility," we need to examine how Kagawa's message in the letter was accepted from a theological perspective. See now the president's reply letter.

The Reply Sent by President Rhee

My dear Doctor Kagawa: I wish to thank you most sincerely for the open letter of December 13 that you addressed to me. You are one Japanese leader I have respected and admired from a distance for years. Your flattering letter makes me feel very humble.

Forgive and Forget You mentioned the historical fact that a large portion of the Japanese people have Korean blood, and this relationship should assure permanent peace between the two countries. This is the spirit in which I went to Japan six years ago at the news as General MacArthur's guest. I frankly started at a news conference in Tokyo although I was known as no friend of Japan. I was willing to forgive and forget the past and start anew if the Japanese would show the same spirit of cooperation. I had hoped for a favorable response from an official Japanese spokesman, but there was no reaction of any sort to my keen disappointment.

On my next visit to Japan, at the invitation of General Clark and Ambassador Murphy, I pointed out that it was American magnanimity that had restored Japan to a favorable position, and that, by the same token, Japan should show magnanimity to her weaker neighbor, Korea, for that is the way to establish permanent peace on earth. A sincere act or even gesture of friendship or respect by the Japanese has gone a long way toward mitigating the bad feelings resulting from nearly forty years of Japanese military rule of Korea. But Mr. Yoshida and Mr. Okazaki, then prime minister and foreign minister, both present as I spoke, simply smiled at my suggestion and said nothing.

First Such Apologized Good Feelings and Trust. In fact, your apology for "Japan's forty years' rule of Korea" is the first utterance by a prominent citizen of Japan to come to my attention. It is understandable that in the absence of such expression, we Koreans would conclude Japan's interest in Korea was not to gain Korean friendship but to regain Korean territory.

When the Korean-Japan Conference opened in Tokyo four years ago we tried to show our magnanimity by presenting our minimum requirements, which included Japan's return of our old books, art treasures, gold reserves, the recognition of the Peace Line, and the cancelation of the so-called treaties of Protectorate and Annexation. After forty years of subjugation, these requests are comparatively small, but they mean much to the Korean people, and Japan's acquiescence would have created good feelings and trust. We had expected our position to be approved wholeheartedly as evidence of Japan's penitent heart. To our disappointment, the Japanese representatives presented a preposterous claim to what amounts to 85 percent of all Korean property belonging to Japan. By solemn oath, Japan signed the Peace Treaty, which fully settled all these questions, but almost before the ink was dry on the Treaty, Japan was ignoring its terms and reasserting her aggressive designs on Korea. A short time later she publicly proclaimed that the establishment of an independent government in Korea by the people in a United Nations-supervised election was illegitimate.

No Reassuring Words As you know, this has been mentioned by us repeatedly, but to date, no Japanese official has sought to placate our fears with reassuring words without retracting them in the next breath.

These days much is being made of the Peace Line being a unilateral project, As you know, the Japanese had as little respect for its predecessors, the MacArthur Line and the Clark Line, because they preferred to recognize no rights of others, only their self-interest. But we envisaged the Peace Line as the best guarantee of peace in the absence of mutual understanding with Japan.

Our fishermen and our marine resources needed protection from Japanese operations. As a nation at war—which we still are—we must guard our shores against infiltrations, spies, enemy agents, and smugglers. Our security must be protected at all costs. The Peace Line also averts possible clashes between our two countries, and safeguarding this peace means more to Japan and Korea than all the fish in Korean waters.

Instead of showing a willingness to sit down with us and reach an agreement on matters of controversy, Japan denounces us and discourses about alleged violations of international law, threatening to solve everything when militarily strong enough. This is not the proper attitude of a nation that truly represents that it was misled by military leaders determined by aggression. Nor can we overlook the overtures being made to Soviet Russia, Red China, and Communist-ruled North Korea by Japanese missions comprised of government representatives, business leaders, and cultural delegations, with the intention of disrupting our security.

We cannot be blamed for anticipating a liaison between the Communists and Japanese leaders who deny the legality of our government's existence. All evidence indicates Japan was not cured of the aggressive spirit, at least toward Korea.

No Hatred for Japan For more than two years we have stated and restated our minimum requirements by which Japan could show good faith and come to a full understanding with us, that we might live in peace. If Japanese government circles consider them arbitrary, they can discuss them with us even now and come to an agreement.

Pardon me, my dear Doctor Kagawa, for replying at such length to your sincere message which was full of the Christian spirit for which you are known. But I want you to know that my heart, too, holds no hatred for my fellowmen, though my disappointment at the Japanese government's firm adherence to aims supposedly repudiated under America's influence is great. We long for peaceful relations with all our neighbors, particularly Japan.

With my heartiest Christmas wishes for you and yours.
Yours sincerely,
Syngman Rhee[44]

Though Kagawa sent the letter of petition for considering Japanese fishermen's fishing rights within the so-called Peace Line, he delivered the message of Japan's atrocities during the annexation of Korea. As long as the letter concentrated primarily on gaining fishing rights in Japan, it was an issue of politics to be discussed diplomatically. It was not a matter for one of the citizens involved.

Notwithstanding, the president did not fail to respond to Kagawa's message, although Kagawa had to wait. It seems that the president, representing Korea, was waiting for an official Japanese apology for the

---

44. *Korean Information Bulletin*, "Korea and Japan."

injustice Japan did against Koreans, which could not have been paid in any compensation.

The president's message was "I was willing to forgive and forget the past and start anew." As Kagawa stated to the American people in 1950, "American Christians should forgive and forget as all Japan is doing."[45]

Thus, I conclude that Korean President Rhee accepted Kagawa's apology.

SHIN SEIKATSU NO DOHYOU
(新生活の道標, DIRECTION FOR NEW LIVES)

The Japanese people were seized by the unknown state of the country, as we can recognize in the chronological table below. In particular, the postwar social and political system changed rapidly with the IEEW, the Japanese Instrument of Surrender, the Imperial Declaration of Humanity, and the International Military Tribunal for the Far East. Amid these changes, Kagawa pointed out the causes of defeat in the war in *Direction for New Lives* and proposed the path the Japanese should take.

Table 7.2: Chronology related to *Direction for New Lives*[46]	
Aug. 1945	IEEW
Sept. 1945	Japanese Instrument of Surrender
June 1946	Imperial Declaration of Humanity
1946–48	Tokyo Trial (International Military Tribunal for the Far East)
June 1946	*Direction for New Lives* is published.
Nov. 1946	New Constitution of Japan is promulgated.
1946–48	NJCCM

---

45. Bradshaw, *Unconquerable Kagawa*, 32.

46. Kagawa, *Complete Set*, 13:31–56.

1949	People's Republic of China is established.
1950–55	Korean War

What is noteworthy is that in *Direction for New Lives*, Kagawa used metaphors that were easy for Japanese readers to understand and uses universal words found in religion, such as *conscience*, to explain to his readers. However, as Kagawa stated at the beginning of *A Reexamination of Oriental Thought*, there is no redemptive love in all Oriental thought and religion, but the central theme of the Bible is redemptive love. Only redemptive love was used without pandering to the Japanese spiritual or religious context.

Kagawa stated that Japan ruled the countries of Greater East Asia by force, and Kagawa harshly criticized its rule in Korea, Manchuria, the Philippines, and Indonesia. Also, the causes of defeat were moral corruption; failure to conduct the country, politics, and governance with love; social neglect of the working class; disordered monogamy; lack of loyalty to the emperor by the military; etc.

Kagawa commented in *Direction for New Lives*:

> Fortunately, General MacArthur was a spiritual man. He promoted policies with a considerable understanding of Japan's defeat in the war, so Japan's collapse was prevented to a certain extent. Still, as a Japanese citizen, the task of reconstruction was not easy.[47]

Reconstruction of nation and restoration of conscience. Both were required because, Kagawa said, Japan had been against God's will through the war, and God had judged the Japanese people with wrath:

> The wrath of Heaven has fallen on the Japanese people, who are ignorant of the power of religion, and whose ungodly and arrogant attitude has been to ignore Heaven and enslave God to humans.[48]

Kagawa concluded by exhorting redemptive love for the Japanese people who were in desperate hopelessness, as follows.

> Defeat does not necessarily mean destruction. If the Japanese use defeat as an opportunity to turn to conscience, they will even discover new steps to courage.[49]

47. Kagawa, *Complete Set*, 13:32.
48. Kagawa, *Complete Set*, 13:51.
49. Kagawa, *Complete Set*, 13:32.

> The Japanese people have come back to the original mission of humanity and have grasped the path to open the eternal ways through spiritual evolution that does not rely on weapons. . . . Having discovered a passage to peaceful East Asia, Japan discovered a heavenly rope ladder that would lead to victory.[50]

CONCLUSION

In a July 1945 speech at SHP headquarters in Tokyo, Kagawa confessed to God Japan's sins in the war, as well as the West's sins. Kagawa confessed moral decline as the reason for Japan's defeat in the war and prayed for forgiveness through Christ's atonement. To Japanese people who had completely lost hope due to their defeat, Kagawa exhorted them to live a life based on the teachings of Christ.

Kagawa's confession of responsibility for the war and his message of redemptive love with Christian brotherhood economics were addressed to Japan and the world. His message was the same as the one given when he went to the United States in 1936, except for his criticism of the West and confession of responsibility for the war.

Finally, Kagawa's religious stance, which advocated transforming society and the world by eliminating the weak from the world and respecting individualism, is still reflected in many people's fantasies even in the twenty-first century. Many scholars in the world, especially in Japan, have criticized Kagawa's thought as too idealistic, and full of illusions and dreams.

Christian Leaders in the World: Statements after the War

First, I introduce the statement of Reinhold Niebuhr (1892–1971), Kagawa's contemporary and a non-pacifist scholar. On February 27, 1960, at Union Theological Seminary in the city of New York, Niebuhr delivered a message entitled "The Wheat and the Tares," in which he stated:

> We will not have justice if the powerful man simply goes after his interest at the expense of the weak.[51]

---

50. Kagawa, *Complete Set*, 13:31.
51. Niebuhr, *Justice and Mercy*, 58.

Niebuhr, a realist theologian, denied the justice of prioritizing the interests of the strong at the expense of the weak, while Kagawa criticized the sins of the West and Japan in colonizing Asian countries by force in the war. Furthermore, Kagawa was not advocating an illusory opinion when he claimed that world peace cannot be achieved unless Christians and the church recognize, through Christian brotherhood economics, that the economic system itself benefits the powerful. The proof of this is not just Niebuhr's personal opinion, but the following statement from the World Council of Church in 1948:

> We must frankly acknowledge our deep sense of perplexity in the face of these conflicting opinions [between pacifism and non-pacifism], and urge upon all Christians the duty of wrestling continuously with the difficulties they raise and of praying humbly for God's guidance.... The churches, for their part, have the duty of declaring those moral principles which obedience to God requires in war as in peace.... They must teach the duty of love and prayer for the enemy in times of war and of reconciliation between victors and vanished after the war.[52]

---

52. World Council of Churches, *Office Report*, 55.

8

Conclusion

CONFESSION OF WAR RESPONSIBILITY OF KAGAWA

We have learned that after Kagawa's became a Christian, God gave Kagawa the gifts that remained throughout his life, such as evangelism; supporting the socially disadvantaged; working toward transformation in local communities, countries, and the world; patriotism toward Japan as a country sent by God; and reverence for the emperor and the imperial family. We should recognize that Kagawa's commitment to the above works was based on redemptive love.

In February 1904, at sixteen, Kagawa was baptized by Harry White Meyers, a missionary sent from the American Southern Presbyterian Mission, ten days after Japan had declared war on Russia. After that, Kagawa experienced WWI (1914–18), the Fifteen Years War (1931–45; the Pacific War broke out in 1941), and the Korean War (1950–53). He died in 1960 at the age of seventy-one. In other words, Kagawa lived a life in which he was forced to encounter modern wars that Japan, the West, and Asia had never experienced before, and he continued to focus on the sins of humanity in wars that rebelled against the will of God.

In the above war-engaging content, we have seen how Kagawa, as one of the pastors of a church in Japan, in which God selected him to live, Kagawa saw the universal evils of the war of both the Japanese Empire and Western countries that unilaterally colonized Asian countries that unilaterally colonized Asian countries.

Kagawa's War Responsibility Confession from SHP Prison

In July 1945, Kagawa was detained at the SHP headquarters in Kudanshita, Tokyo, for nine days. Kagawa prayed repentance of humankind's sin of war to God:

> One month before the defeat [July 1945], I was interrogated for nine days at the military police headquarters in Kudanshita, Tokyo. At that time, if we lost the war, I did not want to go to war, but [1] I was prepared to burn to death and sacrifice myself for my country. I alone had no intention of rebelling against the state. [2] I thought it was a mistake to go to war with the Allies, but I also thought that the foreign countries occupying the East were at fault. [3] I thought I had to prepare a bottle of tears and "repent" the sins of Japan, the sins of other countries, and the sins of humanity's rebellion against God. I am saddened that there are still many people on earth crucifying Christ in the twentieth century.[1]

In review, regarding point 1, Kagawa decided to share the war sufferings of the defeated Japan, convinced that God was calling him to live with the Japanese people. Regarding points 2 and 3, his lament for the evils committed by mankind in Japan and the West took the form of a bottle of tears ("You have kept count of my tossings; put my tears in your bottle. Are they not in your record?" [Ps 56:8 NRSV]). Point 3 can be understood as humankind's sin being rebellion against God, and a prayer of confession seeking the redemptive love of Jesus.

Kagawa Prayed Repentance of the War of Japan in Sapporo

Kagawa committed to the NJCCM from July 1947 to December 1949. As he started visiting the northern part of the Tohoku region and Hokkaido, Kagawa prayed as follows, giving the date as "the year of Christ." It is noteworthy that Kagawa did not use the imperial era of Japan but clearly stated that it was the era of Christ. Through this, Kagawa declared that the new Japan would move forward with Christ as its center, rather than using the official imperial order. It was the twenty-first year of the Showa era.

> [1] The Japanese people, who refused to accept the God of the creation of the universe as their god and loved myths and idols,

---

1. Kagawa, *Complete Set*, 24:354.

were forced to fall into the depths of defeat, albeit fragile. [2] And it became clear that the only thing that could save Japan from its rotten destiny was God's great love and sacrifice, which is the driving force behind the re-creation of life.

[3] There is no crisis as difficult as today for Japan and its people. If we do not now discover that the path to Japan's re-creation lies at the cross, Japan will forever be reduced to a barbarian tribe living on an island in the Pacific Ocean.

The Year of Christ August 26, 1946, in Sapporo[2]

In the opening, point 1, Kagawa confessed and declared God's judgment of wars because Japan did not God but trusted the gods of myths. In point 2, Kagawa exhorted his readers to follow God, who redeems the Japanese people who had been in the depths of helplessness in the calamity of war. Though Kagawa stated the above prayer as a preface, in the main body of his statement, he introduced the story of the prodigal son, the story of God's love for the man who had been living without trusting God. Without commenting on the story, Kagawa related the prodigal son to Japan in the past.

The above testimony by Kagawa can be expressed in the following diagram (cf. chart 7.1):

2. Kagawa, *Complete Set*, 4:4.

KAGAWA TOYOHIKO'S WAR RESPONSIBILITY CONFESSION

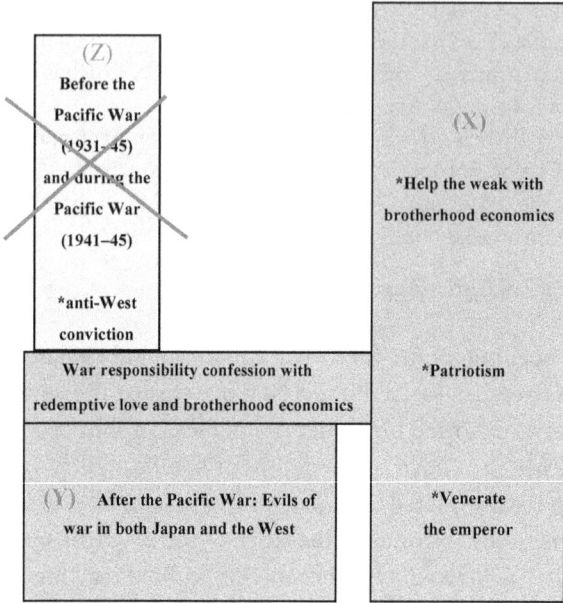

Reverence to the Emperor

Regarding the emperor issue, Christians under the military regime were legally forced to worship the emperor, so Kagawa understood that they should follow the orders of the military regime based on Rom 13. However, during the war, Kagawa's testimony criticizing the government's idolatry was recorded by the SHP in 1942, during the Pacific War, in Kochi Prefecture:

> Those of us who believe in Christianity never worship idols, and of course, we do not do so even now. However, the Japanese nation bows down to shrines and temples. While this may formally amount to idolatry, the ministry of the Minister of Home Affairs has said that the shrines and temples worshiped by our ancestors are worshiped by the Minister of Home Affairs. It is argued that the people must worship in the sense of ancestor worship. The Bible clearly states that they should obey their superiors, and there is no difference between them and ordinary people, but in short, it is a matter of belief.
>
> It is a well-known fact that Christians are generally pacifists, especially as individuals; my pacifism remains unchanged from

beginning to end. The reason for this goes without saying: war is a grave sin.³

AFTER KAGAWA'S CONFESSION OF WAR RESPONSIBILITY

During Kagawa's lecture tour in the United States in 1950, some Americans felt betrayed by Kagawa's criticism of the United States through his radio broadcast statement. Still, they transcended Kagawa's criticism of the United States and responded to Kagawa's faith, and Kagawa's lecture moved many American people.

The above story suggests that there was a divine work within Kagawa. It goes beyond the coexistence of work to serve the weak and patriotism within Kagawa and recognizes that God is involved in history. In other words, God unilaterally accepted Kagawa's and the Americans' response to God, and God's work atoned for the sins within Kagawa.

We recognized that Kagawa confessed a personal war responsibility through the open letter addressed to Korean president Syngman Rhee, who accepted Kagawa's confession by faith in 1955. It was 1955, almost five years before Kagawa passed away in 1960. As the open letter was reported by the nationwide newspaper *Mainichi Shimbun*, in Japanese, Kagawa might have intended to make a testimony of Christianity, which had been regarded as a traitor to the state. Japanese newspapers, Korean newspapers, and *The Korean Information Bulletin* in the US reported the open letter to President Rhee and valued Kagawa's confession based on the Korean and Japanese political context.

Kagawa was labeled as a nationalistic person by the GHQ of the Supreme Commander for the Allied Powers, which wanted to eradicate such a feudalist as he.⁴ Yoshitake Nobuhiko, in an article entitled "International

---

3. Institute for the Study of Humans and Society, *Movement of Christianity*, 2:150–51.

4. SCAP memorandum: "Despite the technical non-permeability of the subject, Kagawa's thinking is obviously confirmed in the ideology of feudalism and ultranationalism, the very concepts that SCAP is committed to eradicate from the Japanese mind. Occupation policies cannot hope to be realized if the leadership of Japan is bestowed on pseudo-liberals like Kagawa, who exploit the trappings of democracy for political purposes. Kagawa is considered the type of a person who would tend to obstruct rather than promote the development of individual initiative on the part of the people and retard the establishment of social and political democracy in Japan" (Schildgen, *Toyohiko Kagawa*, 260).

Politics of the Nobel Prize: The Nobel Peace Prize and Japan, Toyohiko Kagawa, a Japanese Nominee after World War II," commented, "The Norwegian Nobel Committee in 1955 stated that Kagawa's influence in Japan had decreased because of his following the Japanese military authority."[5] Kagawa lost worldly honors before he confessed war responsibility to Korean president Rhee.

We also should not forget that the American population accepted Kagawa beyond his patriotic nature as an evangelist. When Kagawa died in 1960, Richard H. Drummond contributed his report titled "Kagawa: Christian Evangelist" in which he stated that "he was both servant and leader of his people, a man of peace who sought to prevent war between his nation and the United States. . . . Kagawa was perhaps more appreciated outside Japan than within. At the funeral, foreign correspondents were more in evidence than Japanese."[6]

Kagawa Was a Pastor, While Yanaihara Was a Prophet

In 1947, Kagawa stated:

1. The gospel of Christ cannot be spread to Japan simply by doctrine or dissemination. It must be a religion of life that can save people's lives. Since the religion of Christ is a religion of life, love, and blood, we must promote the religion of the cross as the gospel of society as well as of personal salvation.

2. This time, for the first time in recorded history, Japan suffered a crushing defeat in war. Now we are a full-fledged person. Until then, Japan had boasted that it was great and great. However, he kept repeating his foolishness of being like a frog in a well and not knowing the ocean, and in the end, he fell into an unavoidable catastrophe. We must look at world history. I can't help but read about the great events of judgment and love, destruction, and salvation that are taking place before the absolute God.

3. Japan can't receive special treatment before the God of absolute fairness. God's judgment lies in the rise and fall of history. People with a

---

5. Yoshitake, "Nobel Prize," 17.
6. Drummond, "Kagawa," 823.

heart can see God through history. We must become enlightened and know what God throughout human history has done.

4. Jesus is a redemptive love, not to use people, but to serve and be used by people. Jesus's political consciousness lies in his desire to be a redeemer rather than a ruler, accepting people's weakest points, their shortcomings, and forgiving them for their mistakes. He comes down from above and lifts the fallen. . . . Herein lies the key to Jesus's love of neighbor.[7]

Kagawa's above statement confuses Christians who might criticize that Kagawa did not exhort the attendees of the NJCCM to repent, when we recognize that Japan, during the war, committed atrocities against Asian people. Kainou Nobuo criticized Kagawa's statement while he led the NJCCM as follows:

> The New Japan Construction Christian Movement does not follow the style of traditional evangelism meetings. It is not an evangelistic meeting that preaches the gospel of sin and its forgiveness and urges each member of the congregation to repent and convert. Above all, it is a call to stand together for the rebuilding of a new Japan, and an appeal to those who are crouching in the chaos immediately after the defeat to seek comrades in rebuilding Japan. This is precisely where we can say that Kagawa's message for the New Japan Construction Christian Movement was so convincing. It is also true that Kagawa had very little development of ideas that could only be deepened and refined through the experience of that war. The issue of war responsibility, not just whether one was complicit in the war or not, but also the deepening development of ideas that are questioned only in a war like that, was something Kagawa hardly ever saw during this period.[8]

I cannot accept Kainou's criticism against Kagawa for the following reasons:

Kagawa claimed that God warned against pride. Thus, God destroyed Japan. Therefore, by trusting in God, Japan would be rebuilt. This is not a sermon that *tells* us to repent of our proud hearts, but rather a sermon that *leads* us to repentance.

Nonetheless, I am convinced that Kagawa's method was to preach repentance not to all those who attended the movement but to those who

7. Kainou, *Immediately after the War*, 370–73.
8. Kainou, *Immediately after the War*, 375–76.

filled out the decision card, because Japan was not a Christian nation but a nation of Buddhism and Shintoism, where people could not understand the meaning of repentance to God. Kagawa did not lead the NJCCM alone, but after giving a lecture, Kagawa worked with a local church, following those who had made up their minds.

Kagawa's Patriotism against Yanaihara's Prophetic Exhortation

Immediately after the war, in June 1946, Yanaihara Tadao, in his book *Nihon Seishin to Heiwa Koka* (The Japanese spirit and a peaceful nation), stated:

> God has now given the Japanese people an opportunity to reconsider Christianity. Today, we must make every effort to save the Japanese spirit, raise the morality of the Japanese people and the academic standard, and build Japan as a new nation. The flaws in the Japanese spirit have now been revealed through the war and its resulting defeat. If the Japanese people change their traditional arrogant attitude toward Christianity, abandon their prejudices and misunderstandings, stop hating them, become humble, listen to the gospel of Christ, and study the Christian Bible, this will save Japan. This is a path that makes use of the Japanese spirit. Many people question the relationship between the God of Christianity and the God of Japan. The God that Christians believe in is absolute, so it is the God of Japan, the God of foreign countries, and the God of the universe. God has given Japan a mission that only Japan can fulfill. In that sense, Japan has absolute value as a country chosen by God. The same applies to other countries. Although Japan does not look down on other countries, it does not look down on other countries by saying that other countries are barbarians or that Japan is the only divine country. Each country has an absolute value of existence due to the one and only absolute God. Perfect universal peace can only be achieved based on this understanding.
>
> "Lamentation" [poem by Yanaihara]
> God, as we have sinned, we have turned away, and you will not forgive us. Thou shalt tremble with wrath. Thou shalt cover thy wrath, pursue us, slay us, have no mercy upon us, and all our enemies shall speak against us.[9]

---

9. Yanaihara, *Japanese Spirit*, 59.

CONCLUSION

Yanaihara's statement continues as follows:

> If we humbly and truthfully learn our faith in the one God, the Creator of all things, God will surely bless the nation of Japan, give it new life, and make it the light of the world. Disarmament is something to be celebrated, and while the destruction of economic power is painful, it is not a fatal blow to the ideals of the people. His Majesty [the emperor] said that we should respect faith and strive to establish a peaceful nation, and I heard these words as the emperor's will as the ideal model of the Japanese spirit. If Japan truly repents and starts a new nation, Japan will be a blessing for the new nation even if it must pay the great price of the war of the past ten years and its consequences.[10]

Though the above statement of Yanaihara is a message straightforward and understandable to Christians, it was hard to accept by common Japanese people who were not familiar with Christian theology, because Yanaihara used lamentation, which declared God's wrath and punishment of Japan because of its sin. When Yanaihara's book was published first in June 1946, the International Military Tribunal for the Far East, the so-called Tokyo Trial, had just occurred in May 1946; citizens recognized the A-, B-, and C-class war criminals who should have taken responsibility for the war, but they did not recognize complicity in themselves, the citizens.

> In the time of political crisis, the prophet, rather than the priest, was better suited to be Yahweh's spokesperson. A priest could officiate at sacred rites, teach the people the sacred traditions, and manipulate the sacred lot in answer to yes-or-no questions.[11]

Though Anderson values the prophet "at the time of political crisis," that is, here, the political crisis in Japan during the war, he does not reject the ministry of priests, who are always with a congregation, at the time of crisis and in good times. Nevertheless, Kagawa excused his own going too close to the military government; giving Rom 9:3 as an excuse should not be permitted before God and the people we sacrificed during the war.

The churches of nearly all Japanese Christians after the war, starting with the UCCJ, issued the confession of war responsibilities as follows:

---

10. Yanaihara, *Japanese Spirit*, 59.
11. Anderson, *Understanding The Old Testament*, 228.

Table 8.1: Japanese churches' war responsibility confessions

1967	UCCJ
1988	Japan Baptist Convention
1992	Japan Baptist Union
1995	Catholic bishops of Japan
1995	Meiji Gakuin University (Presbyterian)
1995	Cumberland Presbyterian Church (Japan Presbytery)
1996	Nippon Sei-Ko-Kai (NSKK, Anglican Episcopal Church in Japan)
1997	Japan Holiness Church
1997	Presbyterian Church in Japan
2015	Japan Christ Church Alliance

Though it seems that the number of churches that confessed war responsibilities is small, we should recognize that almost all Protestant churches were unified to the UCCJ in 1941 due to the ROL; some denominations later departed from the UCCJ, such as both Baptist denominations, the holiness movement, Presbyterians, etc. However, large numbers of denominations, such as Congregationalists, Methodists, and Presbyterians, remained in the UCCJ.

FUTURE ISSUES REGARDING KAGAWA'S CONFESSION OF WAR RESPONSIBILITY

This time, my perspective on Kagawa's war responsibility was to discuss by focusing on how Kagawa struggled with Japanese society and the nation, as well as his words and deeds in opposition to the West, especially Britain and America, from a theological perspective. However, Kagawa stood on

Presbyterianism, to which I belong. I understand that Kagawa was saved to survive in Japan, an anti-Christian nation, as Kagawa gained a theological perspective of personalism from Bowne (Boston University School of Theology, a Wesleyan school) at the library of Meiji Gakuin Preparatory School, a Presbyterian seminary.

Despite the many challenges Kagawa encountered in stubborn exclusivity towards a non-Christian spiritual climate, Bowne's theology, which demanded the necessity to face an anti-Christian spirituality in Japan, was a significant theology for my theory in this book. Nonetheless, I pointed out that we should not forget that Bowne's personalism might have led the Japanese churches to pander to the national polity of the Japanese government, which demanded worship of the emperor.

I expect that the subject of Kagawa's war responsibility will be discussed critically against my point of view in the future by scholars from the Asian countries that Japan militarily invaded and colonized during the war, as well as scholars from the West, especially Britain, America, Australia, and other Allied powers against whom Japan fought, with their sociopolitical contexts and theological perspectives.

Bibliography

Amemiya Eiichi (雨宮栄一)_.「青春の賀川豊彦」 [Kagawa Toyohiko in youth]. Tokyo: Sinkyo, 2003.

Anderson, Bernhard W. Understanding, The Old Testament. 4th ed. Englewood Cliffs, NJ: Prentice-Hall, 1998.

Arakuni, Keisuke (荒邦啓介).「明治憲法に於ける国務と統帥： 統帥権の憲法史的研究」 [Minister of state and commander-in-chief in the Meiji Constitution: A constitutional historical study of the power of commander-in-chief]. Tokyo: Seibundo, 2017.

Asia for Educators. "The Edicts of the Tokugawa Shogunate: Excerpts from the Edict of 1635 Ordering the Closing of Japan: Addressed to the Joint Bugyō of Nagasaki." Asia for Educators, n.d. https://afe.easia.columbia.edu/ps/japan/tokugawa_edicts_foreigners.pdf.

———. The Edicts of Toyotomi Hideyoshi: Excerpts from Limitation on the Propagation of Christianity, 1587; Excerpts from Expulsion of Missionaries, 1587." Asia for Educators, n.d. http://afe.easia.columbia.edu/ps/japan/tokugawa_edicts_christianity.pdf.

Asonuma, Haruna (阿曽沼春菜).「日本の関税自主権回復問題に見るもう一つの日英関係ー小村条約改正交渉とイギリス」 _[Japan's demand for tariff autonomy and the Anglo-Japanese relations, 1910–11]. Kyoto Law Review 163 (May 2008) 65–81.

Bowne, Borden Parker. Personalism. Boston: Houghton Mifflin, 1908.

Bradshaw, Emerson O. Unconquerable Kagawa. St. Paul, MN: Macalester Park, 1952.

Bradshaw, Emerson O., et al., eds. *Kagawa in Lincoln's Land*. Brooklyn, NY: National Kagawa Co-ordinating Committee, 1936.

Calvin, John. *Commentary on Psalms II*. [In Japanese.] Translated by Demura Akira. Tokyo: Shinkyo, 1983.

———. *Commentary on Romans*. Christian Classics Ethereal Library, n.d. https://ccel.org/ccel/c/calvin/calcom38/cache/calcom38.pdf.

———. *The Institutes of the Christian Religion*. Christian Classics Ethereal Library, n.d. Translated by Henry Beveridge. https://ccel.org/ccel/calvin/institutes/institutes.

Church of Christ in Japan Editing Committee (日本基督教会).「日本基督教会の歴史」 [The history of the Church of Christ in Japan]. Church of Christ in Japan, n.d. https://dl.ndl.go.jp/pid/824961/1/3.

Committee of the Fiftieth Anniversary Japanese Protestant Mission Conference. 「開教五十年記念講演集ー附祝典記録」 [The lecture collection of the fiftieth anniversary of introducing Protestant Christianity in Japan: Supplementary celebration records]. Tokyo: Keisei, 1909.

Doi Akio (土肥昭夫). 「日本プロテスタントキリスト教史」 [The history of Japanese Protestant Christianity.] Tokyo: Shinkyo, 1987.

Drummond, Richard H. "Kagawa: Christian Evangelist." *Christian Century* (July 13, 1960) 823–25.

Ebina Danjo (海老名弾正). 「世界と共に目覚めよ」 [Awakening with the world]. Tokyo: Kobundo Shoten, 1917.

———. 「基督の福音と民本主義」 [Gospel of Christ and democracy]. 「新人」 [New man] (Aug. 1918) 20.

———. 「新時代の曙光を望みて」 [Hoping for the dawn of a new era]. 「新人」 [New man] (Mar. 1919) 16.

Miyagawa Tsuneteru (宮川経輝) 「国民道徳と基督教」 [National morality and Christianity]. 「時事瑣言」 [Current events] (1916) 49–84.

Ebina Danjo (海老名弾正) 「愛国心の最高潮」 [Patriotism at its peak]. 「新人」 [New man] (June 1904) 3.

Fey, Harold E. "Kagawa Revisits America." *Christian Century* (May 21, 1941) 684–86.

Fukushima Kiyonori. (福島清紀) 「明治期における政治・宗教・教育」 [Politics, religion, and education in the Meiji period]. *Bulletin of Toyama University of International Studies* (Mar. 2009) 17–35.

Furuya Yasuo (古屋安夫). *History of Japan and Christianity.* Theology of Japan Monograph Series 3. Saitama: Seigakuin University Press, 2006.

Gandhi, Mohandas Karamchand. *The Collected Works of Mahatma Gandhi.* 90 vols. New Delhi: Minister of Information and Broadcasting, 1977.

Gayn, Mark. *Japan Diary.* Rutland, VT: Tuttle, 1948.

Hatakeyama Keiichi (畠山 圭一). 「第二次世界大戦後半期: における米軍部内の対ソ戦略と対日政策への影響」 [The US military's strategic debate on the USSR in the last half of WWII (1943–45): Implications in policy toward Japan]. *Bulletin of Gakushuin Women's College* 3 (2011) 144–77.

Hatano Sumio (波多野澄雄). 「重光葵と大東亜共同宣言: 戦時外交と戦後構想」 [Shigemitsu Mamoru and the Greater East Asia Joint Declaration: Wartime diplomacy and postwar plans]. *Japanese Political Science Association* 109 (1995) 38–53.

Hayashida Kojun (林田康順). 「明治期における宗教の自由の獲得の受容: 浄土宗を中心として」 [Acquisition and acceptance of freedom of religion in the Meiji era: Focusing on Jodoshu.] *Journal of Research Society of Buddhism and Cultural Heritage* 3 (1995) 187–227.

Hirano Yukikazu (平野敬和). 「帝国改造の政治思想：世界戦争期の吉野作造」 [Political thought on reconstruction of imperial Japan Yoshino Sakuno in World War I]. *Machikaneyama Ronso* [Osaka University] 34 (2000) 1–30.

Honda Itsuo (本田逸夫). 「明治末年以降のローマ書十三章論: 海老名弾正・内村鑑三・山室軍平を中心として」 [Interpretation of Romans 13:1–7 after the last years of the Meiji era: Mainly focusing on the cases of Ebina Danjo, Uchimura Kanzo, and Yamamuro Gumpei]. *Joint Journal of the National University in Kyushu, Education and Humanities* 5 (2017) 1–20.

Hong Yipyo. 「海老名弾正の「会衆主義」理解とデモクラシー論の展開」 [Ebina Danjo's interpretation of Christian congregationalism and the path toward his theory of democracy]. *Asia & Religious Plurality* [Kyoto University] 19 (2021) 5–21.

Hopper, Helen H. "Constitutional Affair." University of Pittsburgh: Japan, n.d. https://www.japanpitt.pitt.edu/essays-and-articles/history/constitutional-affair.

House of Representatives. 「明治憲法と日本国憲法に関する基礎資料」 [Basic materials of the Meiji Constitution and the Constitution of Japan]. *Material* 27 (2003) 1–72.

Huffman, James. "Peace Preservation Law of 1925." Japan Society, 2024. https://aboutjapan.japansociety.org/content.cfm/peace_preservation_law_of_1925#sthash.T6aHFWow.dpbs.

Institute for Advanced Studies on Asia [University of Tokyo]. "Greater East Asia Declaration." [In Japanese.] World and Japan, Nov. 6, 1943. https://worldjpn.net/documents/texts/pw/19431106.T1J.html.

Institute for the Study of Humans and Society [Doshisha University]. 「戦時下のキリスト教運動: 特高資料による2」 [The movement of Christianity during the war: Documents of the special higher police]. Vol. 2. Tokyo: Shinkyo, 1973.

———. 「戦時下のキリスト教運動: 特高資料による3」 [The movement of Christianity during the war: Documents of the special higher police]. Vol. 3. Tokyo: Shinkyo, 1973.

Japan Center for Asian Historical Records. "Hull Note." Japan Center for Asian Historical Records, Dec. 8, 2005. https://www.jacar.go.jp/nichibei/word/index7.html.

———. "National Spiritual Mobilization Committee." Japan Center for Asian Historical Records, 1971. https://www.jacar.archives.go.jp/aj/meta/term-en/00002127.

Kagawa Toyohiko (賀川豊彦). *Across the Deathline* [死線を超えて]. Translated by I. Fukumoto Ichiji and Thomas Satchell. Kobe: n.p., 1922. https://dl.ndl.go.jp/pid/1679802.

———. *Brotherhood Economics*. Rauschenbusch Lectures. New York: Harper & Brothers, 1936.

———. *Christ and Japan*. Translated by William Axling. New York: Friendship, 1934.

———. 「賀川豊彦全集 _4_」 [*A complete set of Kagawa Toyohiko*]. Edited by A Complete Set of Kagawa Toyohiko Publishing Committee. vol. 4. Tokyo Kirisuto Shimbun, 1981.

———. 「賀川豊彦全集 _1_0_」 [*A complete set of Kagawa Toyohiko*]. Edited by A Complete Set of Kagawa Toyohiko Publishing Committee. vol. 10. Tokyo Kirisuto Shimbun, 1982.

———. 「賀川豊彦全集 _1_3_」 _[*A complete set of Kagawa Toyohiko*]. Edited by A Complete Set of Kagawa Toyohiko Publishing Committee. vol. 13. Tokyo Kirisuto Shimbun, 1982.

———. 「賀川豊彦全集24」 [*A complete set of Kagawa Toyohiko*]. Edited by A Complete Set of Kagawa Toyohiko Publishing Committee. 24 vols. Tokyo: Kirisuto Shinbun, 1981–97.

———. *Cosmic Purpose*. Edited by Thomas John Hastings. Translated by James W. Heisig. Eugene, OR: Cascade, 2014.

———. 「国難に殉ずるもの」 [Dying as a martyr in the national crisis]. 「火の柱」 [Pillar of light] 169 (1943) 1–4.

———. "Friends of Jesus." *Tsinan* 4 (1931) 24.

———. "Plea for Sympathetic Treatment Made to MacArthur by Nippon Social Worker." *Nippon Times*, Sept. 2, 1945.

———. "An Open Letter to President Rhee." *Mainichi*, Dec. 13, 1955.

———. 「聖書の社会運動」 [The social movement of the Bible]. Osaka: Nichiyou Sekai Kankou, 1928.

Kainou Nobuo (戒能信生). 「終戦直後の賀川豊彦: 新日本建設キリスト運動を中心として」 [Kagawa Toyohiko immediately after the war: Focused on new Japan construction of the Christian movement]. 「日本キリスト教史における賀川豊彦の思想と実践」 [Toyohiko Kagawa in the history of Christianity in Japan]. Tokyo: Shinkyo, 2011.

Kee, Howard Clark, et al. *Christianity: A Social and Cultural History*. 2nd ed. Upper Saddle River, NJ: Prentice-Hall, 1998.

Keijo Nippo. "The First Time in 14 Years." [In Japanese.] *Keijo Nippo*, June 19, 1938.

Kirisuto Shinbun. *Christianity Yearbook* 1960. [In Japanese.] Tokyo: Kirisuto Shinbun, 1960.

Kitamori Kazoh (北森嘉造). 「日本基督教団 信仰告白 解説」 [Commentary on the confession of faith of the United Church of Christ]. Tokyo: United Church of Christ in Japan, 1955.

Korean Information Bulletin. "Korea and Japan." *Korean Information Bulletin* 2 (Feb. 1956) 1–2.

Kramer, Hand Marin. "How 'Religion' Came to Be Translated as Shukyo: Shimaji Mokurai and the Appropriation of Religion in Early Meiji Japan." *Japan Review* [International Research Center for Japanese Study] 25 (2013) 89–111.

Kuramochi Kazuo (倉持和雄). "Confession on the Responsibility during World War II by the United Church of Christ in Japan and the Exchange between Christians in Japan and Korea." *Annals of the Institute for Comparative Studies of Culture* [Tokyo Woman's Christian University] (2020) 37–56.

Kuroda Shiro (黒田四郎). 「私の賀川豊彦研究」 [My research on Kagawa Toyohiko]. Tokyo: Kirisuto Shinbun, 1983.

Kurokawa Tomobumi (黒川知文). 「日本におけるキリスト教宣教の歴史的考察 3」 [Historical study of Christian mission in Japan, pt. 3]. *Bulletin of Aichi University of Education* (2004) 58–68.

———. 「賀川豊彦による神の国運動と戦争」 [Kingdom of God movement by Toyohiko Kagawa and the war]. *Liberal Arts Review* [Chuo Gakuin University] 1 (2019) 21–41.

Laverge, A. T. "Peace Preservation Law." International Military Tribunal for the Far East, Mar. 14, 1947. http://imtfe.law.virginia.edu/collections/tavenner/4/3/peace-preservation-law.

Lee Sunhye. 「賀川豊彦の社会福祉実践・思想が勧告に及ぼした影響に関する研究」 [Research on the influence of Toyohiko Kagawa's social welfare practices and ideas on Korea]. PhD diss., Doshisha University, 2014.

Mainichi Shimbun. 「日韓友好のために: 賀川への李大統領の返答」 [For Japan-Korea friendship: President Syngman Rhee's reply letter to Mr. Kagawa.] *Mainichi Shimbun*, Dec. 21, 1955.

———. "Government Cautious about Specific Methods, Resolve Issue with Spirit of Compromise: President Syngman Rhee's Reply to Mr. Kagawa." [In Japanese.] *Mainichi Shimbun*, Dec. 22, 1955.

Marra, Claudia. 「廃仏毀釈」 [Anti-Buddhism movement at the beginning of Meiji era]. *Journal of Nagasaki University of Foreign Studies* (Dec. 2014) 173–84.

Maruyama Masao (丸山眞男). 「日本のナショナリズム」 [Japanese nationalism]. In 「日本近代史叢書」 [History of modern Japan] 1. Tokyo: Kawaide, 1953.

Matsutani Yosuke (松谷曄介). "Crossing the Bamboo Curtain: The Background and Meaning of the Japanese Christian Delegation to the Chinese Church in 1957." [In Japanese.] *Bulletin of the Institute for Christian Studies* [Meiji Gakuin University] (2015) 249–78.

Meiji Jingu Shrine. (明治神宮). 「五箇条の御誓文」 [Enshrined Kami]. Meiji Jingu Shrine, n.d. https://www.meijijingu.or.jp/en/about/enshrined/.

Ministry of Education, Culture, Sports, Science and Technology—Japan. 「国民精神総動員運動の展開」 [Development of the national spiritual mobilization movement]. Ministry of Education, n.d. https://www.mext.go.jp/b_menu/hakusho/html/others/detail/1317713.htm.

———. 「国民精神作興ニ関スル詔書」 [Imperial edict on the promotion of national spirit]. Ministry of Education, n.d. https://www.mext.go.jp/b_menu/hakusho/html/others/detail/1317939.htm.

———. 「明治初期における宗教行政」 [Religious administration in the early Meiji period]. Ministry of Education, n.d. https://www.mext.go.jp/b_menu/hakusho/html/others/detail/1317735.htm.

Ministry of Education of the Meiji Government. 「教育勅語」 [The imperial rescript on education 1907]. Meiji Jingu Shrine, 1907. https://www.meijijingu.or.jp/about/3-4.php.

Mishima City Local Museum. 「明治新政府の法令 太政官高札: 五榜の掲示」 [Laws and regulations of the new Meiji government: The high plate of the Great Council of State; five public notices]. Mishima, n.d. https://www.city.mishima.shizuoka.jp/kyoudo/publication/pub_kobako001849.html.

Miyagawa Tsuneteru (宮川経輝) Current Events 「時事瑣言」 Tokyo: Keiseisha, 1916.

Miyata Mitsuo (宮田光雄). *Authority and Obedience: Romans 13:1–7 in Modern Japan.* Translated by Gregory Vanderbilt. American University Studies. New York: Lang, 2009.

Mori Yasuo (森 靖夫). 「軍部大臣文官制の再検討: 年代の陸軍と統帥権」 [Reexamination of the civilian minister system in prewar Japan: The Japanese Army in the 1920s and the Supreme Command]. *Japanese Political Science Association* 59 (2008) 241–62.

Muto Tomio, ed. *Biography of Kagawa by One Hundred and Three Persons.* [In Japanese.] Tokyo: Kirisuto Shimbun, 1960.

National Archives of Japan. 「太政官布告第68条1873年(明治6年2月24日)」 [Grand Council of State Proclamation 68 of February 24, 1873]. National Archives of Japan, Feb. 24, 1873. https://www.archives.go.jp/ayumi/kobetsu/m06_1873_02.html.

———. "The Imperial Rescript Ending the War." National Archives of Japan, Aug. 14, 1945. https://www.digital.archives.go.jp/gallery/en/0000000002.

———. 「大日本帝国憲法の発布」 [Promulgation of the Constitution of the Empire of Japan]. National Archives of Japan, n.d. http://www.archives.go.jp/exhibition/digital/modean_state/contents/constitutional-law/index.html.

National Diet Library. "The 2.26 Incident of 1936." National Diet Library, n.d. https://www.ndl.go.jp/modern/e/cha4/description07.html.

———. "The Constitution of the Empire of Japan." National Diet Library, n.d. https://www.ndl.go.jp/constitution/e/etc/c02.html.

———. "Percentage of Population by Status at the Beginning of the Meiji Era." Kodomo, 1868. https://www.kodomo.go.jp/yareki/theme/theme_07.html.

National Graduate Institute for Policy Studies, and Institute for Advanced Studies on Asia [University of Tokyo]. 「五箇条の御誓文」 "The charter of oath." World and Japan, n.d. https://worldjpn.net/documents/texts/pw/18680314.O1E.html.

———. 「五榜の掲示」 [Five public notices]. World and Japan, n.d. https://worldjpn.net/documents/texts/pw/18680315.O1J.html.

———. "Imperial Rescript [of Surrender], August 14, 1945." World and Japan, Aug. 14, 1945. https://worldjpn.net/documents/texts/docs/19450814.O1E.html.

———. "Treaty of Amity and Commerce between the United States of America and the Empire of Japan (Treaty of Amity and Commerce, Harris Treaty)." World and Japan, 1858. https://worldjpn.net/documents/texts/pw/18580729.T1E.html.

National WWII Museum. "The Path to Pearl Harbor." National WWII Museum, n.d. https://www.nationalww2museum.org/war/articles/path-pearl-harbor.

Niebuhr, H. Richard. "The Disorder of Man in the Church of God." In *Man's Disorder and God's Design*, edited by World Council of Churches, 1:78–88. Amsterdam Assembly Series. New York: Harper & Brothers, 1948.

Niebuhr, Reinhold. *Justice and Mercy*. Edited by Ursula M. Niebuhr. New York: Harper & Row, 1974.

Niebuhr, Reinhold, and Angus Dun. "God Wills Both Justice and Peace." *Christianity & Crisis* 15 (June 13, 1955) 75–78.

Nitobe Inazo (新渡戸稲造). 「武士道」 [The spirit of Japan: An exposition of Japanese thought.] Tokyo: Shokabo, 1904.

Nunokawa Hiroshi (布川 弘). 「戦間期における国際実所構想と日本:太平洋問題調査会における議論を中心として」 [The concept of international order and Japan in the interwar period: Focusing on discussions at the Institute of Pacific Relations]. Paper written for Hiroshima University Graduate School of Humanities and Social Science, 2007.

Obinata Sumio (大日方 純夫). 「明治新政府とキリスト教: 諜者の動向を中心に」 [The early Meiji government and Christianity: Spying activities on Christianity]. *Bulletin of the Graduate School of Literature of Waseda University* 4 (1999) 3–17.

Office of the Historian. "740.00119 P.W./8-1045: Telegram." Office of the Historian, Aug. 10, 1945. https://history.state.gov/historicaldocuments/frus1945v06/d405.

Ogata, Sadako N. (緒方貞子). *Defiance in Manchuria: The Making of Japanese Foreign Policy, 1931–1932*. Los Angeles: University of California Press, 1964.

Ohki Hideo (大木英夫). *A Theology of Japan*. [In Japanese.] Edited by Huruya Yasuo. Tokyo: Yorudan, 1989.

Saito Motoko (齋藤 元子). 「メソジスト監督派教会女性海外伝道運動への来日宣教師夫人の貢献」 [The contribution of missionaries' wives in Japan to the foreign mission movement of the Methodist Episcopal Church]. *Wesley Methodist Studies* 10 (2009) 85–97.

Sasaki Yuichi (佐々木雄一). 「明治憲法体制における首相と内閣の再検討「割拠」論をめぐって」 [Reexamination of the prime minister and cabinet under the Meiji constitutional system: Regarding the "divided basis" theory]. *Japanese Political Science Association* 70 (2019) 248–70.

Schildgen, Robert. *Toyohiko Kagawa: Apostle of Love and Social Justice*. Los Angeles: Centenary, 1998.

Statistics Japan. *Statistical Yearbook of the Empire of Japan*. [In Japanese.] Tokyo: Ministry of Internal Affairs and Communications, 1996. https://www.stat.go.jp/museum/toukei150/shiryo/shiryo22.html.

Suma Yakichiro (諏磨弥吉郎). 「韓国の主張変らない 誤解もあるが、希望もある」 [South Korea's claims will not change. There are misunderstandings, but there is also hope.] *Mainichi Shimbun*, Dec. 22, 1955.

Syukyo Shinbun. 「西洋に学び明治の宗教政策を主導」 [Learned from Western Europe and led religious policy in the Meiji period]. Religion News, Mar. 18, 2023. https://religion-news.net/2023/03/18/tada797/.

Tae-Ryong Yoon. "Historical Animosity Is What States Make of It: The Role of Morality and Realism in Korea-Japan Relations." *Korean Journal of International Studies* 9 (2011) 1–37. https://pdfs.semanticscholar.org/0920/58ac8d1ac856640325e1189d3312cffd99fe.pdf.

Takeda Kiyoko (武田清子). *The Dual-Image of the Japanese Emperor*. London: Macmillan Education, 1988.

———. "'Man' in the Taisho Democracy: Focusing on Sakuzo Yoshino's Thought." *International Christian University Educational Studies* 8 (1961) 34–71.

Takenaka Katsuo. "Kagawa as a Pacifist." *World Tomorrow* (Dec. 1931). Page range unavailable.

Takeuchi Masaru (武内 勝). 「賀川豊彦とそのボランティア: 新生田川地区に於ける賀川豊彦とその事業」 [Kagawa Toyohiko and volunteers for him: Work by Kagawa Toyohiko in the Shinikutagawa District]. Edited by Murayama Moritsugu. Kobe: Committee of Publication of Takeuchi Masaru's Verbal Statement, 1973.

Tamamuro Fumio (圭室文雄). "Local Society and Temple-Parishioner Relationship within the Bakufu's Government Structure." [In Japanese.] *Japanese Journal of Religious Studies* (2001) 261–92.

Thorp, Gerald R. "Religious Leader Sees No Early Rebirth of Christianity in Japan." *Chicago Daily News*, Sept. 11, 1945.

Totani Yuma (戸谷由麻). *The Tokyo War Crimes Trial: The Pursuit of Justice in the Wake of World War II*. Cambridge, MA: Harvard University Asia Center, 2008.

UCCJ [United Church of Christ in Japan]. "Confession on the Responsibility during WWII." UCCJ, Mar. 26, 1967; rev. Eng. trans. Jan. 20, 1982. https://uccj.org/confession.

———. 「日本基督教勘の成立過程」 [The formation process of the United Church of Christ in Japan, 1930–41]. Vol. 1 of 「日本基督教団史資料集1」 [History of the United Church of Christ in Japan]. Tokyo: United Church of Christ in Japan, 1997.

———. 「日本基督教会の再編」 [Reorganization of the United Church of Christ, 1945–54]. Vol. 3 of 「日本基督教団史資料集3」 [History of the United Church of Christ in Japan]. Tokyo: United Church of Christ in Japan, 1998.

———. 「戦時下の日本基督教団」 [The United Church of Christ in Japan during the war, 1941–45]. Vol. 2 of 「日本基督教団史資料集4」 [History of the United Church of Christ in Japan]. Tokyo: United Church of Christ in Japan, 1998.

———. "What We Believe." UCCJ, Oct. 26, 1954; Eng. trans. Oct. 24, 1968. https://uccj.org/faith.

Uchimura Kanzo (内村鑑三).「ロマ書の研究」 [Study of the book of Romans]. Tokyo: Kyobun Kan, 2012.

Uemura Masahisa (植村正久).「神」 [God].「植村伝道叢」 [Evangelism series] 1. Tokyo: Shinkyo, 1947.

Wesley, John.「ジョン・ウェスレー信仰日誌」 [John Wesley's diary of faith]. Translated by Kagawa Toyohiko and Kuroda Shiro. Tokyo: Kyobunkan, 1929.

———. "Notes on the Second Book of Moses Called Exodus." Wesley Center Online, n.d. http://wesley.nnu.edu/john-wesley/john-wesleys-notes-on-the-bible/notes-on-the-second-book-of-moses-called-exodus/#Chapter+XXXII.

World Council of Churches, ed. *Man's Disorder and God's Design*. 5 vols. Amsterdam Assembly Series. New York: Harper & Brothers, 1948.

———. *The Office Report*. Amsterdam: WCC, 1948.

Yanaihara Tadao (矢内原忠雄).「聖書講義VII」 [The book of Isaiah]. Vol. 7 of *Bible Commentary*. Tokyo: Iwanami, 1978.

———.「矢内原忠雄全集18」 [Complete works of Yanaihara Tadao]. Vol. 18. Tokyo: Iwanami, 1964.

———.「国家の理想」 [The ideal of the nation]. *Chuo Koron* (Sept. 1937) 4–22.

———.「日本精神と平和国家」 [The Japanese spirit and a peaceful nation]. Tokyo: Iwanami, 1946.

Yasujima Hisashi (安嶋 彌).「教育勅語をめぐって: 明治前期の開明思想と伝統思想」 [On the imperial rescript on education: Civilization thought and traditional thought in the early Meiji era]. *Gakushikai* 798 (1993). https://www.gakushikai.or.jp/magazine/article/archives/archives_798_2/.

Yokoyama Haruichi (横山春一).「賀川豊彦伝」 [The biography of Kagawa Toyohiko]. Tokyo: Kirisuto Shinbun, 1951.

———. *A Warrior of Love for His Neighbors: Kagawa Toyohiko*. [In Japanese.] Tokyo: Shinkyo, 1952.

Yoshinare Akiko (吉馴明子), "Civilization, War and Christianity: On Articles Concerning the Russo-Japanese War by Masahisa Uemura." International Christian University, Institute for the Study of Christianity and Culture(2016) 139–67.

Yoshitake Nobuhiko (吉武信彦).「ノーベル賞の国際政治学: ノーベル平和賞と日本：第二次世界大戦後の日本人候補、賀川豊彦」 [International politics of the Nobel Prize: The Nobel Peace Prize and Japan, Toyohiko Kagawa, a Japanese nominee after World War II]. *Regional Policy Study* 15 (2013) 17–29.

Yoshino Sakuzo (吉野作造).「憲政の本義を説いて其有終の美を済〈な〉すの途〈みち〉を論ず」 [Explaining the true meaning of constitutional government and discussing the way to achieve its final beauty]. *Chuokoron* (1916) 3–142.

———.「満韓を視察して」 [Inspection of Manchuria and Korea]. In「近代日本思想体系17吉野作造集」 [Modern Japanese thought system] 17:145–81. Tokyo: Chikuma, 1976.

———.「吉野作造選集_1_」 [Yoshino Sakuzo omni]. Vol. 1. Tokyo: Iwanami, 1995———.「吉野作造選集3」 [Yoshino Sakuzo omnibus]. Vol. 3. Tokyo: Iwanami, 1995.

———.「吉野作造選集9」 [Yoshino Sakuzo omnibus]. Vol. 9. Tokyo: Iwanami, 1995.

Index
(Omitted: Kagawa Toyohiko)

Name & Subject	Japanese	Page Number
A Warrior of Love for His Neighbors: Kagawa Toyohiko	隣人愛の闘士賀川豊彦先	115
Abe Yoshimune	阿部義宗	xiv, 127
Acquisition and acceptance of freedom of religion		22
Across the Deathline	死線を越えて	2
Akashi Shigetaro	赤司繁太郎	27
Amemiya Eiichi	雨宮栄一	3-4, 108, 110
American Southern Presbyterian	合衆国長老教会	3, 157
Anti-Immigration Act of 1924	排日移民法 1924	6-7, 46
Aoyama Gakuin University	青山学院大学	55
Arakuni Keisuke	荒邦啓介	94
Asonuma Haruna	阿曽沼春菜	46
Assimilation Policy	同化政策	80, 84
Awakening with the world	世界と共に目覚めよ	78
Axis Powers	枢軸国	61
Ballagh James Hamilton.	バラ宣教師	7
Book of Isaiah Vol 7	聖書講義VII イザヤ書	75, 98
Boston University STH personalism		108, 110-11, 121, 167
Bowne, Borden Parker		110-11, 167

Name & Subject	Japanese	Page Number
Bradshaw, Emerson O.		2, 13, 42, 45–46, 140, 142–45, 153
Brotherhood Economics		14–15, 28, 87, 108–9, 124–27, 155–56, 160
Buddhism	仏教	xiv, 17–19, 21, 23–24, 26, 57, 59–61, 111, 132, 164
Bushido	武士道	64, 70
Calvin, Commentary on Romas		116–18, 120
Catholic bishops of Japan		166
Charter Oath in Five Articles (COFA)	五ヶ条の御誓文	xviii, 93, 99, 100
China's Reconstruction and Japan	中国復興と日本	14, 53, 55, 124
chitsuroku shobun	秩禄処分	100
Christ and Japan		113–4
Chuokoron Sha	中央公論社	73, 85
colonial polycy	植民地政策	5, 19, 36, 55, 79, 80
Commentary on the confession of faith of the United Church of Christ]. Tokyo: United Church of Christ in Japan	日本基督教団信仰告白解説	71, 127
Committee of the Fiftieth Abiversary Japanese Protestatn Mission Conference.	開教五十年記念講演集	67
Complete works of Yanaihara Tadao]. Vol. 18.	矢内原忠雄全集18	105
Confucianism	儒教	xiv, 18–19, 57, 111
Conglegationist	会衆主義(日本では組合教会)	xiv, 65
Cosmic Purpose	宇宙の目的論	14–15, 124

Name & Subject	Japanese	Page Number
Cumberland Presbyterian Church (Japan Presbytery)		166
Daijokan (Grand Council of State)	太政官	21
Danka (temple Parishoner system)	檀家制度	5, 19
Defiance in Manchuria: The Making of Japanese Foreign Policy, 1931–1932	満州事変　政策の形成過程	95
Direction for New Lives	新生活の道標	xi, 153–4
Doi Akio	土肥昭夫	26–7
Drummond Richard H.		162
Dying as a martyr in the national crisis	国難に殉ずるもの	109, 116, 119, 120
Ebina Danjo	海老名弾正	xiv, xvii, 64, 65, 76, 77, 78, 86
Edict of ordering the closing of Japan	鎖国令	20
Edict of Toyotomi Hideyoshi: Expulsion of Missionaries	豊臣秀吉バテレン禁止令	viii, 5, 19
Edinburgh Missionary Conference	エディンバラ宣教会議	33–4
Explaining the true meaning of constitutional government and discussing the way to achieve its final beauty	憲政の本義を説いて其有終の美を済すの途〈みち〉を論ず	81
Fey, Harold E		129, 130, 131
Fifteen-Year War (1931–1945)	十五年戦争	5, 8–9, 15–16, 36, 71, 92, 96, 98, 106, 126, 157
Five Public Notices	五榜の掲示	viii, xviii, 23, 78
Francisco de Xavier	フランシスコ　ザビエル	18

Name & Subject	Japanese	Page Number
Fukoku Kyouhei Seisaku	富国強兵政策	4, 33
Fukushima Kiyonori	福島清紀	99–101
Furuya Yasuo	古屋安雄	104
Gandhi, Mohandas Karamchand		116
Ganghwa Island Incident	江華島海兵隊銃乱射事件	63
Gayn, Mark		97
General Headquarters, the Supreme Commander for the Allied Powers (GHQ)	連合国軍最高司令官総司令部	161
God Evangelism series 1	神　植村伝道叢	70, 131
Great East Asia Co-prosperity Sphere	大東亜共栄圏	31, 62
Great Kanto Earthquake	関東大震災	viii, 1, 34, 36
Hatakeyama Keiichi	畠山圭一	61
Hayashida Kojyun	林田康順	22
Heimindo	平民道	64
Hirano Yukikazu	平野敬和	80, 87
Hirohito		102
His Imperial Highness Higashikuninomiya	東久邇宮稔彦王	62
His Imperial Highness Mikasa	三笠宮崇仁親王	62
Historical Animosity Is What States Make of It: The Role of Morality and Realism in Korea-Japan Relations		149
History of Japanese Protestant Christianity	日本プロテスタント・キリスト教史	26, 27
History of the UCCJ 1 (fmormation)	日本基督教団史資料集 1 (成立)	128

Name & Subject	Japanese	Page Number
History of the UCCJ 2 (During the war)	日本基督教団史資料集 2 (戦時下)	92
History of the UCCJ 3 (Reorganization)	日本基督教団史資料集 3 (再編)	55-6
Hokuriku Eiwa School	北陸英和学校	3
Honda Itsuo	本田逸夫	69
Hong Yipyo	洪, 伊杓	76, 77
Huffman, James.		128
Hull Note	ハル・ノート	30
Ideal of the nation	国家の理想	73-74, 86
Imperial Edict of the End of the War (IEEW)	終戦の詔書	xi, xviii, 14, 30, 125, 132-36, 139, 153
Imperial Edict on the Promotion of National Spirit 1923	国民精神作興ニ関スル詔書	xviii, 33, 37
Imperial Edict Rescript Ending War (IEEW)	終戦の詔書	xi, xviii, 14, 30, 125, 132-36, 139, 153
Inspection of Manchuria and Korea	満韓を視察し	79, 82
Institute for the Study of Human and Society, Movement of Christianity 2	戦時下のキリスト教運動 2	11, 107, 114, 161
Institute for the Study of Human and Society, Movement of Christianity 3	戦時下のキリスト教運動 3	9, 11, 40, 89, 101, 115, 131-2
International Military Tribunal for the Far East	極東国際軍事裁判	133, 153, 165
Inukai Tsuyoshi	犬養 毅	96
Ito Hirobumi	伊藤博文	94, 99

Name & Subject	Japanese	Page Number
Japan Baptist Convention		118, 166
Japan Baptist Union		166
Japan Christ Church Alliance		166
Japan Diary		97
Japan Holiness Church		166
Japan-Korea Annexation	韓国併合ニ関スル条約	64
Japanese Christian Delegation to the Chinese Church in 1957		12
Japanese Nationalism	日本のナショナリズム	8, 9
Japanese Spirit and a Peaceful Nation	日本精神と平和国家	28–30, 75, 86, 133, 164
Japanized Christianity		105–6, 132
Jodo Shinsyu Honganjiha (true pure land Hinganji sect)	浄土真宗本願寺派	21, 24
John Wesley's diary of faith. Translated by Kagawa Toyohiko and Kuroda Shiro	ジョン・ウェスレー信仰日誌	117
Joseph Hardy Neesima	新島襄	63
Justice and Mercy		155
Kagawa in Lincoln's Land (1936)		42, 45–6
Kagawa Revisits America		129–31
Kagawa Toyohiko	賀川豊彦	Omitted: whole pages related
Kagawa Toyohiko and volunteers for him	賀川豊彦とそのヴォランイア	47
Kagawa Toyohiko Complet Set 4	賀川豊彦全集 4	58, 59, 60, 62, 159
Kagawa Toyohiko Complet Set 10	賀川豊彦全集 10	48

Name & Subject	Japanese	Page Number
Kagawa Toyohiko Complet Set 13	賀川豊彦全集 13	12, 53–55, 98, 112, 153–54, 155
Kagawa Toyohiko Complet Set 24	賀川豊彦全集 24	7, 100, 123, 133, 140–41, 143, 158
Kagawa Toyohiko immediately after the war: Focused on new Japan construction of the Christian movement	終戦直後の賀川豊彦: 新日本建設キリスト運動を中心として	57, 162–3
Kagawa Toyohiko in youth	青春の賀川豊彦	3–4, 108, 110
Kagawa: Christian Evangelist		162
Kainou Nobuo	戒能信雄	57, 163
Kamino Kuni Sinbun (newspaper for (KGM)	神の国新聞	xviii, 44
Kashiwagi Gien	柏木義円	27
Katsura Taro	桂 太郎	67
Kawasaki Mitsubishi Shipyard Strike	川崎・三菱造船所ストライキ	34
Lee Sunhye	李 善惠	48–50
Kingdom of God Movement (KGM)	神の国運動	ix, xviii, 2, 32, 39–40, 43, 44–45, 56, 69–71, 76–77, 108, 113
Kingdom of God movement by Toyohiko Kagawa and the war	賀川豊彦による神の国運動と戦争	45, 1088
Kitamori Kazo	北森 嘉蔵	71, 127
Kobe Church	神戸教会	89, 101
Kochi Church	高知教会	114
Kokutai (National Polity)	国体	6, 41, 45
Komatsubara Eitaro	小松原 英太郎	67
Korea and Japan." Korean Information Bulletin 2 (Feb. 1956)		152, 161

Name & Subject	Japanese	Page Number
Korean Information Bulletin		152, 161
kosatsu (official bulletin board)	高札	23
Koube Seminary	神戸神学校	4, 50
Koukoku Shinminka Seisaku	皇國臣民化政策	48, 49
Kramer, Hand Marin		21
Kumagai Naozane	熊谷直実	60
Kuroda Shiro	黒田四郎	2, 37, 43–44, 56, 109
Kurokawa Tomobumi	黒川知文	33–35, 39, 40, 45, 108
League of Nations	国際連盟	xviii, 36, 40, 46, 64
Leserach on the Influence of Toyohiko Kagawa's social welfare	賀川豊彦の社会福祉実践	48–50
Less-Majeste Incident	不敬事件	64, 67
Mainichi Simbun		147, 148, 161
Man in the Taisho Democracy: Focusing on Sakuzo Yoshino's Thought."	武田清子	81
Man's Disorder and God's Design 5 vols		xix, 156
Manchurian Incident in 1931	満州事変 1931	36, 39, 44, 47, 92, 95 98
Marra, Claudia		21, 31
Maruco Polo Bridge Incident	盧溝橋事件	10, 71, 73, 86
Maruyama Masao	丸山眞男	8–9
Matsutani Yosuke	松谷曄介	12

Name & Subject	Japanese	Page Number
Meiji Gakuin	明治学院	4, 50, 110, 166–7
Meiji Jingu Shrine	明治神社	93
Meiji Restoration	明治維新	xiv, 9, 13, 18, 23, 78, 90, 92
Meyers, Harry White		157
Mikado system		102
Minister of state and commander-in-chief in the Meiji Constitution: A constitutional historical study of the power of commander-in-chief	明治憲法に於ける国務と統帥: 統帥権の憲法史的研究	94
Ministry of Education, Japanese Government	文部省	xviii, 25–26, 33, 37, 91, 99
minpon shugi	民本主義	76–78, 80–1
Miyagawa Tsuneteru	宮川経輝	78, 79
Miyakawa Tsuneteru	宮川経輝	78–9
Miyata Mitsuo	宮田光雄	11
Mori Yasuo	森 靖夫	94, 95
Mori Yasuo	森 靖夫	94–5
Mott John R.	モット 世界宣教への指導者	33
Movement 3.1. (March First Movement in Korea in 1919).	3.1.独立運動	34
My Research on Kagawa Toyohiko	私の賀川豊彦研究	2, 37, 44, 56, 109
Nagao Hachinomon	長尾八乃門	3
Nagao Maki	長尾 巻	3–5
Nambara Shigeru	南原繁	133
Nation		102

Name & Subject	Japanese	Page Number
National Archives of Japan	国立公文書館	3, 30-31, 94
National Diet Library	国立国会図書館	13, 80, 90, 94, 96-7
National Ecumenical Missionary Movement (NEMM)	全国協同運動	ix, xviii, 32-6
National Graduate Institute for Policy Studies and Institute for Advanced Studies on Asia	政策研究大学院大学・東洋文化研究所	23, 25, 66, 135
National Morality and Christianity, Current Ivents	国民道徳と基督教 時事瑣言	78-9
New Japan Construction Christian Movement (NJCCM)	新日本建設キリスト教運動	ix, xviii, 2, 32, 41, 55-56, 58-60, 109, 112, 153, 158, 163, -4
New York Herald Tribune		102
New York Times		102
Niebuhr, Reinhold		155-56, 185
Nihon Kirisuto Kyokai	日本基督教会	3, 50
Nippon Sei-Ko-Kai (NSKK, Anglican Episcopal Church in Japan)		166
Nitobe Inazo	新渡戸稲造	xiv, 6, 46, 64-65, 67, 69, 70, 77
Nobel Peace Prize	平和ノーベル賞	162
Non-Church movement	無教会主義	xiv, xvii, 65, 71
Notes on the Second Book of Moses Called Exodus		117
Obinata Sumio	大日方純夫	24
Office of the Historian, Aug. 10, 1945.		132
Ogata, Sadako N.	緒方貞子	95
Okada Keisuke	岡田 啓介	96

Name & Subject	Japanese	Page Number
On the imperial rescript on education: Civilization thought and traditional thought in the early Meiji era	教育勅語をめぐって: 明治前期の開明思想と伝統思想	99
Onomura Rinzo	小野村林蔵	44-5
Open Letter to General MacArther	マッカーサーへの公開書簡	xi, 97, 132, 134, 136-38, 139
Oriental Thought	東洋思想	98, 109, 111-12, 121
Patriotism at Its Peak (Shinjin: 1904)	愛国心の最高潮（新人 1904）	76-7
Peace Line	李承晩ラインを指す	151
Peace Preservation Law (PPL)	治安維持法	xix, 6, 10, 33-34, 36, 82, 88, 89, 109, 113, 128
Pearl Harbor	真珠湾攻撃	61, 102
Plea for Sympathetic Treatment Made to MacArthur by Nippon Social Worker		136-8
Political thought on reconstruction of imperial Japan Yoshino Sakuno in World War I	帝国改造の政治思想：世界戦争期の吉野作造	80, 87
Politics, religion, and education in the Meiji period	明治期における政治・宗教・教育	100
Potsdam Declaration	ポツダム宣言	xviii, 132
Presbyterian Church in Japan		166
Prophecy of America's Demise	米国滅亡の予言	14, 123-4
Quaker	クエイカー	65

Name & Subject	Japanese	Page Number
Records of General Headquarters Supreme Commander for the Allied Powers (SCAP)	連合国最高司令官総司令部文書	161
Reexamination of the civilian minister system in prewar Japan: The Japanese Army in the 1920s and the Supreme Command	軍部大臣文官制の再検討: 年代の陸軍と統帥権	94-95
Reexamination of the prime minister and cabinet under the Meiji constitutional system: Regarding the "divided basis" theory	明治憲法体制における首相と内閣の再検討—「割拠」論をめぐって	96
Reformed Church in America (Dutch)	アメリカ改革派教会 (和蘭)	xix, 7
Religious Leader Sees No Early Rebirth of Christianity in Japan		103, 138, 140
Religious Organization Law (ROL)	宗教団体法	xix, 88, 89
Rescript of Education	教育勅語	xviii, 6, 98
Riverside Japanese American Christian Leaders Conference (RJACLC))	リバーサイド日米キリスト者会議	xix, 14, 40-41, 124, 126-7
Roams 9:3	ロマ書9章3節	69, 115
Roosevelt Franklin	フランクリン・ルーズベルト	61, 119-20, 130
Russian Revolution of 1917	ロシア革命 1917	6, 33-34, 88, 113
Russo-Japanese War (1904-5)	日露戦争 (1904-5)	4, 18, 26, 34, 47, 64, 67, 72-73, 77, 78, 86
Saionji Kinmochi	西園寺公望	94-6
Saiton Makoto	斎藤 実	96
Sankyo Godo (Three Religions Association: Shinto, Buddhism, and Christianity)	三教合同 (神道、仏教、基督教: 政府主導)	18, 26-7
Sasaki Yuichi	佐々木雄一	96

Name & Subject	Japanese	Page Number
Schildgen, Robert		73
Shimaji Mokurai	島地黙雷	21, 26
Shintoism	神道	6, 17, 18–19, 28, 57, 61, 89–90, 111 114–15, 129, 164
Shirabe Masaji	調　正路	118
Sino-Japanese War (1894–95)	日清戦争	14, 34, 37, 64, 78, 98, 106
Special Higher Police	特別高等警察	xix, 9
Stalin Joseph	ジョゼフ・スターリン	61
Study of the book Romans	ロマ書研究	68, 69
Suma Yakichiro	須磨弥吉郎	148
Tae-Ryong Yoon		140, 149
Tairano Kiyomori	平清盛	60
Taisho democracy	大正デモクラシー	82
Takagi Mizutaro	高木壬太郎	27
Takahashi Korekiyo	高橋 是清	96
Takeda Kiyoko	武田清子	81, 101–5
Takenaka Katsuo		51
Tanaka Giichi	田中義一	96
the 2600th anniversary celebration of the Japan Empire	皇紀二千六百年奉祝全国基督教信徒大会	100
The biography of Kagawa Toyohiko	賀川豊彦伝	115
The Consitution of Japan	日本国憲法	93, 153
The Consitution of the Empire of Japan	日本帝国憲法	13, 18, 20, 80, 89–91, 93

Name & Subject	Japanese	Page Number
the Pillar of Light	火の柱	33, 109, 118
The social movement of the Bible	聖書の社会運動	97, 103, 108, 119
The Tokyo War Crimes Trial: The Pursuit of Justice in the Wake of World War II		132
The University of Tokyo	東京大学	98
Theology of the Pain of God	神の痛みの神学	71
Thorp, Gerald R.		103, 138, 140
Tokugawa Bakufu	徳川幕府	xiv, 3, 5, 17–20, 23–25, 100, 110, 169
Tokyo-Asahi Simbun	東京朝日新聞	73, 74
Totani Yuma	戸谷由麻	132
Toyohiko Kagawa: Apostle of Love and Social Justice	賀川豊彦 愛と社会正義を追い求めた生涯	73, 102, 120, 144, 161
Toyotomi Government	豊臣政府	viii, 5, 17–21, 24, 28, 101, 110
Treaty of Amity and Commerce between the US and Japan	日米修好通商条約	63, 66
Truman Harry S.	トルーマン	132, 137
UCCJ's Confessioin	教会規則	92
Uchimura Kanzo	内村鑑三	vxii, xvii, 6, 27–28, 64–65, 67–69, 71, 73, 75, 77, 86
Uemura Masahisa	植村正久	xiv, xvii, 6, 32–33, 55, 63–64, 65, 69, 70–73, 77
Unconqurable Kagawa		2, 13, 42, 140, 142–43, 145, 153
Understanding of The Old Testament. 4th ed		165

Name & Subject	Japanese	Page Number
United Church of Christ in Japan (UCCJ)	日本基督教団	xiv, xix, 10, 12, 23, 26, 40, 55–56, 88–89, 91–92, 114, 118–19, 121, 123–24, 126–29, 132, 144 165–6
USSR	ソビエト連邦共和国	30, 61
Washington Post		102
Wesley, John.		117–8
Winn C. Thomas	ウィン宣教師	3
World Council of Churches	世界教会協議会	xix, 156
WWII	第二次世界大戦	ix, xiv, xv, 12, 41, 61, 104
Yanaihara Tadao	矢内原忠男	ix, 10–11, 28–30, 63–65, 71, 73–75, 86–87, 98, 105–6, 133–34, 136, 162, 164–5
Yasujima Hisashi	安嶋　彌	99
Yokoyama Haruichi	横山春一	115, 118
Yomiuri Hochi Shimbun		102–3, 139
Yoshinare Akiko	吉馴明子	72
Yoshino Sakuzo	吉野作造	34, 36, 63–65, 76, 79, 80, 81–87
Yoshino Sakuzo omnibus. Vol. 1	吉野作造選集1巻	81
Yoshino Sakuzo omnibus. Vol. 3	吉野作造選集3巻	80, 82
Yoshino Sakuzo omnibus. Vol. 9	吉野作造選集9巻	82–66

www.ingramcontent.com/pod-product-compliance
Lightning Source LLC
Chambersburg PA
CBHW062036220426
43662CB00010B/1524